On the MOVE Plus

Course Book

von
Kate Tranter

Ernst Klett Sprachen
Barcelona Budapest London Posen Sofia Stuttgart

Plus

von
Kate Tranter

Beratung
Christine Reichelt, Fachbereichsleiterin
an der Volkshochschule Berlin-Neukölln

Janice Probert, Studienleiterin für Sprachen
an der Volkshochschule Düsseldorf

Inga Schröder, Fachbereichsleiterin Sprachen
an der Volkshochschule Wedel

The European Language Certificates
Beratung: Geoff Tranter
Chief Co-ordinating Examiner
for the Certificate in English

1. Auflage   1 ⁵ 4 ³ | 2007   06   05

Alle Drucke dieser Auflage können im Unterricht
nebeneinander benutzt werden, sie sind unter-
einander unverändert.
Die letzte Zahl bezeichnet das Jahr dieses Druckes.

© Ernst Klett Sprachen GmbH, Stuttgart 2003.
Alle Rechte vorbehalten.
Internetadresse: http://www.klett.de

Redaktion: Pauline Ashworth, David Shallis

Druck: Aprinta, Wemding
Printed in Germany.
ISBN 3-12-524135-9

Introduction

Willkommen bei *On the MOVE Plus*, dem praktischen Englischkurs für Fortgeschrittene!

Das vorliegende **Kursbuch** *(Course Book)* beginnt mit einer kurzen **Einstiegslektion** *(Unit 0 Starter)* und gliedert sich im Folgenden in vier Blöcke von je drei regulären Lektionen und einer kurzen **Wiederholungslektion** *(Revision Unit)*. Der **Abschlusstest** *(The Test)* bietet Ihnen die Möglichkeit, die wichtigsten grammatischen Strukturen sowie nützliche Redewendungen und Wortschatz noch einmal zu überprüfen.

Im **Anhang** befinden sich eine Grammatikübersicht *(Grammar Overview)* und sämtliche Hörtexte *(Tapescripts)*. Ein lektionsbegleitendes Wörterverzeichnis *(Unit Vocabulary)*, in dem alle neuen Wörter chronologisch aufgelistet sind, sowie ein alphabetisches Wortregister *(Alphabetical Word List)* schließen den Anhang ab.

Das **Tonmaterial** zu *On the MOVE Plus* ist sowohl auf Kassetten als auch auf CDs erhältlich.

Das *On the MOVE Plus* **Arbeitsbuch** *(Workbook)* enthält eine Vielfalt von zusätzlichen Übungen und Texten zum Festigen, Vertiefen und Erweitern Ihrer Kenntnisse.
Last but not least finden Sie einige nützliche Redewendungen für die Unterrichtsstunden auf der Innenseite des vorderen Buchdeckels.

Und jetzt wünschen wir Ihnen viel Freude und Erfolg mit *On the MOVE Plus!*

- **Course Book**
  ISBN 3-12-524135-9
- **1 Kassette zum Course Book**
  ISBN 3-12-524139-1
- **2 CDs zum Course Book**
  ISBN 3-12-524141-3
- **Teacher's Book**
  ISBN 3-12-524136-7
- **Workbook**
  ISBN 3-12-524138-3

Contents

UNIT 0	*Starter*	7

UNIT 1	*Lifestyle*	8
Functions	Speculating; talking about likes and dislikes	
Grammar	Present Simple vs. Continuous; *have got*; *used to*	
Pronunciation	Wordstress	
Vocabulary	Daily routines; hobbies and interests	

UNIT 2	*From here to there*	16
Functions	Asking for information; explaining regulations	
Grammar	Polite questions; short responses; the *going to* future	
Vocabulary	Public transport; city features and facilities	

UNIT 3	*Buy it!*	24
Functions	Shopping; dealing with problems and complaints	
Grammar	Conjunctions; relative clauses; relative pronouns	
Pronunciation	Wordstress (2-word expressions)	
Vocabulary	Online shopping; advertising; supermarkets	

UNIT 4	*Revision*	32

UNIT 5	*You are what you wear*	34
Functions	Describing clothes; compliments; giving advice	
Grammar	Verbs of sense + adjectives; Past Simple vs. Perfect; 2-word verbs	
Pronunciation	Linking sounds (catenation)	
Vocabulary	Clothes; body decorations; valuables	

UNIT 6	*Enjoy!*	42
Functions	Explaining recipes; invitations; dinner with friends	
Grammar	Adverbs of time/place; *ought(n't) to/needn't/may*; Past Perfect	
Vocabulary	Food: meals, nutrition, ingredients, recipes	

UNIT 7	*The media and me*	50
Functions	Suggestions; giving opinions	
Grammar	Passives; reported speech	
Vocabulary	Types of media; TV programmes; news	

Contents

| UNIT 8 | *Revision* | 58 |

UNIT 9	*House and home*	60
Functions	Speculating; saying that something is important; dis/agreeing
Grammar	Causative; reporting offers, promises, requests, commands
Vocabulary	Furniture and furnishings; types of home; risks and insurance

UNIT 10	*Learning for life*	68
Functions	Talking about ways of learning; qualities and skills
Grammar	Question tags (*do/don't you?*); *wish*; reporting questions
Vocabulary	Education systems; school subjects; qualifications

UNIT 11	*The world around us*	76
Functions	Talking about worries; expressing regret; sympathizing
Grammar	Question tags (other forms); Perfect modals; Present Perfect Continuous
Pronunciation	Intonation (question tags)
Vocabulary	Weather & climate; landscapes; land use

| UNIT 12 | *Revision* | 84 |

UNIT 13	*It takes all sorts*	86
Functions	Describing appearance; greetings cards/conventional messages
Grammar	Conditionals 1 and 2; *whose*; Past Conditional
Vocabulary	Means of identification; appearance; names; families; friends

UNIT 14	*A balanced life*	94
Functions	Describing regular activities; asking for detailed information
Grammar	Futures: *going to* vs *will*; verb + infinitive
Pronunciation	Reading a text: sentence stress, pauses
Vocabulary	Housework activities; sports; unusual holidays

UNIT 15	*Come together*	102
Functions	Expressing surprise; suggesting; invitations; a thank-you letter
Grammar	Definite article; verb + *ing*; Present Simple and Present Continuous as future forms
Vocabulary	Body language; events, festivals

The On the MOVE test   **110**

The On the MOVE poster   **111**

Appendix
Anhang

Grammar overview   **112**
Grammatikübersicht

Tapescripts   **120**
Hörtexte

Unit Vocabulary   **136**
Kapitel-Wörterverzeichnis

Alphabetical Word List   **159**
Alphabetisches Wortregister

Starter

UNIT 0

1 English and us

A Find someone in your class who:

1. learned English at school.
2. is learning English for their career.
3. has friends or relatives in an English-speaking country.
4. has been to an English-speaking country recently.
5. can sing a song in English.
6. sometimes reads an English newspaper or magazine.

B Report something interesting.

2 The book tour

Look through this book. Where can you find the following things?

1. The contents of the book.   Page ____
2. Important language that comes up in Unit 1.   ____
3. How to pronounce one of the words in Unit 5.   ____
4. A list of all the important vocabulary in the book. ____
5. An overview of the grammar in the book.   ____
6. Some useful phrases to use in class.   ____

3 Effective language learning

A Tick the statements you agree with.

1. Don't say anything if you aren't sure about the grammar. ☐
2. Forget the grammar. The important thing is to speak. ☐

3. You should never make mistakes. ☐
4. Making mistakes can be helpful. ☐

5. The teacher should correct every mistake. ☐
6. The teacher should only correct important mistakes. ☐

7. When people are talking, try to understand everything they say. ☐
8. Try to get a general idea of what people say. ☐

9. Translate to check that you understand. ☐
10. Don't try to translate. You can't, because languages are different. ☐

B Compare with a partner. Does he/she have any useful tips?

UNIT 1 Lifestyle

1 Around the world

A Pairwork. Look at the pictures and answer the questions.

1. Where do you think the pictures were taken?
2. What time of day or year is it?
3. What are the people doing?

1.
2.
3.

It looks like …
He's probably …
I'm not sure, but it could be …

B Listen and check, then complete these sentences.

1. That's my dad. He _____ a nap. Most people _____ a siesta after lunch.

2. We _____ breakfast at a local restaurant. We always _____ for breakfast on Sundays and I always _____ pancakes.

3. They _____ in the sea. My friend Jim _____ swimming every day.

> a nap = a short sleep

C Mark the correct information.

> **The present tenses**
> The Present Simple is used to talk about current or temporary / routine or regular activities: *Most people **have** a siesta after lunch.*
> The Present Continuous is used to talk about current or temporary / routine or regular activities: *We're **having** breakfast at a local restaurant.*

D Look at 1B again. Do people do the same things where you live?

E Think of three people you know. What are they probably doing now? Compare with a partner and report.

> (Annette) says her sister is probably watching television.

2 Early birds and night owls

A Angie and Kevin Bailey are being interviewed for a radio programme. Read the interview. What do you think the questions were?

Interviewer: Angie, what _____?

Angie: Well, I don't like getting up early but I'm most energetic at about eight o'clock in the morning, so I usually get up before then. About half six most days.

Interviewer: _____?

Angie: Oh, when I've had a shower, I feel awake straightaway.

Interviewer: _____?

Kevin: Well, I'm not really a morning person – especially in winter. It takes me ages to wake up properly then. It's much better in summer, though, when it's light outside.

Interviewer: _____
_____?

Angie: Oh, yes! Sundays. I like to have a nice long lie-in, a proper breakfast …

Kevin: I prefer Friday evening. There's the whole weekend ahead of you.

Interviewer: _____?

Kevin: Monday mornings! I don't know why, but I always seem to be in a bad mood …

Angie: Yes, you are!

> half six = half past six

B Listen and complete the interview.

C Pairwork. You have to find out if someone is a morning person or a night person. Think of some more questions you could ask.

When …?
Do you …?
How long …?
Why …?

at six o'clock
in the morning
on Monday mornings

D Choose a different partner and interview them. How many "early birds" and "night owls" are there in your class?

 In Britain most people start work between about eight thirty and nine o'clock. Children usually start school about the same time, so people typically get up between seven and eight o'clock. Anything before that is early. The morning rush hour usually lasts from around seven thirty to nine and in the afternoon it is from about four thirty to six. Most people go to bed between eleven o'clock and midnight.

3 I've got a radio alarm

 A Listen. Which of these things do you hear?

☐ stopwatch   ☐ radio alarm   ☐ alarm clock

☐ grandfather clock

☐ timer   ☐ watch   ☐ electronic organizer

(desk) diary
calendar

B Listen. How many times did the speakers use the verb *have got*?

Speakers

1. [2] 2. [ ] 3. [ ] 4. [ ] 5. [ ]

C Complete the box.

Have got
The verb *to have got* means the same as *to have*, but is less formal.

to have	to have got
Do you have …?	_____ you got …?
I have …	I _____ got …
I don't have …	I _____ got …

D Pairwork. Ask a partner about the things in 3A.

Have you got …?

Yes, I have. / No, I haven't.

E Listen to the song. What does the singer say he's got?

In pop songs
I've got is often shortened to *I got*.

F Pronunciation. *Timer* has got two syllables (*ti-mer*). It is stressed on the first syllable (Oo). Say the words below and mark the correct stress symbols.

1.	Oo / oO	timer
2.	oO / Oo	alarm
3.	ooO / Ooo	calendar, diary, grandfather, radio
4.	oooO / Oooo	organizer
5.	ooOo / oOoo	electronic

● **TALKING POINT**
There is an English saying: "A watched pot never boils".
Is there a similar saying in your language? Does time ever go too fast or too slowly for you?

4   A life of leisure?

A   Add some hobbies to these diagrams.

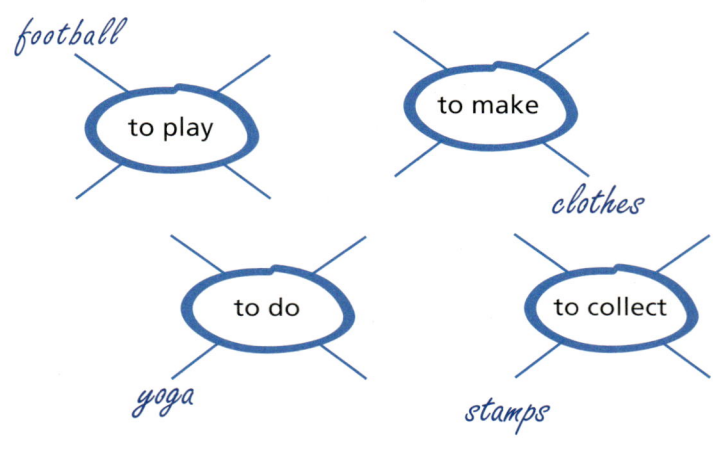

football — to play
to make — clothes
to do — yoga
to collect — stamps

billiards
chess
coins
DIY
furniture
models
postcards
sport

B   Pairwork.
How many more hobbies can you think of in three minutes?

to go to …
to read …
to watch …

C   Group work. Find three things that everyone in your group likes doing and three things that they don't. Compare with another group.

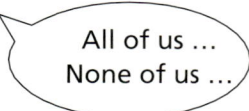

All of us …
None of us …

😊😊 I love danc**ing**.
😊 I like / enjoy collect**ing** stamps.
😐 I don't mind do**ing** DIY.
☹ I don't like play**ing** cards.
☹☹ I hate / can't stand garden**ing**.

D   What are the most popular hobbies in your country? Why do you think they are so popular?

5 I used to collect stamps

A Listen and number the pictures.

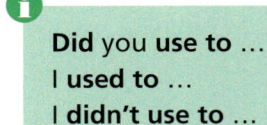

B Listen again and complete these sentences.

1. I _____ collect stamps when I was a teenager.

2. There _____ be colour TV when we were growing up. My brother and I _____ watch "The Lone Ranger" every week.

3. She _____ wash all our clothes by hand.

4. Most people _____ go abroad for their holidays. Our family _____ _____ go camping at the seaside.

> **Did** you **use to** …?
> I **used to** …
> I **didn't use to** …

C Complete the box.

> **used to**
>
> This form describes something that was usual in the _____ . It is followed by the _____ form of the verb: *I used to live in Manchester, but I live in Bristol now.*

infinitive
past

D On a piece of paper write 50–75 words about how things used to be when you were younger. Don't write your name on it.

E Put all the the texts on a table or pin them up on the wall. Read the other texts and guess who wrote them.

6 The time of your life

A Read these quotes. Which do you like best, and why?

"I like my wrinkles – they show that I've lived." *(Actress Shirley McLaine)*

"Youth is wasted on the young." *(From a song by Cahn & van Heusen)*

"Your schooldays are the best days of your life." *(Traditional)*

"Life begins at forty." *(Singer Sophie Tucker)*

B Read this text and mark the words that fit best, then listen and check.

Life-long learning at the U3A

I used to think that it would be wonderful / terrible to be old but I'm 66 now and I'm having the best / worst time of my life. I retired four years ago and so I've got lots of time to do what I want. Of course, I'm lucky / unlucky – I'm still healthy and I've also got enough money. I travel a lot nowadays and I'm learning French at the University of the Third Age. It's not really a university – it's a kind of school for people over 50. They offer lots of boring / interesting courses in the afternoons and evenings. You can learn languages or do painting or pottery courses. And you make lots of friends with similar / different interests. I didn't have time when I was younger. I used to work all day and then I was fresh / tired in the evening. Now I often go out in the evening. In fact, my daughter has just bought me an answering machine because she says I'm always / never there when she tries to phone me!

C Read the text again and answer these questions.

1. What has changed in her life?
2. What is the University of the Third Age?
3. How does she feel about life now?

D Group work. Decide which is the best age to be. Now tell the other groups what you think and why. Which group has the best arguments?

> ● **TALKING POINT**
> What age do people usually retire at in your country?
> Do you know anyone who is doing something interesting in their retirement?

Checklist!

Grammar

A Present Continuous and Present Simple

1. He's _____ a nap.
2. Most people _____ a siesta after lunch.

B have got

1. ❓ Have I/you/we/they got …?
   _____ he/she/it got …?
2. ✔ I/you/we/they have ('ve) got ….
   He/she/it _____ ('s) got …
3. ✘ I/you/we/they _____ (haven't) got …
   He/she/it _____ (hasn't) got …

C used to

1. ❓ Where did you _____ to live?
2. ✔ I used _____ collect stamps.
3. ✘ Most people _____ use to go abroad for their holidays.

Phrases

A Speculating

1. It looks _____ somewhere in the Mediterranean.
2. I'm not _____, but it could be Greece.
3. He's probably having a nap.

B Talking about likes and dislikes

1. I love dancing.
2. I like/enjoy collect_____ stamps.
3. I _____ mind doing DIY.
4. I don't like playing cards.
5. I hate/can't _____ gardening.

Grammar: A1 having, A2 have, B1 Has, B2 has, B3 have not – has not, C1 use, C2 to, C3 didn't
Phrases: A1 like, A2 sure, B2 ing, B3 don't, B5 stand

UNIT 2 *From here to there*

1 **This one means that …**

A Where could you see these signs?

 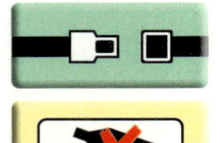  

a. b. c. d. e.

B Complete these explanations and match them with the signs.

This one means that:
1. you ___have to___ fasten your seat belt. ☐
2. you ___aren't allowed to___ use a mobile phone here. ☐
3. you _____ throw anything out of the window. ☐
4. you _____ buy a ticket and put it behind your car window. ☐
5. you _____ eat anything here. ☐

C How would you explain these signs?

This compartment is reserved for passengers with first class tickets only

Please give up this seat for elderly or disabled people

D Think of another sign that you often see. Explain it a partner.
Listen to your partner's explanation and draw the sign.

16

2 Can you tell me … ?

A Look at the pictures and listen. Which of the things do the speakers mention?

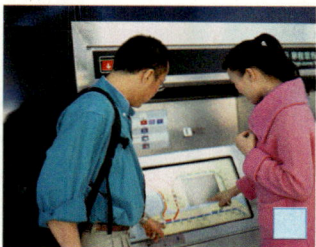

From here to there — UNIT 2

B Complete the questions, then listen again and check.

1. Excuse me, do you know where I _____ find a timetable?
2. Can you tell me where I can _____ a ticket, please?
3. Excuse me, do you know how this machine _____?
4. Can you tell me which platform the train to Victoria _____ from, please?

C Complete the box.

> **Polite questions**
>
> To make a _____ more polite, change it into a _____
> and add a _____ at the beginning:
>
> Where can I buy a ticket? → **Can you tell me** where **I can buy** a ticket?
> How does this machine work? → **Do you know** how this machine **works**?

statement
question phrase
question

Trains in Britain

The world's first railway was the "Stockton and Darlington", which opened in north-east England in 1825. Dozens of other railway companies were founded in the following years and Britain quickly became an exporter of railway technology to Europe and the rest of the world.

The British railway companies were nationalized in 1948 and privatized again in the 1990s. Train services in Britain are now operated by 26 different companies. The infrastructure – stations, tracks, signals, tunnels, etc. – is managed in the public interest by Network Rail, a "not-for-profit" company.

Britain also has many historic trains which run on private lines, and the National Railway Museum at York is a must for all enthusiasts.

D Listen to someone asking for information about public transport and mark the sentences true (T) or false (F).

1. You can buy return tickets. **F**
2. There are ten single tickets in a carnet. ☐
3. You can't use a day ticket after three o'clock the next morning. ☐
4. A monthly season ticket is always valid until the last day of a calendar month. ☐
5. There are no reductions for families. ☐
6. Senior citizens pay half price. ☐
7. Three adults and two children are allowed to use the family ticket. ☐
8. Zones 1 and 2 cover the city centre. ☐

E How is public transport organized in your country? Collect information in groups and then tell your teacher.

3   The best way to get there

A You want to get from central London to Heathrow Airport by underground. Write five polite questions.

1. _____
   _____
   _____

2. _____
   _____
   _____

3. _____
   _____
   _____

4. _____
   _____
   _____

5. _____
   _____
   _____

Trains: how often?
First train: what time?
Journey: how long?
Tickets: where?
Single: how much?

UNDERGROUND   **Piccadilly Line**

Piccadilly Circus
Green Park
Hyde Park Corner
Knightsbridge
South Kensington
Gloucester Road
Earl's Court
Barons Court
Hammersmith
Turnham Green
Acton Town
South Ealing
Northfields
Boston Manor
Osterley
Hounslow East
Hounslow Central
Hounslow West
Hatton Cross
✈ Heathrow Terminal 4
   Heathrow Terminals 1, 2, 3

B Pairwork. Now read some information about other ways to get to Heathrow.
Partner A: Read the "Airbus" ad and answer your questions.
Partner B: Read the "Heathrow Express" ad and answer your questions.

From here to there — UNIT 2

Take the **Airbus**
between Central London and Heathrow Airport.
What better way to catch your first sight of London than from the top of a traditional red double-decker bus?
The journey takes 1 hour 40 minutes. The buses run every 30 minutes at peak times and the first bus leaves at 5.30 a.m. You can purchase Airbus tickets on the bus or you can buy online or through our Telephone Sales Centres - Just ring 08705 747777.

Fares
Adults: £ 7.00 single
£10.00 return trip

Heathrow Express
is the revolutionary, non-stop train service between London's Paddington station and Heathrow airport. The journey takes 15 minutes and the trains run every 15 minutes from 5 a.m. until midnight. You can buy tickets online, by phone, at our ticket desks in Paddington Station and Heathrow or from our new, easy-to-use, touch-screen ticket machines which accept cash and all major credit and debit cards.

Fares
Express Class
single: €18.00
return: € 32.00
carnet (12 singles): €195.00
First Class
single: € 30.00
return: € 60.00
carnet (12 singles): € 330.00

C Ask your partner about the other method of getting to Heathrow and take notes. Use the questions you wrote in 3A. Which method would you choose, and why?

The Airbus   *The Heathrow Express*

D What's the best way to get to your nearest international airport?

● **TALKING POINT**
Traffic in London moves just as slowly now as it used to 100 years ago. What do you think is the best method of transport in a city?

4 Travel talk

A What do you do when you're travelling? Compare with other people in the class.

> I like talking to people. It passes the time.

> I just doze. I don't go to sleep properly. I'm always afraid of missing the stop!

I just doze.	I don't go to sleep.
– So do I. / Me too.	– Neither do I. / Nor me.
– I don't.	– I do.

B Listen and make notes. Where are the people travelling to, how and why?

- France, the USA, Wales, India, Austria
- ferry, plane, coach, train
- return home, family visit, holiday, business trip, student exchange

	Destination	Method of travel	Reason for journey
1.			
2.			
3.			
4.			
5.			

C Choose one of the people from 4B. You are travelling with him or her. Think of some things you could talk about.

> What's it like?
> Have you been to … before?
> Do you speak … ?

D Write a destination and a means of transport on a piece of paper. Talk to your partner who is a fellow traveller.

5 What are you going to see there?

A Which of these places would you like to visit most? Why?

Kennedy Space Center

View launches & landings
Space shuttle
International Space Station

WaterWorld
Thrilling rides and unforgettable animal encounters including killer whales, dolphins, sealions, stingrays and more

The Everglades National Park

Alligator wrestling
Bird watching
Fishing
Swamp buggy rides

B Listen. Which of the places is the woman going to visit?

C Listen again and complete these sentences.

1. What are you _____ there?
2. We're _____ a trip to Disneyworld.
3. I don't know what we're _____ yet.
4. I'm _____ that. I wouldn't feel safe.

D Complete the box.

> **Going to**
>
> This form of the _____ is used for talking about things you intend to do. It is formed with *be going to* and the _____ form of the verb:
>
> - What are you **going to see** there?
> - We're **going to start off** with a trip to Disneyworld.

infinitive
future

E Pairwork. Think of some interesting places to visit in your area. Plan a two-day programme for a Japanese couple and their 15-year-old daughter. Tell the class what you are going to do with them.

Are you going to …?
We're going to …
We aren't going to …

From here to there

UNIT 2

6 Three cities

 A Read these texts. Which cities do they describe?
Listen and check.

Two cities for the price of one! Old ....., with its colourful bazaars, busy streets and narrow lanes, is full of historic monuments. New ....., by contrast, is the modern capital of India and has wide tree-lined avenues, elegant official buildings and beautiful parks. .....: a perfect introduction to the exotic sights and smells of India and the ideal starting point for your visit to some of India's finest tourist attractions, such as Agra and the Taj Mahal.

Less than 2 hours from London, ... (....... in Welsh) is a city with an international reputation and a lively atmosphere. ....'s attractions include its busy commercial centre, a world-class opera house, home to the Welsh National Opera, and the Millennium Stadium for top sporting events. Its excellent shops, superb museums and its exciting nightlife all help to make the Welsh capital one of Britain's favourite cities.

Welcome to ....., a cosmopolitan city with a superb climate, world-class shopping and excellent conference facilities. .....'s seven miles of beaches, three golf courses and 20 parks make it one of the world's favourite tourist destinations. ..... International Airport is the gateway to Latin America and the city has one of the fastest-growing economies in the country. With its rich mix of cultures and perfect natural setting, ... is the city you won't want to forget.

B Complete these expressions from the texts.

1. _____ commercial centre
2. _____ city
3. _____ monuments
4. _____ reputation
5. _____ atmosphere
6. _____ mix of cultures

C Look at the texts again. How many words can you find that describe something positively?

D Write 100 – 150 words about a town you know. Use at least three expressions from the texts.

> ● **TALKING POINT**
> What makes a city attractive to visitors?

Checklist!

Grammar

A Polite questions

1. Where's the ticket office?
   Can you tell me _____ , please?
2. How does this machine work?
   Excuse me, do you know _____ ?

B Short responses

1. I just doze.
   ✓ So do I. / Me _____.
   ✗ I don't.

2. I don't go to sleep.
   ✗ Neither do I. / _____ me.
   ✓ I _____.

C The future with *going to*

1. ❓ What are you going _____ do there?
2. ✓ We're _____ to start off with a trip to Disneyworld.
3. ✗ I'm not _____ try that.

Phrases

A Asking for information

1. What does this sign _____?
2. What's the best _____ to get to the airport from here?
3. _____ Delhi like?

B Explaining regulations

1. You have ____ buy a ticket, but you _____ have to have a first class one.
2. You're _____ to use a mobile phone on a train, but you _____ allowed to use one on a plane.

Grammar: A1 where the ticket office is, A2 how this machine works B1 too, B2 Nor – do, C1 to, C2 going, C3 going to
Phrases: A1 mean, A2 way, A3 What's, B1 to – don't, B2 allowed – aren't

UNIT 3 — Buy it!

1 At the shops

A Find people in your class who have bought the following things recently. Why did they buy them?

> Something to wear
> Something to read
> Some furniture
> Something to listen to
> A present for someone

When did you last buy …?

 B Listen. What sorts of shop do you think the people are in?

 C Listen again. What did the salespeople say?

1. ■ I'd prefer yellow.
   - ● Yes. _____?

2. ■ Could you gift-wrap it for me, please?
   - ● Yes, _____.

3. ■ Can I exchange them if they don't match my dress?
   - ● Yes, _____.

4. ■ Have you got anything for backache?
   - ● You _____.

5. ■ I need one with an internal modem.
   - ● We _____
     _____.

Can I help you?

How much is that, please?

I'll take that, please.

D Pairwork. One of you is a customer and the other is a salesperson. Work out a shopping dialogue, including some phrases from 1C. Play it for the rest of the class.

2 Online shopping

A Look at the website and answer the questions.

1. What can you buy on the website?
2. What do you have to do with the shopping basket?
3. What are the advantages of shopping at Wiltons.com?

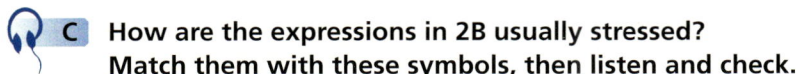

B Look at the website again and complete these "word partnerships".

1. shopping *basket*
2. _____ quality
3. weekly _____
4. special _____
5. _____ service
6. _____ store
7. _____ prices
8. delivery _____

C How are the expressions in 2B usually stressed?
Match them with these symbols, then listen and check.

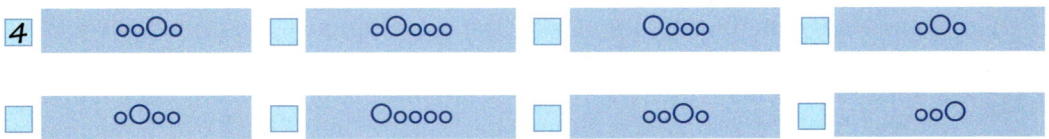

D   Some people are talking about online shopping. Look at these sentences from their conversation. What sort of words are missing?

1. I suppose it's very helpful _if_ you live a long way from the shops, _or_ you can't get out of the house.
2. There aren't any good shops where I live, ____ I often order clothes online, ____ I prefer going to a shop ____ I like to see things before I buy them.
3. I wouldn't use my credit card to shop online, ____ everyone says it's safe.
4. I think it's safe ____ it's very convenient. My son always books his holidays online ____ he doesn't have to go to the travel agent's. It's cheaper too.
5. I don't think I'd book a holiday online ____ it was cheaper. Think of the risk – all that money!

E   Complete the sentences with these conjunctions, then listen and check.

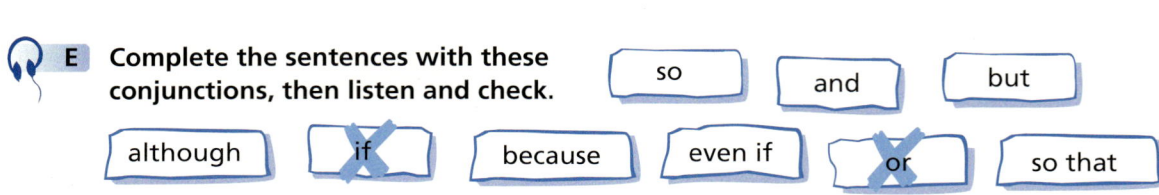

F   Interview a partner. Find out if they shop online. Why? Why not?

24-hour shopping

The way people shop in English-speaking countries has changed a lot in recent years. You can find supermarkets that are open 24 hours a day, seven days a week, and department stores, clothes and bookshops are often open on Sundays and late in the evening. The internet has also had a major impact on shopping habits. Internet shops are always open and this is one of the reasons people give for shopping online. Reports vary about how many people shop online, but everyone agrees that online shopping is growing. According to one report, 39% of American shoppers used the Internet for shopping last year, up from 19% twelve months earlier. In second place were the Australians at 20%, ahead of Britain and Canada, where 15% of consumers bought things online. In the USA the most popular online shopping item is clothes. In Britain, by contrast, books are top of the list, while in Hong Kong most people shop online for food.

3 What's the problem?

> bad   broken   damaged
> doesn't work   too small

A Label the pictures.

1. It's _____
2. It's _____.
3. It _____.
4. It's _____.
5. It's _____.

> It's **too** small.
> It is**n't** big **enough**.

B Listen and mark the correct information.

1. a. Two of the glasses are missing / broken.
   b. The company offers / doesn't offer to replace the glasses.
2. a. The shoes are too big / too tight.
   b. The customer wants / doesn't want to exchange the shoes.
3. a. The salesperson can / can't repair the camera.
   b. The customer would like a refund / a credit note.

C Pairwork. Think of something that you've bought and what the problem is. Do you want a refund or would you like to exchange it? Now take it back to the shop. Your partner is the salesperson.

- Have you got the receipt, please?
- I'm afraid we don't give refunds.
- I can give you a credit note.
- We'll replace them straightaway.

● **TALKING POINT**
Think of a shop that you go to where the service is always good. Tell the rest of the class about it.

4 It's a brilliant ad

A Look at these advertisements. What do you think they could be advertising? Who are they aimed at?

> It could be an ad for (a car) because …

- teenagers
- young single adults
- young families
- middle-aged people
- retired people

B Organize these words into positive and negative.

boring
brilliant
clever
effective
funny
horrible
interesting
offensive
sexist
stupid

Positive	Negative
_____	_____
_____	_____
_____	_____
_____	_____
_____	_____

C Group work. Think of an ad you particularly like or don't like. Tell the group about it.

> There's a really (brilliant) ad for … . It shows …

5 How influenced are we by advertising?

A Listen to some people talking about the influence of advertising. Which of these statements do you hear?

"I don't think advertising makes any difference." ☐
"I just choose the clothes which fit best." ☐
"I probably buy products with names which I recognize." ☐
"When someone well-known advertises something, it definitely makes a difference." ☐
"I look for the best value for money." ☐

B What do you think about the statements in 5A? Compare with a partner.

C Read the information in the box, then mark the relative clauses in the sentences below.

> *Relative clauses*
> A relative clause is a part of a sentence which gives more information about people or things: *an ad **which** you've just seen on TV.*

1. I buy the one which is cheapest.
2. If it's someone who I respect, then I think the product is probably OK, too.
3. I probably buy products with names which I recognize.
4. I know some people who only buy clothes with the right brand names.
5. I just choose the clothes which fit best.

D Now read this information. Can you leave out any of the relative pronouns in 5C?

> *Relative pronouns*
> A relative clause usually starts with a relative pronoun:
> • people **who** only buy clothes with the right brand names.
> • an ad **which** you've just seen on TV.
>
> The relative pronoun is not necessary if it refers to the **object** of the clause:
> *an ad (which) you've just seen on TV.*

E Write two sentences about products you often buy. Include relative clauses!

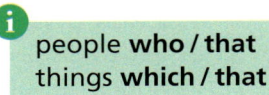

people **who** / **that**
things **which** / **that**

Unit 3 Buy it!

6 Shopping in a supermarket

A Look at this plan of a supermarket. Listen and number the rest of the products.

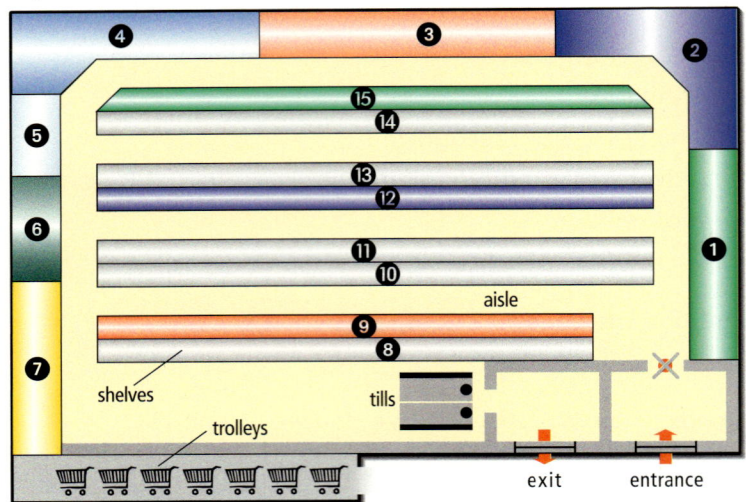

Shelf Products

- ❷ dairy products
- ❹ fish
- ○ frozen foods
- ○ fruit and vegetables
- ○ meat
- ❻ mineral water, soft drinks
- ❾ tea, coffee
- ○ tinned foods
- ⑫ toiletries
- ○ wines and spirits

B Pairwork. Where would you place these products in the supermarket? Why?

- ○ breakfast cereals
- ○ confectionery
- ○ rice and pasta
- ○ cleaning products
- ○ herbs, spices, sauces

C You are at the entrance to the supermarket. Ask a different partner where you can find two of these things.

spaghetti
chocolates
salt
cornflakes
washing powder

They're in the next aisle but one.

It's on the shelf above/below the coffee.

It's next to/opposite the fish counter.

D Which is the best supermarket in your area?

● **TALKING POINT**
Some people say that the small local shop is dying. Is it true? Does it matter?

Checklist!

UNIT 3

Grammar

A Conjunctions

1. There aren't any good shops where I live, _____ I often order clothes online.
2. I wouldn't use my credit card online, _____ everyone says it's safe.
3. My son always books his holidays online _____ he doesn't have to go to the travel agent's.
4. I don't think I'd book a holiday online _____ it was cheaper.

B Relative clauses

1. I buy the one _____ is cheapest.
2. I know some people _____ only buy clothes with the right brand names.

Phrases

Shopping

1. _____ I help you?
2. _____ you got anything for backache?
3. I'll _____ that, please.
4. Could you gift-_____ it for me, please?
5. Can I _____ them if they don't match my dress?
6. You could _____ this. It's very good.
7. These are very _____ value.
8. We haven't got any in stock, but I can _____ one for you.
9. Please _____ the receipt.
10. If you'd like to return them to us, we'll _____ them straightaway.
11. I'm afraid we don't _____ refunds.
12. I can _____ you a credit note.

Grammar: A1 so, A2 although, A3 so that, A4 even if, B1 which/that, B2 who/that

Phrases: 1 Can, 2 Have, 3 take, 4 wrap, 5 exchange, 6 try, 7 good, 8 order, 9 keep, 10 replace, 11 give, 12 give

UNIT 4 Revision

A Personal adjectives

1 Look at the three diagrams. Choose five adjectives to go with each diagram.

- A day in your life
- A person you know
- A place you've been to

boring	early	fashionable	horrible	pleasant
brilliant	effective	favourite	lovely	ridiculous
busy	elderly	forgetful	mad	superb
colourful	energetic	healthy	narrow	terrible
convenient	exciting	helpful	natural	thrilling
cosmopolitan	exotic	historic	perfect	well-known

2 Compare with a partner. Explain your choices.

B Odd one out

1 Four of the words in each line are stressed on the same syllable. Which is the odd one out?

     Oo   Oo   oO   Oo   Oo
1. busy • narrow • superb • thrilling • pleasant

2. effective • ridiculous • exotic • fashionable • forgetful

3. convenient • favourite • natural • colourful • healthy

2 Look through Units 1-3 again and collect another set of five words. Write them on the board. Can the rest of the class find the odd one out?

C Grammar dice

1 Pairwork. Look at the first card and shake the dice to select a verb form, then look at the second card and use the dice to get a conjunction. Write a true sentence with your words.

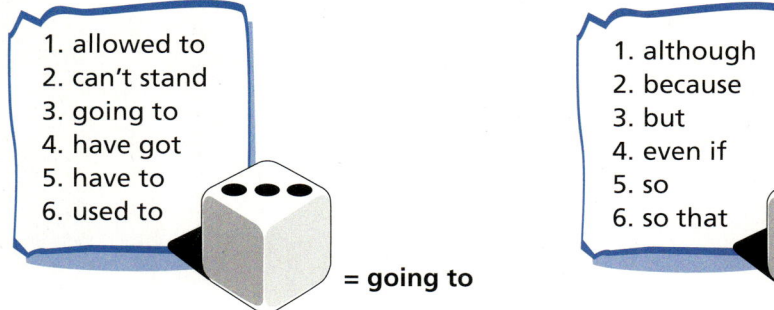

1. allowed to
2. can't stand
3. going to
4. have got
5. have to
6. used to

= going to

1. although
2. because
3. but
4. even if
5. so
6. so that

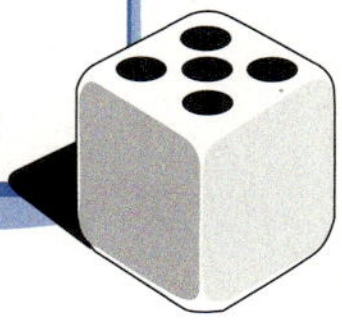

= so

2 Repeat the procedure twice. Give your sentences to another pair to check.

D Who's buying what?

1 Who says what? Mark these sentences C for customer or S for salesperson.

☐ Can I exchange it if …?
☐ Can I help you?
☐ Could you gift-wrap it for me, please?
☐ Have you got anything for …?
☐ Have you got them in a bigger size?
☐ Have you got your receipt, please?
☐ I can order one for you.
☐ I'd like a refund, please.
☐ I'll give you a credit note.
☐ We'll replace them straightaway.
☐ We've haven't got any in stock.

2 Choose a product and work out a dialogue. Play it for the rest of the class, but don't say what the product is. Can they guess?

E Picture story

1 Pairwork. Look through Units 1 – 3 again and find a picture you like.

2 Work out a story about the picture and tell it to the class.

UNIT 5 *You are what you wear*

1 What do you wear?

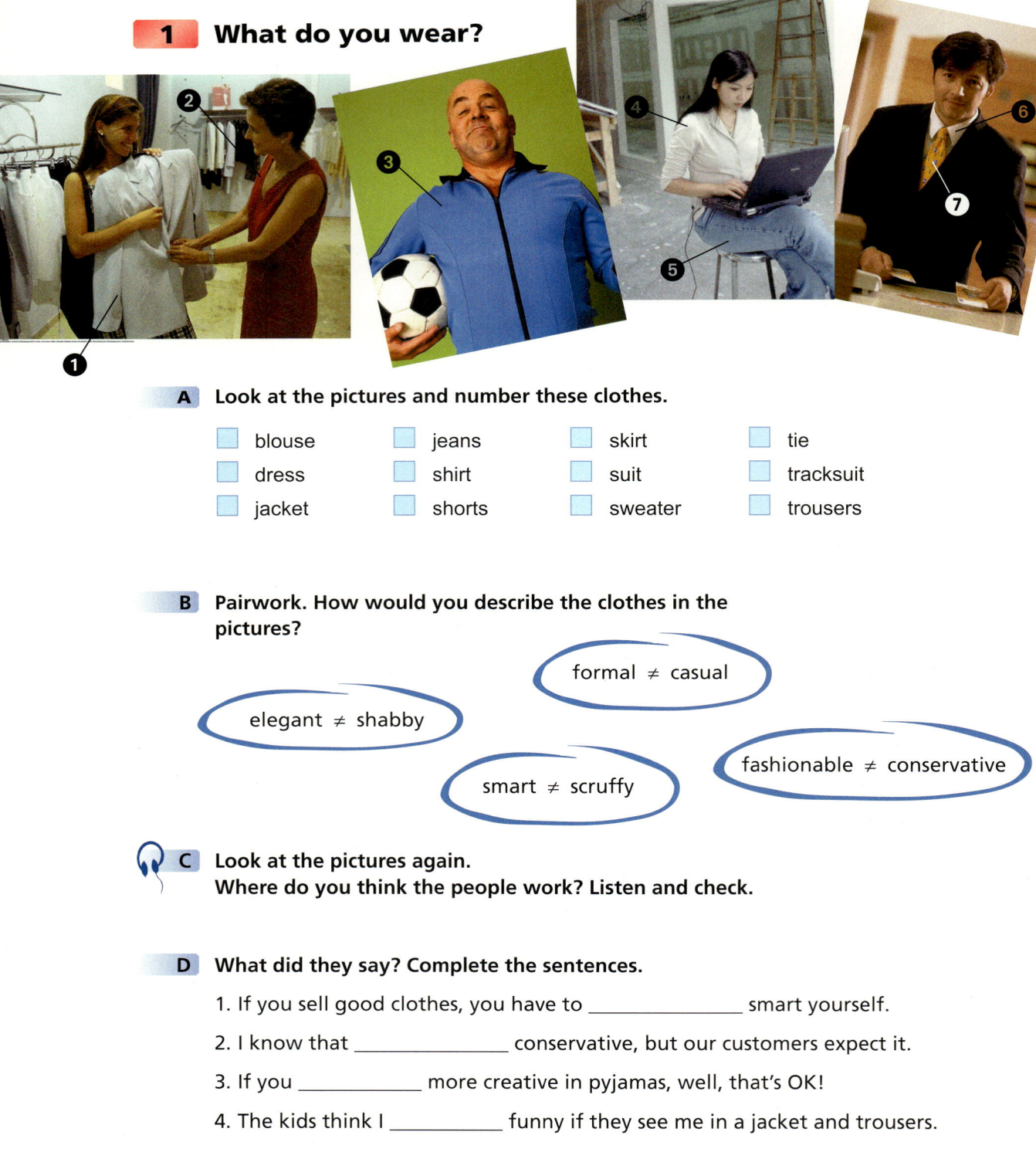

A Look at the pictures and number these clothes.

- ☐ blouse
- ☐ jeans
- ☐ skirt
- ☐ tie
- ☐ dress
- ☐ shirt
- ☐ suit
- ☐ tracksuit
- ☐ jacket
- ☐ shorts
- ☐ sweater
- ☐ trousers

B Pairwork. How would you describe the clothes in the pictures?

- formal ≠ casual
- elegant ≠ shabby
- smart ≠ scruffy
- fashionable ≠ conservative

C Look at the pictures again. Where do you think the people work? Listen and check.

D What did they say? Complete the sentences.

1. If you sell good clothes, you have to _____ smart yourself.
2. I know that _____ conservative, but our customers expect it.
3. If you _____ more creative in pyjamas, well, that's OK!
4. The kids think I _____ funny if they see me in a jacket and trousers.

E Complete the box.

> **The verbs of sense**
> The five verbs of sense (feel, look, smell, sound, taste) are followed by _____: She looks smart.
> Other verbs are followed by _____: She dresses smartly.

adjectives
adverbs

F Read the text and mark the correct words.

Women and trousers

If you asked a modern western woman why she wears trousers, she would probably be surprised by your question. Trousers are practical when you're working, they're warm, they feel comfortable / comfortably and can look smart / smartly. Well, only a century ago things were different. Women wore skirts and men wore trousers and that was that. It was only in the First World War that many women began to wear trousers because they had to do men's work. After that women began to wear them for sports or if they wanted to dress casual / casually. But they didn't wear trousers when they had to dress formal / formally until the 1970s. Even now there are still companies and schools in Britain and the United States which prefer their female employees and students to wear skirts.

G Interview a partner.
What do they normally wear in these situations? Why?

at work
at home in the evening
outside in cold weather
for sightseeing on a hot day
when visiting friends

> He wears …
> because he needs to feel comfortable.

You are what you wear — UNIT 5

2 I've got nothing to wear!

A Read the descriptions, then write the catalogue numbers under the pictures.

Floral blouse
100% silk
Colours: blue/cream, green/cream
Sizes: S, M, L
Cat. no.: TL 5873   € 35.99

Plain cardigan with buttons and belt
50% wool, 50% acrylic. Machine washable
Colours: beige, burgundy, green
Sizes: 8/10, 12/14, 14/16
Cat. no.: BT 4342   € 38.50

Striped trousers with side pockets
75% linen, 25% viscose
Colour: black, grey. Sizes: 12, 14, 16, 18
Cat. no.: RA 8692   € 41.99

Checked shirt, short-sleeve
100% Cotton
Colours: blue/white, brown/white, red/white
Sizes: M, L, XL
Cat. no.: AF 2465   € 26.25

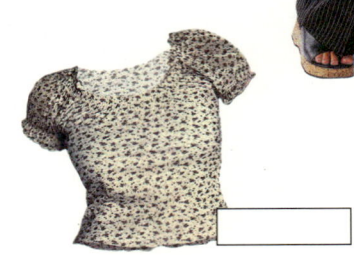

B Find more words in 2A.

Materials: cotton, _____

Colours: blue, _____

Patterns: checked, _____

C Listen and complete this order form.

Cat. No.	Item	Colour	Size	Qty	Price
	shirt			2	
R A 8 6 9 2		black			€41.99
			M	1	

D How could you say these things in other words?

"Blue **suits** you."
"They'll **go with** my new jeans."
"If they don't **fit**, we can always send them back."

> too tight ≠ too loose

E Describe a favourite item of clothing. Why do you like it?

3 Uniforms

A What sorts of people wear uniforms in your country? Why do they wear them?

You are what you wear

UNIT 5

B Read the following opinions. Match each one with an opposite point of view.

1. "When you get up in the morning, it's nice if you don't have to think about what you're going to put on," says Julie (14). She wears exactly what everybody else wears at her school in Washington, DC. Each school day, she wears a white shirt, black shoes, and a red skirt.

2. "I think it lowers the cost of clothes. Kids don't think about clothes as much when they're all wearing the same thing," an education official in the USA says.

3. "I don't like wearing my uniform because it's not the latest fashion, and it makes me look like a little kid," says 12-year-old Anthony, and most school children in the UK agree, according to a BBC report.

4. "It costs hundreds of dollars to buy school uniforms for two or three children. If they don't have the newest school uniform, other children will laugh at them." (A mother in Canada)

C There are a lot of "two-word verbs" in English. How many can you find in 3B? Do you know any more?

get up, _____

D Group work. Write down arguments for or against uniforms. Compare with another group. Who has the best arguments?

- **TALKING POINT**
  The title of this unit is "You are what you wear". What do you think it means? Do you agree?

"You can't judge a book by its cover!"

37

4 Body decorations

- perfume
- piercing
- tattoo
- make-up
- jewellery

A Match the pictures and the definitions. Write the missing definition.

1. ornaments which are often made of valuable metals and precious stones
2. a piece of metal or precious stone which is attached to the skin or a part of the body
3. coloured substances which are used on the face to change the appearance
4. a design which is made by pricking little holes in the skin and filling them with dye
5. _____

B Are these sentences true (T) or false (F)? Listen and check.

1. People have probably always used make-up. ☐
2. They have used perfume for at least 5000 years. ☐
3. Tattooing first became popular in the 20th century. ☐
4. Sailors wore earrings to help them see better. ☐

> B.C. = before Christ
> A.D. = Anno Domini

C Complete the box.

> The **Past Simple** is used to talk about things that happened in the _____:
> Egyptians **had** tattoos four thousand years ago.
>
> The **Present Perfect** is used to connect the past to the _____:
> People **have decorated** their bodies for thousands of years / since 3000 B.C.

D Pairwork. Think of someone who has changed their appearance. Write some questions for them on a piece of paper.

Have you ...?
Why did you ...?

> to change your hairstyle
> to dye your hair
> to have a facelift
> to lose / to put on weight

38

5 I like your scarf!

A Answer the questions.
Compare with a partner.

What sorts of compliment do people pay each other in your country?

Do men pay women compliments about the way they look? Why? Why not?

Do women pay men compliments? If not, why not?

Wow!

B Organize these sentences into two different conversations, then listen and check.

No, I bought it on holiday last year.
Oh, do you like it?
Yes, it's really neat, isn't it?
I like your scarf. Is it new?
Wow, that's a trendy mobile!
Thanks. I'm glad you like it.
Yes, it is. It's very practical, too.
It's lovely. That colour really suits you.

I like your scarf.
Is it new?

Wow, that's a trendy mobile!

C Pairwork. Choose one of the conversations and change some of the details. Pay compliments to your partner.

D Complete this pronunciation rule.

If one word in a sentence ends in a _____ (e.g. *is*) and the next begins with a _____ (e.g. *it*), then there is no break between the two words (*is͜ it*).

vowel
consonant

E Say these sentences aloud. Mark the words which sound connected, then listen and check.

1. It lowers the cost of clothes.
2. Other children will laugh at them.
3. They started using perfume.
4. How often have you changed your hairstyle?
5. I bought it on holiday.

UNIT 5

You are what you wear

6 Valuables

A Which of these things do you normally take with you when you go out? Where do you normally keep them?

- diary ☐
- driving licence ☐
- glasses ☐
- ID card ☐
- keys ☐
- mobile phone ☐
- passport ☐
- umbrella ☐
- walkman ☐
- watch ☐

> briefcase
> handbag
> pocket
> purse
> rucksack
> wallet

B Listen and mark the correct information.

1. The woman knows / doesn't know where she lost her purse.
2. Her purse is / isn't at the lost property office.
3. She has reported / is going to report the loss to the police.
4. She left her purse in a park / a shop.

In Britain people do not have identification cards. People who want to travel have to have passports. When they need to show identification, they use their driving licence or birth certificate.

C Look at these problems. What advice would you give?

"I can't find my glasses."
"Oh no! I've lost my key!"
"Someone's stolen my passport."

> You'd better …
> If I were you, I'd …
> Why don't you …?

● **TALKING POINT**
Have you ever lost anything important and found it again?
Do you have any tricks to stop yourself losing things?

Checklist!

Grammar

A The verbs of sense

1. to feel / to l_____ / to smell / to s_____ / to taste
2. She looks smart. She dresses smart_____.

B Past Simple

1. I bought it on holiday _____ year.
2. The Egyptians had tattoos four thousand years _____.

C Present Perfect

1. People _____ probably always used make-up.
2. People have decorated their bodies _____ thousands of years.
3. They've used perfume _____ at least 3000 B.C.

D Two-word verbs

1. When you get _____ in the morning, …
2. You don't have to think _____ what you're going to put _____.
3. It make me look _____ a little kid.
4. Other children will laugh _____ them.

Phrases

A Giving and receiving compliments

1. That colour really _____ you.
2. Thanks. I'm _____ you like it.

B Giving advice

1. You'd _____ phone the lost property office.
2. If I were you, I _____ cancel your credit card.
3. Why _____ you ask the ice cream man?

Grammar: A1 look – sound, A2 ly, B1 last, B2 ago, C1 have, C2 for, C3 since, D1 up, D2 about – on, D3 like, D4 at

Phrases: A1 suits, A2 glad, B1 better, B2 'd, B3 don't

UNIT 6 *Enjoy!*

1 Eating habits

A Pairwork. How many kinds of food can you think of in three minutes?

B Listen to someone talking about what they eat, when and where. Make notes and compare with a partner.

	Breakfast	Lunch	Afternoon	Evening meal
What?				
What time?				
Where?				

C Complete the box.

> **Time and place**
> Adverbs of frequency (always, often, never, etc.) normally come _____ the main verb in a sentence: *I **usually** have breakfast at work*. Other time expressions usually come _____ of the sentence: *I **always** go out **at lunchtime***. The time phrase usually comes _____ the place: *I have another coffee in my office **in the afternoon***.

after
at the end
before

D Add words or phrases to these sentences to make them true for you.

I have a cup of coffee.   I have breakfast.   I eat a hot meal.

I always have a cup of coffee at work at about eight o'clock in the morning.

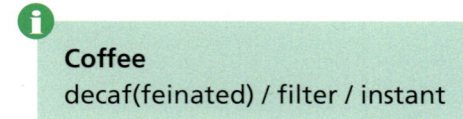

Coffee
decaf(feinated) / filter / instant

Unit 6 — Enjoy!

2 A little bit of what you fancy does you good

A Look at the diagram. Which foods go where?

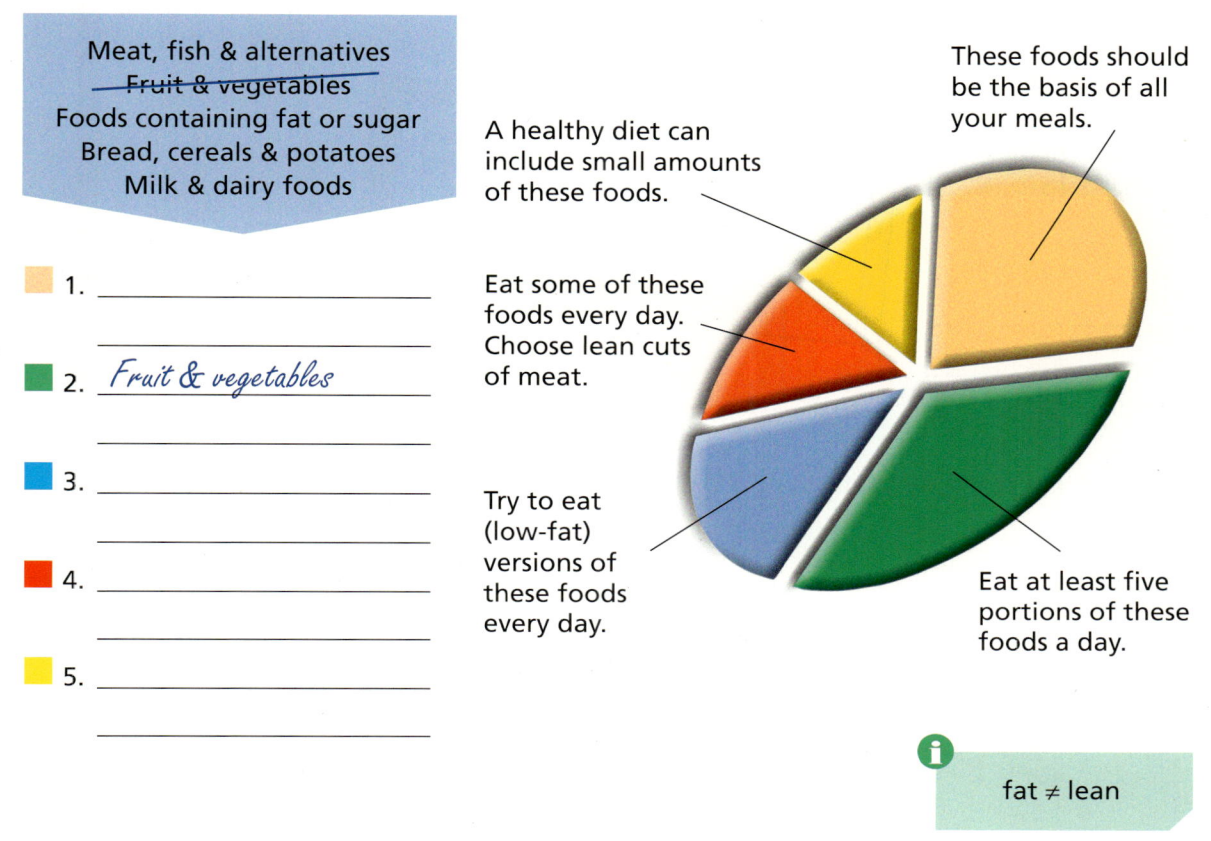

> Meat, fish & alternatives
> ~~Fruit & vegetables~~
> Foods containing fat or sugar
> Bread, cereals & potatoes
> Milk & dairy foods

1. _____
2. *Fruit & vegetables*
3. _____
4. _____
5. _____

- These foods should be the basis of all your meals.
- A healthy diet can include small amounts of these foods.
- Eat some of these foods every day. Choose lean cuts of meat.
- Try to eat (low-fat) versions of these foods every day.
- Eat at least five portions of these foods a day.

ℹ️ fat ≠ lean

B Read the text and check.

For your daily health, you need to eat a lot of food that is rich in carbohydrates, for example rice and potatoes. You should also make sure you eat plenty of vegetables and fruit as they are particularly rich in vitamins and roughage. You do not need much protein; you can get enough by eating dairy products, meat or meat replacements like tofu, and legumes such as beans and peas. The diagram also shows that it's important not to eat too much fat or sugar. In fact we do not need to eat any cakes or chocolate at all but, as the saying goes, "A little bit of what you fancy does you good!"

C Read the text again. Underline all the "quantity expressions".

For example:
… you need to eat <u>a lot of</u> food that is …

D Interview a partner. How does their diet compare with the experts' advice?

3 Recipes

A Match the food and the instructions.

1. soup
2. sausages
3. apple pie

Fry or grill until brown. Serve with chips or mashed potatoes and peas.

Best before 12.09

Pour 900 millilitres of water into a saucepan and boil it. Empty the contents into the boiling water and stir. Cover and simmer for five minutes.

Suitable for vegetarians

* Bake in a microwave for six minutes or place in the centre of a preheated oven and bake for 30 minutes at 180°C.

STORE IN A COOL DRY PLACE

B Look at the instructions again. How many cookery verbs can you find?

C You are going to hear part of a cookery programme. Listen and complete the list of ingredients.

Classic recipes

Chicken, leek and ham pie

• *For the pastry*
250 g flour

_____ g butter
1 egg

____ tbs water
a pinch of salt

• *For the filling*

_____ g chicken
2 medium-sized leeks
1 thick slice ham

_____ ml white wine
300 ml milk
salt and pepper

"250 grammes **of** flour"
"300 millilitres **of** milk"
"3 tablespoons **of** water"
"one slice **of** ham"

D Number these instructions in the correct order, then listen to the rest of the recipe and check.

1	Preheat the oven to 180° C.
☐	Pour the sauce over the chicken and add the ham. Put the mixture into a flat pie dish.
☐	Cut the chicken and ham into 2 cm cubes. Fry the chicken until it is brown all over, then add the wine and cook for 10 minutes.
☐	Serve with new potatoes and fresh spring vegetables such as peas or asparagus.
☐	Make the pastry and cover the filling with it. Brush the pastry with egg and bake the pie for 35-40 minutes.
☐	Now cut the leeks into thin slices and cook them in butter for 5-6 minutes. Add some flour, milk, salt and pepper to make a thick sauce.
7	Enjoy!

E Listen to the recording for 3D again. Which of these "sequencers" did the speakers use?

☐ after that   ☐ lastly   ☐ then
☐ before we do that ☐ next   ☐ to finish it off
☐ first / first of all ☐ now

F Pairwork. Tell your partner how to cook or make something. Use at least five of the sequencers in 3E.

According to a recent survey of British eating habits, the average Briton's favourite food is not the traditional "roast beef and two veg", nor the famous fish 'n' chips, nor even the world-conquering hamburger. No, the one dish that the Brits would really miss is … curry. Which explains why there are so many good Indian restaurants in the country. Or is it the other way round?

> ● **TALKING POINT**
> "Too many cooks spoil the broth." What do you think this saying means? Do you agree with it? Is it true in everyday life?

Enjoy! **UNIT 6**

4   Invitations

A Some friends are going to invite you to their home. What would you like to be invited for and why?

- afternoon tea
- a barbecue
- dinner
- morning coffee
- Sunday brunch

tea [ti:] *n*
1. a drink made by pouring hot water onto dried and cut leaves.
2. a light meal eaten in the late afternoon, usually with sandwiches, cakes and tea to drink.
3. an informal cooked meal eaten in the evening. Also called *supper*.

B Read this dialogue. What do you think the missing words could be? Listen and check.

Jackie: _____ come over to our house on Sunday? We're having a few friends round for a barbecue at about six.

Lisa: Oh, _____, but I'm afraid we can't.

Rod: We've promised to go to my parents for the day and we won't be back till late.

Jackie: _____! We'll have to find another time.

Lisa: Yes, that would be nice.

Duncan: _____ coming for dinner the Saturday after instead?

Jackie: Yes, _____ come then?

Rod: _____. What time?

Jackie: Oh, around seven.

Lisa: Fine.

Jackie: Good. _____ seeing you then.

Rod: Yes. Thank you.

C Decide on a day and a time and then invite people in your class to your home. Who can come?

5 Dinner with friends

A Mark the correct information, then listen to an interview about eating out in Canada and check.

1. you ought to = you should / shouldn't
2. you oughtn't to = you shouldn't / don't have to
3. you needn't = you don't have to / shouldn't
4. you may = you can / should

B What advice did the expert give?
Complete these sentences with words from 5A.

1. You _____ arrive a little late.
2. You _____ take a gift.
3. You _____ tell the host before the meal if there's anything you can't eat.
4. You _____ refuse a second helping.
5. You _____ smoke without asking.

C Group work. Write some advice for someone who is visiting your area.

You ought to help with the washing up.

D Match the sentences on the left with the ones on the right, then listen and check.

1. Would you like to try some of this?
2. Could you pass me the salt, please?
3. Would you like some more dessert?
4. Can I get you another glass of wine?
5. I'm afraid we must be going.
6. Thank you very much for a lovely evening.

a. I'd better not, thank you. I'm driving.
b. Thank you for coming.
c. Mm, yes please!
d. Oh, do you have to?
e. It's delicious, but I really couldn't!
f. Yes, of course. Here you are.

1 c   2 ☐   3 ☐   4 ☐   5 ☐   6 ☐

E Group work. Practise three scenes: 1. when the guests arrive, 2. at the meal table and 3. when they leave. Perform one of your scenes for the rest of the class.

6 Intercultural experiences

A Listen and complete the story.

"A few years ago in Australia some students invited me to a party on Christmas Day. I arrived with my bottle at about eight thirty in the evening and then I discovered that the party _____ started at lunchtime and most of the guests _____ already left and gone to the beach.
So, anyway, when I _____ eaten some food I joined them on the beach and went for a swim, too.
It was a lovely Christmas but now I never accept an invitation without asking exactly what time I should come!"

B Complete the box.

> **Past Perfect**
>
> The Past Perfect is formed with *had* + the past _____ of the verb: *(the party)* **had started**. It shows that one thing happened _____ another thing in the _____:
>
> *When I arrived, the guests had already left.*

before
participle
past

C Now read this story. Mark the correct tenses, then listen and check.

One year when he was visiting China, some friends invited / had invited him out to dinner at a local restaurant. They ate / had eaten the starters when the waitress brought / had brought them some bowls of clear soup with lemon. He just tasted / had just tasted a little when he noticed / had noticed that everyone else was washing their fingers in it. He was very embarrassed!

> ● **TALKING POINT**
> What was the most enjoyable meal or evening out which you have ever had? Have you had any embarrassing or interesting experiences?

Checklist! UNIT 6

Grammar

A Quantity

1. You need a lot _____ food that is rich in carbohydrates.
2. Make sure you eat plenty _____ vegetables.
3. You can get _____ protein by eating dairy products.
4. It's important not to eat too _____ fat or sugar.
5. A little bit _____ what you fancy does you good!

B Modal verbs

1. If you're invited to dinner, you _____ to arrive a little late.
2. You _____n't take a gift. / You _____ refuse a second helping.
3. You _____ n't to smoke without asking.

C Past Perfect

When I arrived, the guests _____ already left.

Phrases

A Invitations

1. Would you _____ to come over to our house on Sunday?
2. We'd _____ to, but I'm afraid we can't. / _____ a shame!
3. How _____ coming for dinner the Saturday after instead?
4. _____ don't you come then? / That _____ be great.

B At dinner

1. Would you like to _____ some of this?
2. It's delicious, but I really _____!
3. Could you _____ me the salt, please?
4. Can I _____ you another glass of wine?
5. I'd _____ not, thank you. I'm driving.
6. I'm afraid we must _____ going.
7. Oh, do you _____ to? / _____ you for coming.

Grammar: A1 of, A2 of, A3, enough, A4 much, A5 of, B1 ought, B2 need, B3 may, B4 ought, C had

Phrases: A1 like, A2 love – That's, A3 about, A4 Why – would, B1 try, B2 couldn't, B3 pass, B4 get, B5 better, B6 be, B7 have – Thank

49

UNIT 7 — *The media and me*

1 The media age

A Number these things in the order they were invented.

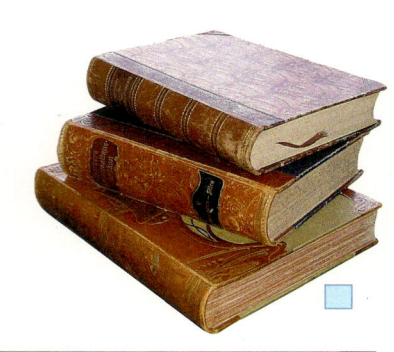

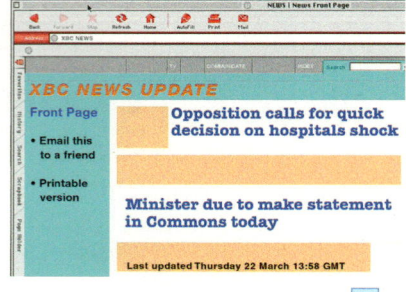

B Complete these sentences with things from 1A, then listen and check.

1. The first real _____ in English was the London Gazette, which was published from 1666.

2. The BBC broadcast its first _____ programme in 1922.

3. The _____ was developed for military communications in the 1960s.

4. _____ were printed in China as early as the 9th century A.D.

5. The first colour _____ programme was broadcast in the USA by CBS in 1951.

C Where would you look for information about these things? Compare with a partner.

the weather forecast	a celebrity scandal
the latest share prices	a TV programme
the traffic news	a local concert
the sports results	last-minute holidays

> **on** TV / the radio / the internet
> **in** the newspaper / a magazine

D Many households now have at least two televisions, a DVD player, two or three radios and CD players, and several computers. Which of these things have you got? Which of them would you miss most, and why?

2 TV and radio programmes

A Match the types of programme with the definitions.

1. A documentary — is an ongoing story about the lives of a group of people.
2. In a quiz show — shows the same characters in amusing situations.
3. A sitcom — is a set of programmes of the same kind with the same title.
4. A soap — people try to answer questions.
5. A series — presents detailed facts about a particular subject.

Nowadays most "soap operas" are shown on TV, but the first ones were broadcast by American radio stations in the 1930s. They were sponsored by soap manufacturers, which is how they got their name. The longest-running soap on British radio is "The Archers", about a farming community in the English Midlands. It has been broadcast since 1951.

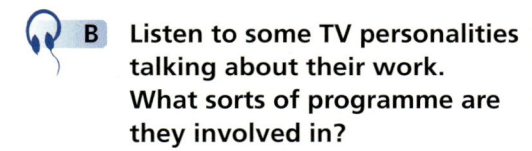

B Listen to some TV personalities talking about their work. What sorts of programme are they involved in?

1. _____
2. _____
3. _____
4. _____
5. _____

C Mark the correct information, then listen again and check.
1. The stories should not sound too depressing / depressed.
2. It's no good if you aren't interesting / interested in it.
3. It's never boring / bored.
4. Sometimes they're so exciting / excited that it takes a while to calm them down.

> The programme is exciting.
> The children are excited.

D Pairwork. Talk about the programmes that you watch on TV and find one you both like or dislike. Write a sentence or two explaining why.

UNIT 7 — The media and me

3 It's your choice

A Answer the questions, then compare with a partner.

How is TV paid for in your country?

How many TV channels do you get?

When are commercials usually shown?

How do you know that the programme has stopped and the commercials have started?

What do you do during the commercial breaks?

> TV
> ad / commercial / spot

B Listen to some other people answering the questions in 3A. Make notes. Are their answers the same as yours?

C Complete the box.

> **The Passive**
> The Passive is used when what happens is more important than who does it. It is formed with the **past participle** of the verb plus the appropriate tense of **to be**:
>
> Most "soap operas" _are_ shown on TV.
>
> The first ones _were_ sponsored by soap manufacturers in the 1930s.
>
> "The Archers" _has been_ broadcast since 1951.

TV in Britain

If you want to have a TV in Britain, you have to pay an annual licence fee. This pays for the programmes which are made by the BBC. Commercial television is financed by advertising. Television advertising in Britain is restricted to an average of between seven and nine minutes per hour. There is no advertising in some programmes, such as short children's programmes. Cigarette advertising on TV was banned in the UK in 1965. Sponsorship of some TV programmes has been allowed since 1991 but this is strictly regulated. Pay TV was introduced in the late 1980s.

D How many Passives can you find in the text above?

E Group work. Choose two pay TV channels to subscribe to.

ORBIT

Subscribe to Orbit Digital TV now

Save 50% !

Choose our Family or Professionals Package today.
Call 0117 586858 for more info.

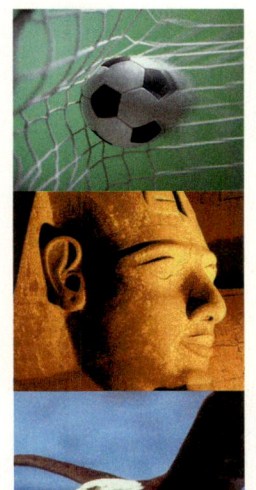

World Sports
World Sports offers full coverage of all major sports events around the world. We cover it all from international athletics to show jumping, and bring you the latest results as soon as they come through.

History Plus
Subscribe to History Plus for high-quality programmes on every aspect of life in the past. You don't have to be a history freak to be fascinated by our colourful and informative programmes, supported by world-class historians. It's history on your doorstep.

The Nature Channel
For just a small sum you could be enjoying our most exciting nature programmes whenever you want. The Nature Channel offers an insight into the fascinating world of nature – swim with the otters or watch the mating pattern of bird-eating spiders as if you were there.

Film 24
How often do you wish you could find a really good film to watch just when you've got time? Now your problem is solved. Our film channel guarantees you top quality feature films 24 hours a day. No more running to the video store or channel-hopping in frustration – just switch on Film 24 and sit back and enjoy.

Globe News
Now you don't need to worry about not being up-to date because you've missed the news. Our news channel offers news and views 24 hours a day, with specialist business sections and background information for the busy working person.

How about subscribing to the … channel?

That's a good idea. Let's do that.

I'd be more interested in the … channel.

I'd prefer the … channel.

> **TALKING POINT**
> "Children must have access to TV in order to grow up normally."

The media and me — UNIT 7

4 What's the news?

A Read these three headlines. Who do you think will be mentioned in the stories?

Drug-related crime still rising

More money for teachers

Dear Britain

B Match the headlines with these stories. Which is good news and which is bad news?

1. The government announced yesterday that they would create 2,000 new teaching jobs this year. A spokeswoman for the teachers' unions welcomed the government's decision but said that it did not solve the real problem. Too many good teachers were still leaving the profession because the pay was too low, she said.

2. New figures show that crime is falling, especially in inner city areas. A police spokesman said that the number of violent crimes had fallen by 6%, burglaries by 8% and car thefts by 6%. Only drug-related crimes had risen in the twelve months before the investigation, he said.

3. The British Tourist Association announced yesterday that tourists were spending record sums in Britain. However, they explained that this was not because more tourists were coming into the country, but because prices for tourist attractions had risen significantly since last year. 51% of those questioned said they would definitely return to Britain in the near future.

C Look at the articles again and complete these sentences.

1. "Tourists are spending more."   They said that tourists _were spending_ more.
2. "Car thefts fell by 6%."   He said that thefts _had fallen_ by 6%.
3. "Prices have risen."   They said that prices _had risen_.
4. "We will create more jobs."   They said that they _would create_ more jobs.

D What's the news today? Who said what?

5 Private and confidential

"I do not believe that the reading public wants nothing but trash and sensationalism. A newspaper ... must inform, entertain and educate ..."
(Lord Kelmsley, Chairman of Allied Newspapers Ltd, June 1937)

UNIT 7 — The media and me

A Do you agree with Lord Kelmsley?

- I (don't) think that …
- In my opinion, … If you ask me, …
- It depends on the paper. If …

B Look at the headlines and answer the questions.

1. Which of the stories do you think most people would read?
2. Which of the stories mentions a person's private life?
3. Which of the stories should be published?

Headlines:
- Minister's new girlfriend
- Pop star sells home
- Priest's drug problem
- TV celebrity's divorce
- 90 die in floods

> They should publish it.
> It should **be** publish**ed**.

C Pairwork. Do you agree with these statements? If not, change them so that you do.

1. A journalist's job is to find out all they can about people who are in the news.
2. Celebrities can't expect to have a private life.
3. Private photographs of famous people shouldn't be published without permission.
4. Politicians and their families should be protected from the media.

6 A news programme

A Do you watch the news regularly?
Do you have a favourite news programme?
Why do you like it?

B What sorts of topic would you expect to find in the national TV news? Which topics are usually given most time?

> politics
> culture

C Look at the news items below. In what order would they normally appear in the TV news?

- ☐ Southern Europe is having its longest drought in living memory, according to EU experts.

- ☐ "I have taken drugs," admits international 100m runner.

- ☐ The heads of five South American states met in Buenos Aires yesterday to discuss ways of improving links between their countries.

- ☐ The economy will grow by about 2% in the next year, according to a recent survey.

- ☐ Senior cabinet minister acknowledges frustration with government policy. "There is a deep split in the party," he says.

D Group work. Design your own five-minute news programme.

Include:
a commercial before the programme starts.
a live report from one of your correspondents.
sponsorship for the weather.

E Present your news programme to the class.

> ● **TALKING POINT**
> "No news is good news." Should there be more good news on TV?

Checklist! UNIT 7

Grammar

A The Passive

1. Infinitive: Private photographs shouldn't _____ published.
2. Present Simple: Commercial TV _____ financed by advertising.
3. Past Simple: Cigarette advertising on TV _____ banned in 1965.
4. Present Perfect: Sponsorship _____ allowed since 1991.

B Reported speech

1. "There is a deep split in the party."
   The minister said there _____ a deep split in the party.
2. "The heads of five states met in Buenos Aires."
   The newsreader said that the heads of five states _____ met in Buenos Aires.
3. "I have taken drugs."
   The runner admitted that he _____ taken drugs.
4. "The econonomy will grow by about 2%."
   The survey forecast that the economy _____ grow by about 2%.

Phrases

A Suggesting and responding to suggestions

How about subscribing to the film channel?

1. That's a good idea. _____ do that.
2. I'd _____ the sports channel.
3. I'd _____ more interested in the nature channel.

B Giving opinions

What do you think?

1. I (don't) think that …
2. In my _____ , …
3. If you _____ me, …
4. It _____ on the paper. If …

Grammar: A1 be, A2 is, A3 was, A4 has been, B1 was, B2 had, B3 had, B4 would
Phrases: A1 Let's, A2 prefer, A3 be, B2 opinion, B3 ask, B4 depends

UNIT 8 *Revision*

A Word search

1 Pairwork. Add words to these lists. Time limit: 5 minutes!

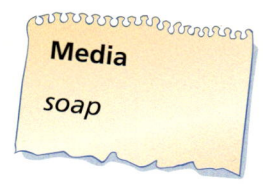

- Clothes: skirt
- Food: cake
- Valuables: handbag
- Media: soap

2 Compare with another pair. You get one point for each word on your list that they haven't got.

B What's the saying?

1 Break this "word wall" up into separate words, then organize them into three English sayings.

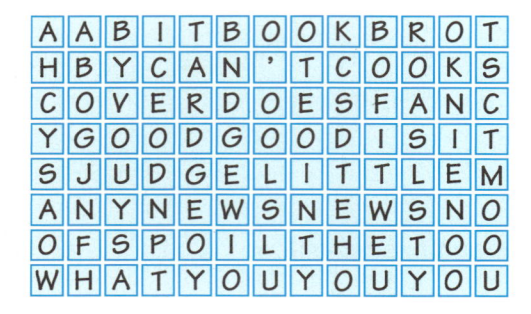

```
A A B I T B O O K B R O T
H B Y C A N ' T C O O K S
C O V E R D O E S F A N C
Y G O O D G O O D I S I T
S J U D G E L I T T L E M
A N Y N E W S N E W S N O
O F S P O I L T H E T O O
W H A T Y O U Y O U Y O U
```

1. *You* _____.
2. *A* _____.
3. *No* _____.
4. *Too* _____.

2 Match the picture with one of the sayings. Think of a picture for each of the other sayings.

C Report them!

1 Think of three things that other people have said during this lesson. Write them down, then report them to the rest of the class.

2 Did anyone report something that you didn't? If so, write it down and change it back into direct speech!

D Rules for dinner guests

1 Complete these rules.

1. YOU OUGHT TO ARRIVE A LITTLE LATE.
2. YOU NEEDN'T TAKE A GIFT.
3. YOU MAY REFUSE A SECOND HELPING.
4. YOU OUGHTN'T TO SMOKE WITHOUT ASKING.

2 Change each of the rules into its opposite.

1. You oughtn't to arrive a little late
2. You need take a Gift
3. You ought to Refuse a second Helping
4. You ought to smoke without Asking

3 Where do you think the changed rules could be good advice?

E Celebrity dinner

1 Choose one of these people.
- a famous sport star
- a well-known politician
- a popular entertainer

2 One of you is the celebrity, who has invited the rest of you to dinner.
- What are you going to wear?
- What do you think will be served for dinner?
- What will you talk about during the dinner?

3 It's dinner-time! Make conversation with your host/hostess.
- Ask them some questions.
- Pay them some compliments.
- Give them some advice.

Revision UNIT 8

UNIT 9 House and home

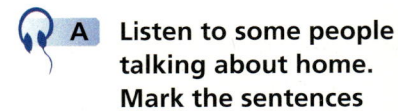

1 What is home?

A Listen to some people talking about home. Mark the sentences true (T) or false (F).

Interview 1
1. She has French citizenship.
2. She spent her childhood in America.
3. She feels that America is no longer home.
4. When she talks about America she says "back home".

Interview 2
1. He did his training 200 miles from his hometown.
2. He says he's only got one home.
3. He says home is more important when you're young and not settled.
4. He feels at home when he stays with his girlfriend at weekends.

B Complete these sentences. Compare with a partner.

Home is the place where my …
Home is the place where I feel …

C Look at the statistics. Why do you think there is such a difference between men and women?

Maybe it's because …
It's probably because …
It must be because …

People still living with their parents between the ages of 25 and 29

	Men	Women
Italy	66%	44.1%
UK	20.8%	10.8%

D What is the situation in your country? Is it more like Italy or the UK?

2 The most important thing is …

A Match these descriptions with the things in the pictures.
1. Brighten any room with these lightweight cotton curtains.
2. Country-style: basketwork armchair with matching coffee table.
3. Keep your bedroom stylish and tidy with this classic wardrobe.
4. Functional: steel-framed dining table with four chairs.
5. Also in this range of bedroom furniture: an elegant chest of drawers.
6. Colourful two-seater sofa makes up into guest bed in minutes.
7. The solution to your storage problems: built-in cupboards.
8. The ultimate luxury: a pure new wool carpet.

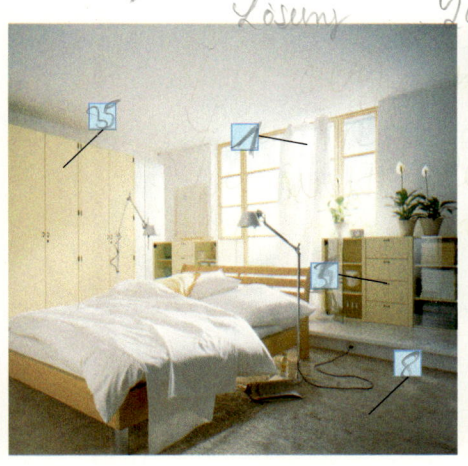

House and home — UNIT 9

B Which of the things in 2A would you expect to find in a living room?

C What makes a living room comfortable, in your opinion? Compare with a partner.

- The most important thing for me is …
- In my opinion, … is essential.
- A living room without … just wouldn't feel right to me.
- Exactly.
- Yes, but what about …?
- Oh, d'you think so?

on the left / on the right
in the corner / in the middle
next to / between / opposite
above / below

D Pairwork. Draw a plan of your living room. Explain it to your partner.

3 Do-it-yourself

A Match the verbs with the nouns.

1. to make _____
2. to strip _____
3. to install _____
4. to paint _____
5. to clean _____

> a carpet
> some curtains
> a socket
> a wall
> wallpaper

B Read the text and check your answers to 2A.

"A few months ago we decided to redecorate our living room. We stripped the old wallpaper and painted the walls and ceiling a nice light cream colour. The TV was in a rather inconvenient part of the room so we had a new socket installed at the same time.

We had the carpet cleaned professionally and Rachel made some colourful floral curtains which really brightened up the room. Our sofa was beginning to look a bit worn, but it was still very comfortable, so we decided to have some new covers made for it and now it looks great.

I found a rather nice antique mirror which we hung above the fireplace. Finally Rachel bought a new white lampshade and a couple of Japanese vases and now the room's as good as new!"

> ⓘ light ≠ dark

C Read the text again. What did Rachel and her husband do themselves? What did other people do for them?

D Complete the box.

> **to have something done**
> This form is used to talk about things which we pay other people to do for us:
> We didn't clean the carpet ourselves. We _____ it _____ by a local firm.

E What have you had done recently? What are you going to have done in the near future? Write some sentences.

> We had our TV repaired last month.
> I'm going to have my car serviced tomorrow.

F Pairwork. Look at these bathrooms. What would you change? What would you do yourself? What would you have done?

- shower curtain
- bath
- washbasin
- tiles
- shelf
- towel rail

"I'd paint the bathroom myself."

"I'd have the tiles replaced."

Seven out of ten homes in Britain, and eight out of ten in Ireland, are owned by the people who live in them. Most people would rather have a home of their own than pay rent to a landlord, so they buy a cheap, small house or flat as soon as they can. To do this they normally have to get a long-term bank loan, called a "mortgage". Sometimes they let a room or two to someone else and the income from the rent helps them to pay the mortgage. It's quite usual to have owned two or three different houses in a lifetime.

landlord/landlady ≠ tenant

- **TALKING POINT**
  What are the advantages and disadvantages of being a home owner and a tenant, in your view?

House and home — UNIT 9

4   A new home?

A   Interview a partner. Report something interesting.

How many times have you moved house?
If you could live anywhere, where would you move to?
If you had to move now, what would you do yourself and what would you have done?

B   Choose one of these flats or houses to move to. Explain why you chose it.

Fully-furnished studio flat 1 bedroom **€460 pcm**
Recently redecorated. South-facing balcony. Lift. Central location. No pets.

Unfurnished flat 2 bedrooms **€795 pcm**
Large sunny living room. Use of garden. 3 mins on foot to shops.

Terraced house 3 bedrooms **€1250 pcm**
Unfurnished, CH, double-glazing. Quiet location. 8 km. from motorway.

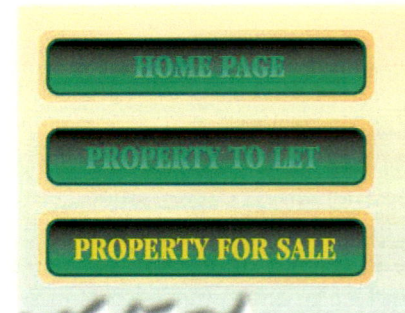

Ground floor flat 2 bedrooms **€115,000**
Stylish open-plan kitchen/living room, guest toilet. Underground garage.

Semi-detached house 3 bedrooms (2 double/1 single) **€180,000** Fitted kitchen, refitted bathroom, loft, patio. Covered parking space for one vehicle.

Detached house 4 bedrooms **€390,000**
Utility room, conservatory, garage, garden. Fine view of city. In need of updating.

C   Pairwork. Write an ad for another home.

pcm = per calender month
CH = central heating

D   When you move, it's a good idea to pack a box with things you will need for the first night in your new home. What would you put in your box?

5 Neighbours

A How many neighbours have you got? Where do they live?

B Look at this survey about neighbours in Britain.
What do you think the figures were? Listen and check.

Good neighbours?	
1. _____ meet their neighbours soon after they have moved.	93%
2. _____ often talk to their neighbours.	81%
3. _____ would trust their neighbours to look after their pets.	78%
4. _____ would trust their neighbours to look after their children.	47%
5. _____ would give their neighbours a spare key.	32%

> **more than/over**
>   three quarters
> **almost/nearly/just under**
>   a third

C Class survey! Which of the things in 5B would the people in your class do?

D Now listen to some people talking about their experiences with their neighbours. Complete the sentences.

1. "Would you like us to look after the children?"
   They _____ look after the children.
2. "You'll have to change the glass in that window."
   She _____ change the glass in the window.
3. "I'll feed it for you while you're away."
   He _____ feed it while we were away.
4. "Could you get rid of them, please?"
   They _____ get rid of them.

E Do you have any interesting stories about neighbours?

> She asked us to …
> He told me not to …

House and home UNIT 9

6 My home is my castle

A What do these things have in common?

> storm   vandalism
> earthquake   flood
> fire   lightning

B Look at the advertisement below and find words that mean:

1. what an insurance policy costs — _premium (Prämie)_
2. what the insurance company will pay for — _cover_
3. when something gets broken or spoilt — _damage_
4. the things in a house — _contents_
5. when someone steals something from a house — _burglary_
6. what a lawyer charges his/her customers — _legal fees_

Destroy = zerstören

C What risks to your home doesn't this insurer cover?

D What other sorts of insurance do you think everyone should have? Why?

> **Some types of insurance**
> health
> liability
> life
> motor
> travel

Castle Rock Insurance

Enjoy all the extras with our new household insurance!
The lowest premiums and the most comprehensive cover available

Buildings
Damage to building – fire, lightning, storm, flood
Accidental damage – windows, doors
Vandalism – walls, windows, doors

Contents
Fire – unlimited
Burglary – unlimited
Accidental damage – TV, audio, video, computer, furniture, mirrors

Extras
Legal fees – unlimited
Helpline – free

> **TALKING POINT**
> If you had to move to a foreign country and you could only take five things with you out of your home, what would they be?

Checklist! — UNIT 9

Grammar

A The Causative

1. I always _____ my windows cleaned. I don't clean them myself.
2. Last year we _____ a new shower put in. We couldn't do it ourselves.

B Reported speech: offers, commands, promises, requests

1. "_____ look after your children?"
   They offered to look after the children.
2. "_____ change the glass in that window."
   She told us to change the glass in one of the windows.
3. "_____ feed your cat for you while you're away."
   He promised to feed our cat while we were away.
4. "_____ get rid of those frogs, please?
   They asked my father to get rid of the frogs.

Phrases

A Speculating

1. Maybe it's because (it's difficult to find a flat).
2. It's _____ because (their mothers do all the housework).
3. It must _____ because (women get married earlier).

B Saying that something is important

1. The _____ important thing for me is a sofa.
2. A living room without a carpet just wouldn't _____ right to me.
3. A TV _____ essential.

C Agreeing and disagreeing

1. Exactly.
2. Yes, _____ what about …?
3. Oh, d'you _____ so?

Grammar: A1 have, A2 had, B1 Would you like us to, B2 You'll have to, B3 I'll, B4 Could you

Phrases: A2 probably, A3 be, B1 most, B2 feel, B3 is, C2 but, C3 think

UNIT 10 *Learning for Life*

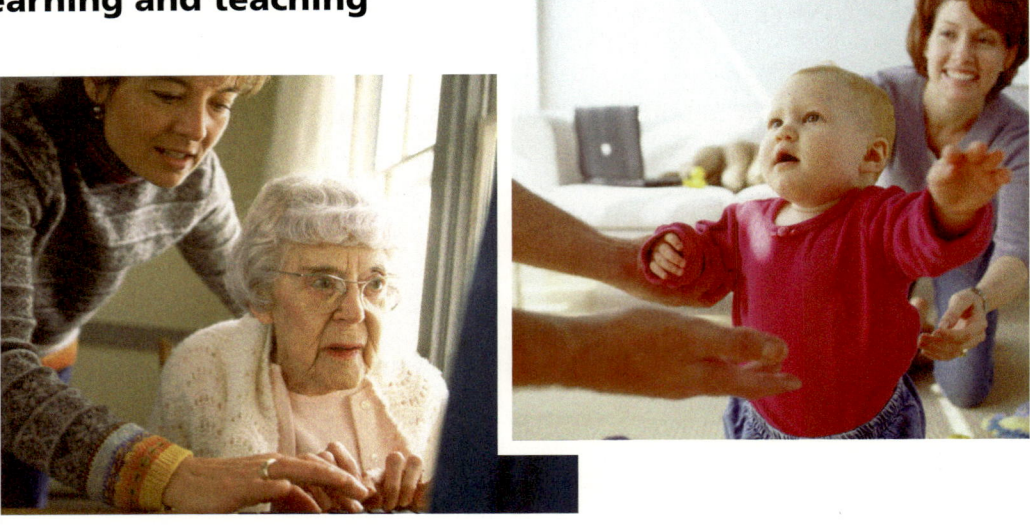

1 Learning and teaching

A Organize these words into three sayings about learning. Are there any similar expressions in your language?

- too late
- before you run
- but for life
- learn to walk
- for school
- to learn
- it's never
- you don't learn

B Pairwork. What order do people normally learn to do these things in?

- to cross the road alone
- to speak
- to eat with a knife and fork
- to ride a bike
- to speak a foreign language
- to drive
- to swim
- to walk
- to write
- to read

> Most people learn to walk **at the age of** one. **when they are about** one (year old).

C Listen. What did the people learn and how?

D Think of five things you have learned. How did you learn them?

> My mother **taught me to** cook.
> My brother **learned to** sing by imitating pop stars.
> I **taught myself** Italian from a book.

2 Education systems

A Read these texts. How many similarities can you find between the different school systems?

Learning for life — UNIT 10

In Finland compulsory schooling begins at the age of seven and continues for nine years. After that students can stay on for three years to specialize in certain areas and take a final examination in four to seven subjects. Lunch is provided free of charge at Finnish schools.

Japanese children begin compulsory schooling at six, but most of them have previously attended a kindergarten. They can leave school at 15 or stay on for another three years. Lunch is served from a school cafeteria and eaten in the classrooms. After their lessons, children spend approximately 30 minutes cleaning the school.

In England many children start school before the compulsory age of five, but cannot leave before they are 16. If they stay on for another two years, they specialize in two or three subjects for their final examinations. School canteens sell meals at lunchtime because school lasts until about 3.45 pm.

B Write about the school system in your country or another country you know (75-100 words).

C What do you think about these things? Compare with a partner.

- NO MORE EXAMS!
- Free education for ALL
- 30 pupils in a class = 15 too **many**
- We want free school lunches
- EMPLOY MORE TEACHERS!
- Scrap afternoon lessons!

I think education should be free, **don't** you?

I don't think education should be free, **do you**?

3 I wish ...

A Pairwork. Which of these subjects did you both do at school? Which ones was your partner good at?

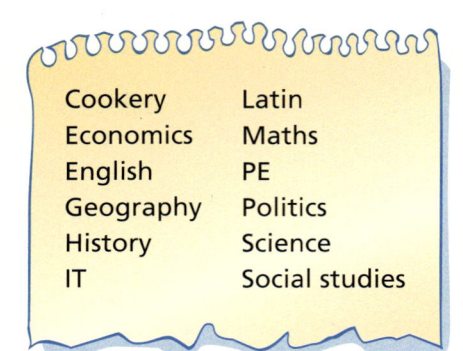

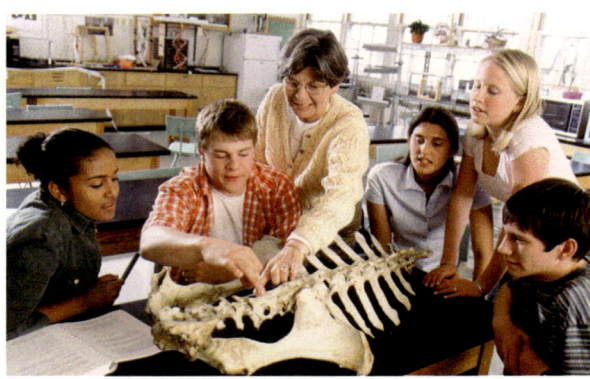

Cookery   Latin
Economics   Maths
English   PE
Geography   Politics
History   Science
IT   Social studies

B Class survey! Which ten subjects should all children do at school? Why?

> PE = Physical Education
> IT = Information Technology

C Now listen to some people talking about their schooldays. What did they say?

1. I wish _____ more about computers.

2. I wish _____ us how to repair cars.

3. I wish _____ Spanish.

4. I really wish _____ swim.

D Look at 3C again and complete the box.

> **Talking about wishes**
>
> For wishes about the present, use *I wish* + the Past _____:
> *I wish I **knew** more about computers.*
>
> For wishes about the past, use *I wish* + the Past _____:
> *I wish they **had taught** us how to repair cars.*

E Pairwork. What do you wish? Compare with a partner.

I wish ...

So do I.

Oh, do you? I wish ...

● **TALKING POINT**
People often say that your school days are the best days of your life. Why do you think they say that? Do you agree?

4 The right person for the job

A Match the headings with the rest of the ads.

JOB CORNER
Tel: 0221 7531 3001

1. **Bored with your desk job?**

c. Three mornings a week. Must be single, honest and good with small children.

a. Must be interested in local culture and have excellent computer skills. A graduate would be preferred.

4. **Wanted: researcher and editor for weekly events magazine**

2. **Nanny required for two-year-old boy**

d. Fit, flexible and keen on gardening? Then why not join our landscaping team? Call us at Nature's Gardens.

b. We are looking for someone who is fond of animals and will exercise our well-trained Queenie while we are on holiday.

5. **Calling all dog walkers!**

3. **Hotel receptionist needed now**

e. Must enjoy working with people and be reliable, efficient and fluent in French or German.

1 ☐ 2 ☐ 3 ☐ 4 ☐ 5 ☐   ☐

B Look at the five jobs again. What sort of people would they suit?

C Choose two of these jobs.
What qualities and skills do you need to do them?

- salesperson
- mother
- fashion designer
- politician
- farmer

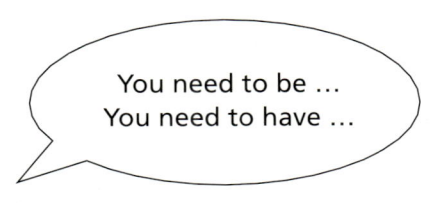

You need to be …
You need to have …

> fluent **in**
> fond **of**
> good **with**
> interested **in**
> keen **on**

Learning for life — UNIT 10

71

D Look at these things that someone says about his job. What do you think it is?

"The most important thing is to be sociable."
"You have to be cheerful, helpful and tactful."
"People expect you to be knowledgeable."
"You need to know the city like the back of your hand."
"You have to have nerves of steel."
"You should be trustworthy, as fit as a fiddle, flexible, easy-going."

E Listen and check.
What shouldn't you do in his job?

1.
2.
3.
4.

F What did the interviewer ask? Complete her questions.

1. _____ makes a good …?

2. _____ well do you need to know …?

3. _____ you need to be …?

4. _____ about your routine? Is it …?

G Interview a partner about their job or another job they know about. Report something interesting.

> So to sum up, a good …
> should be …

Anyone who wants to be a London taxi driver (or "cabby") has to do a course called the *Knowledge of London*. This takes at least two years. Cabbies have to know the exact position of all the sights, museums, churches, hotels, stations, hospitals, law courts and anywhere else a passenger might want to go. They are expected to know details of 25,000 streets in Central London and all the major routes leading into it. Only when candidates have passed a written exam and a series of oral examinations can they collect their hard-earned taxi driver's licence and badge and become a real London cabby.

5 Qualifications

A What would these qualifications be called in your country?

GCSE (General Certificate of Secondary Education) exams in a number of different subjects which you take at the age of 16 in England

NVQ (National Vocational Qualification) a qualification which shows that you have the practical and theoretical knowledge to do a particular job

degree [dɪˈgriː] the qualification which you receive when you complete your studies at a university

A (Advanced) **levels** [ˈeɪˌlevlz] exams in several subjects which you take to qualify for university in England

B What qualifications do you think a police officer needs? Listen to someone talking about her interview with the police. What qualifications has she got?

C What other questions do you think the interviewers asked? Listen to some more of the conversation to check, then report these questions.

1. "Are you afraid of the dark?"

   They asked her *if she was afraid of the dark.*

2. "Why do you want to join the police?"

   They asked her _____.

3. Have you done any self-defence?

   They asked her _____.

4. Have any of your friends ever committed a crime?

   They asked her _____.

D Look at the questions in 5C again, then complete this box.

> **Reporting questions**
> - Questions in the _____ Simple are reported in the Past Simple.
> - Questions in the Past Simple or _____ Perfect are reported in the Past Perfect.

E Have you ever had a job interview? What questions were you asked?

> They asked me …
> I was asked …

Learning for life — UNIT 10

6 It's never too late!

A Why do people go to evening classes? How many reasons can you think of?

B Listen to an adult education director talking about the people who come to her centre. Does she mention the same things?

C Which of these courses would you like to do? Do you know anyone else they might appeal to?

AT 78 The flower garden 2 weekends May 12/13 + July 2/3 11am-3pm
Here you can learn everything you have ever wanted to know about designing a flower garden so that there is always something flowering. Bring a picnic lunch.

VT 261 Office management 10 sessions Mondays 6.30-8pm
Begins March 11
Brush up your office skills: bookkeeping, computer filing, telephone etiquette and anything else you need.

PT 639 Self-defence 5 sessions Wednesdays 7-8.30pm. Begins March 9
Learn the basics of self-defence so that you're not afraid to go out alone. Psychological tips and essential holds will give you the self-confidence you need.

CC 105 Creative writing 5 days April 10-15 10am-4pm
Have you always wanted to write? This course with expert teachers takes you through the steps of planning, writing, correcting and publishing your ideas and opinions.

PT 507 Salsa for beginners Thursdays 6.30-8pm. Begins March 10
Do you enjoy moving to music? Then this course could be for you. Don't worry if you've never learned to dance, it's never too late to start.

D Pairwork. Write an ad for a course you would both be interested in. Sell it to the rest of the class!

- Oriental cookery
- Aromatherapy
- Local History

> **TALKING POINT**
> What do you think are the three most essential skills in the modern world? How can you learn them best?

Checklist!

Grammar

A Question tags

1. I think education should be free, _____ you?
2. I don't think education should be free, _____ you?

B wish

1. I don't know much about computers. I wish I _____ more about them.
2. We didn't learn how to repair cars. I wish they _____ us how to repair them.

C Reported questions

1. "Which of your qualifications are relevant?"
   They asked her which of her qualifications _____ relevant.
2. "Did you come to the interview alone?"
   They asked her if she _____ to the interview alone.

Phrases

A Talking about ways of learning

1. My mother taught me _____ cook.
2. My brother learned to sing _____ imitating pop stars.
3. I taught _____ Italian from a book.

B Talking about qualities and skills

1. My wife's fluent _____ Italian, but I'm not very good _____ languages.
2. My boyfriend works in a hospital. He's very good _____ older people.
3. Our daughter's very fond _____ animals and our son's very keen _____ sport.

Grammar: A1 don't, A2 do, B1 knew, B2 had taught, C1 were, C2 had come
Phrases: A1 to, A2 by, A3 myself, B1 in – at, B2 with, B3 of – on

UNIT 10

UNIT 11 *The world around us*

1 And now the weather

A Pairwork. Add the words in the box to the diagram. What other "weather words" do you know?

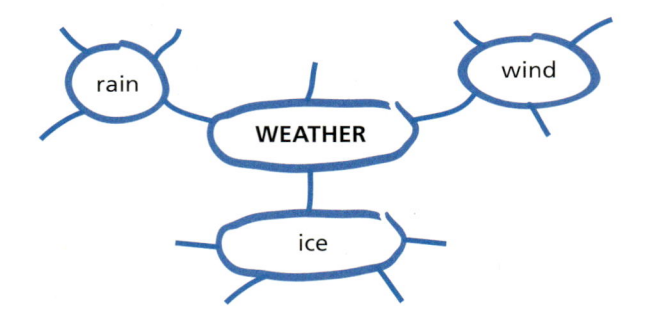

Diagram: WEATHER — rain, wind, ice

drizzle
frost
a breeze
a blizzard
a shower
a gale
hail

B Choose two of the words in the diagram. What does your partner associate with them?

C Listen to a weather forecast and mark these sentences true (T) or false (F).

1. The weather hasn't been very nice lately. ☐
2. It's going to get warmer. ☐
3. Tomorrow will be changeable. ☐
4. We should expect more thunderstorms on Tuesday. ☐
5. Drivers should be especially careful on Wednesday. ☐

D What do you think the weather will be like in your area in the next few days?

People in Britain often talk about the weather, partly because it is very changeable, and partly because it is an easy way of starting a conversation. It is a safe topic which is not too personal and does not offend anybody. So if someone starts talking to you about the weather, they will not expect a weather forecast. They are just being friendly and giving you a chance to talk.

E Listen to some people making small talk. Complete the sentences.

1. It's a lovely day today, _____?
2. That was a terrible storm last night, _____?
3. They didn't forecast it, _____?
4. It hasn't rained like that for ages, _____?
5. No, it really poured down, _____?

F Complete the box.

> **Question tags**
> If the verb is positive, then the question tag is _____:
> *It's a lovely day to day,* **isn't it**?
> If the verb is negative, then the question tag is _____:
> *It hasn't rained* like that for ages, **has it**?

G Look at 1E and listen to the recording again. Do the sentences go up at the end or down?

	1	2	3	4	5
↗					
↘					

H Pairwork. Read the tapescript for 1E with your partner and continue the small talk. How long can you keep it going?

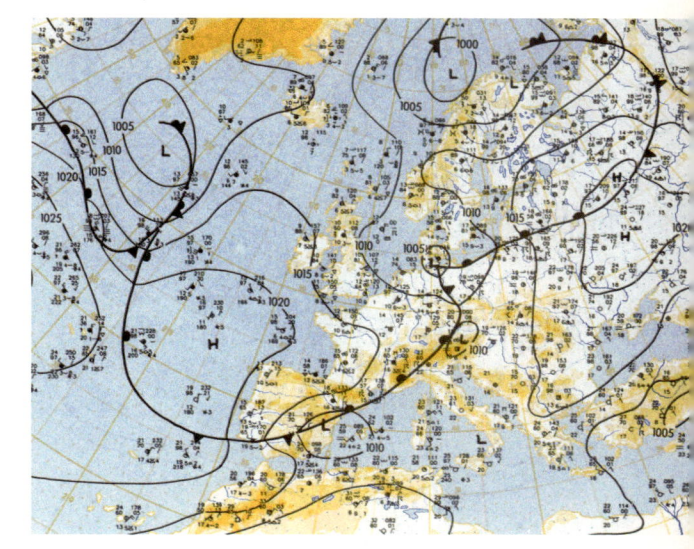

The world around us — UNIT 11

77

2 Landscapes

A Pairwork. Choose one of these texts and think of a title that would make people want to read it.

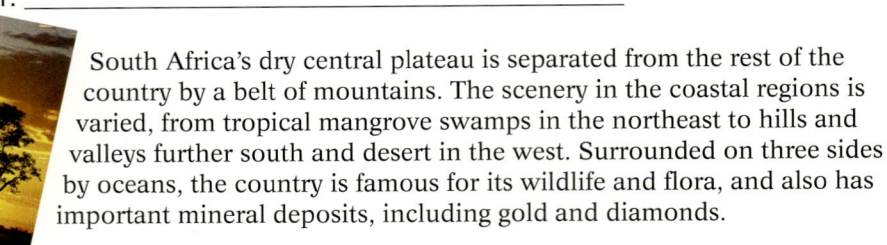

1. _____

South Africa's dry central plateau is separated from the rest of the country by a belt of mountains. The scenery in the coastal regions is varied, from tropical mangrove swamps in the northeast to hills and valleys further south and desert in the west. Surrounded on three sides by oceans, the country is famous for its wildlife and flora, and also has important mineral deposits, including gold and diamonds.

2. _____

New Zealand's spectacular scenery ranges from volcanoes, lakes and waterfalls to rolling farmland and subtropical forest, and its 15,000 km of coast includes many fine beaches. An active seismic region with hot springs, some of which are used for domestic heating, the country also has substantial reserves of coal and natural gas. The weather is changeable, with average temperatures of 18° C in the north and 9° in the south.

3. _____

Most of the island is a plateau around 100 m above sea-level, with a narrow coastal plain. There are two mountain ranges and many small rivers, some of which are used to produce hydroelectric power. Rainfall is high in the north, but the south is usually very dry. Hurricanes can cause serious damage between August and November. Jamaica's exports include sugar, bananas and bauxite.

B Find words in the texts that fit in the categories below. Which could you use about the area where you live?

Landscape	Climate	Natural resources
plateau	dry	gold

C What kind of landscape do you like best? Why? Is there any kind you don't you like? Compare with a partner.

> I don't like being in the mountains – I always feel closed in.

> I love the sea. I get a bit nervous when I'm too far away from it.

3 Traveller's tales

A What would be a reason for you not to visit a country? Why?

dangerous animals

political problems

natural disasters

I'd be worried about …

I wouldn't want to go anywhere where they have …

B Listen to some travellers talking about problems they have had. Mark the correct information.

1. He got ill from drinking / eating something.
2. The island was hit by an earthquake / a hurricane.
3. A bear tried to get into their car / tent.
4. She started an avalanche / landslide.

C Listen again. What did they say?

1. I _____ drunk the water.

2. The travel agents _____ told you.

3. They _____ stored it in the camp.

4. I _____ listened to the locals.

D Group work. Have you ever been in a worrying situation at home or on holiday? Tell your partner about it. Sympathize with your partner.

I would have been …
That must have been …
You could have been …

- **TALKING POINT**
  According to an English saying, travel broadens the mind.
  Do you agree? Why? Why not?

The world around us — UNIT 11

79

4 Changes around us

Land use in the UK
15% urban areas*
74% agricultural activities
10% forest and woodland

* inc. residential, commercial and industrial areas, plus land used for transportation and recreational purposes

A Look at the statistics and find expressions which refer to the following things.

1. farming _____
2. housing _____
3. parks, sports facilities, etc. _____
4. roads, airports, railways, etc. _____
5. towns and cities _____

B Read these texts. Who do you think they were written by?

❶ Local farmers have agreed to sell valuable agricultural land for an exclusive residential development: a handful of luxury houses surrounded by a high security wall with automatic gates. Nice for the rich, perhaps, but what we need is affordable accommodation, so that our young people can stay in the area!

❷ Plans for a second runway at the city's airport have been rejected. Passenger numbers have doubled in the past two years and local residents say the noise has become unbearable. According to the airport authorities, the rejection will mean less business for the region.

❸ Another piece of news: the local council has passed a compulsory purchase order which means that I'll have to sell them some of my garden to complete the coastal path. And I've just planted a dozen rose bushes there!

C Answer the questions.

1. Are there any "gated communities" in your area? Do you think they are a good idea? Why?
2. Should private citizens be able to stop major transport projects?
3. Should local authorities have the right to make compulsory purchases of private land?

5 They've been trying for years

A Listen and complete these sentences.

1. We _____ to accept the developers' offer. It's hard to give up land that we _____ ____ for generations.

2. The number of people employed at the airport _____ _____ by 20%. In the rest of the area jobs _____ _____ since the airport opened.

3. They _____ to complete the path for years. All the other people with houses along the coast _____ _____ their land.

B Complete the box.

> **Have done** vs. **have been doing**
> The Present Perfect Simple is used to focus on _____:
> We **have decided** to accept the developers' offer.
> The Present Perfect Continuous focuses on _____:
> We **have been farming** this land for generations.

an activity
a result

C Choose three of the following verbs and make true sentences with them. Write them down and get your partner to check the the grammar!

| live | decided | increase | buy | try |
| sell | learn | work | go | disappear |

My brother has bought a new car.
He has been saving up for a year.

The world around us — UNIT 11

6 Pros and cons

A Listen to an engineer talking about his company. How many times does he mention these things?

coal mine // ☐
open-cast mine // ☐
coal field // ☐

B What did the speaker say about these things?

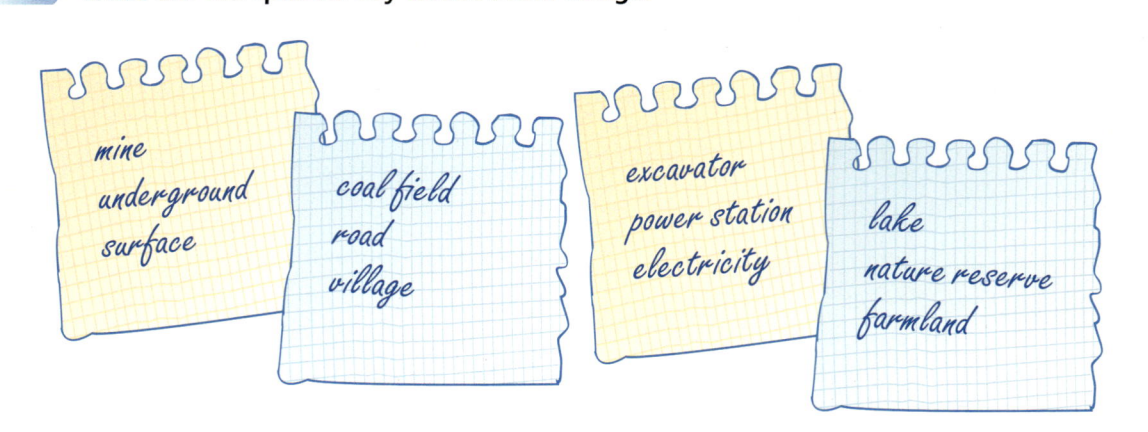

- mine
- underground
- surface

- coal field
- road
- village

- excavator
- power station
- electricity

- lake
- nature reserve
- farmland

C Think of some other uses for a former mine.

D Group work. You are going to be on an environmental programme on TV. Divide into two groups: one for mining and one against it.

1. Collect arguments for your position. How will the other side counter your arguments?

2. Choose an anchorperson and start the programme. Who has the best arguments?

> **TALKING POINT**
> NIMBY stands for "Not in my back yard!" What do you think this means? Is there a similar expression in your language?

Checklist! UNIT 11

Grammar

A Question tags

1. It's nice and sunny today, _____ it?
2. The weather wasn't very nice yesterday, _____ it?
3. It's been a lovely afternoon, _____ it?
4. You slept through the storm last night, _____ you?

B Perfect modals

1. I should _____ listened to the locals.
2. I _____ have drunk the water.

C Present Perfect Simple vs. Present Perfect Continuous

1. The number of people employed at the airport _____ increased by 20%.
2. In the rest of the area jobs _____ disappearing since the airport opened.

Phrases

A Talking about worries

1. I _____ be worried about dangerous animals.
2. I _____ want to go anywhere where they have earthquakes.

B Sympathizing

1. I _____ have been terrified.
2. That _____ have been awful.
3. You _____ have been killed.

Grammar: A1 isn't, A2 was, A3 hasn't, A4 didn't, B1 have, B2 shouldn't, C1 has, C2 have been
Phrases: A1 'd, A2 wouldn't, B1 would, B2 must, B3 could

83

UNIT 12 Revision

A Topic scrabble

1 Group work. Choose one of these topics and write the words on the board.

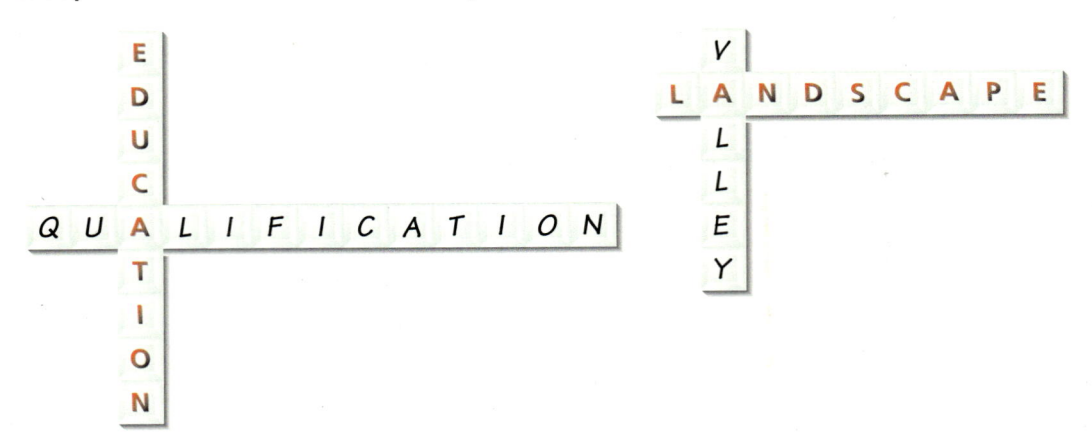

```
        E
        D
        U
        C
Q U A L I F I C A T I O N
        T
        I
        O
        N
```

```
        V
L A N D S C A P E
        L
        L
        E
        Y
```

2 Form two teams. Take it in turns to add words to the puzzle. The last team to add a word wins.

B What's my job?

1 Pairwork. Choose a job.

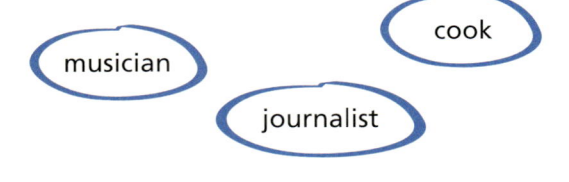

- musician
- cook
- journalist

2 One of you does the job and the other is an interviewer.
- Interviewer: Prepare some questions about the job, but don't name it!
- Interviewee: Prepare some answers, but don't say what the job is!

> What qualities do you need to do your job?

> The most important thing is to be …

> And how well do you need to … ?

> You have to be …
> You shouldn't be …

3 Perform your interview for the rest of the class. Can they guess what the job is?

C The Yes/No game

1 Pairwork. Complete these questions any way you like.

1. You live _____, don't you?
2. You're a good _____, aren't you?
3. You don't really like _____, do you?
8. You aren't _____, are you?
4. You've got _____, haven't you?
5. You can make _____, can't you?
6. You haven't been to _____, have you?
7. You used to like _____, didn't you?
9. You won't be _____ tomorrow, will you?
10. You were good at _____ at school, weren't you?
11. You didn't watch _____ yesterday, did you?
12. You wouldn't move _____, would you?

2 Choose a new partner and ask them your questions.
They have to answer, but they aren't allowed to say "Yes" or "No".
Each time they do, you get one point.

D Design a flat

1 Divide into small groups. Decide how you could turn your classroom into a one-room flat, with a small bathroom and a kitchenette.

- What would you do yourselves? What would you have done?
- How would you decorate the flat? How would you furnish it?

2 Draw a plan of your finished design. Explain it to the other groups.

E In the news

1 Think of three people who are in the news. Complete one of these sentences for each person and write them on a card.

I wish . . .
I've been . . . ing
I shouldn't have . . .
. . . asked me to . . .
I could have been . . .
I wouldn't want to . . .

2 Hand the card to another pair. Can they guess who the people are?

Revision — UNIT 12

UNIT 13   *It takes all sorts*

1 Who are you?

A What do these things have in common? When do people normally use them?

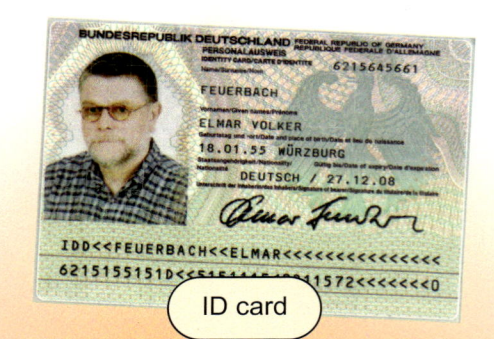

- ID card
- badge
- signature
- fingerprint
- PIN number

B Listen. What's happening?

C Interview a partner. Report something interesting.

How many different cards have you got?
Do you need any passwords?
How many numbers do you have to remember?
How do you remember them?

> cash card
> credit card
> key card
> loyalty card
> membership card
> swipe card

D What would you do if:
you lost your ID card?
you found a credit card lying on the pavement?
you forgot your PIN number?
a salesperson said your signature didn't match the one on your card?
your computer didn't accept your password?

E Complete the box.

The Conditional
Something that you think is _____ : *If I **lose** my key card again, I'll …*
Something that you think is _____, but not _____ : *If I **found** a credit card, I'd …*

> possible
> probable

2 **What does she look like?**

A Match the pictures and the texts.

1. He's got a roundish face with straight brown hair and a moustache – well, I suppose I should say he used to have brown hair because he's rather bald now! Mum says he's a bit overweight, but he's been like that as long as I can remember and …

2. Although my hair is quite thick it's really an ordinary mousy colour and my skin is very pale. Beauty counselling has taught me what sort of clothes and colours make you look slim, and also how to use make-up more effectively, so that …

3. The police are looking for a well-built, clean-shaven man with longish fair hair and blue eyes. The suspect is in his mid-thirties and average height. When he was last seen, he was wearing a red T-shirt and jeans, and driving a white …

4. There was an elderly lady behind me in the queue. She was fairly small and she had grey curly hair. She looked like everybody's idea of a dear old granny. Her face was very lined, but she had a nice smile and I suddenly realized that it was …

roundish
= quite round

B Mark the words in the texts that you can use to describe people. Can you think of any more?

Age: *middle-aged*, …
Face: *beard*, …
Hair: *shoulder-length*, …
Build: *stocky*, …

C How many words can you find in the texts that modify other words? For example: *My hair is quite thick*

quite, _____

D Pairwork. Choose another picture of a person in this unit and write a description of him or her.

"The reason why women take so much trouble with their appearance is that men's eyes are more developed than their brains."

It takes all sorts   UNIT 13

3 What's in a name?

Thomas Cook
From Aramaic *Te'oma*: "twin"

Jennifer Lopez
From Welsh *Gwenhwyfar*, French *Guinevere*: "white, smooth"

A Answer the questions and compare with a partner.

> **The names quiz**
> How many names do people normally have in your country?
> Do you like your first name?
> Do you know what your first name means?
> If you had to change your name, what name would you choose?
> Do people have nicknames in your country?
> What are the most popular children's names at the moment?

- first name *or* given name
- surname *or* family name
- nickname
- pet name

B Listen and complete the table.

Where surnames come from	Some examples		
Appearance			Young
	Bull		Sparrow
Occupations		Farmer	
Patronymics		Peterson	
	Field		
Towns or regions	Burton		Scott

… people **whose** surname is Scott.

C What sorts of surnames do people have in your country?

> ● **TALKING POINT**
> The title of this unit is "It takes all sorts". Is there a similar saying in your language? When would you use it?

4 Blood is thicker than water

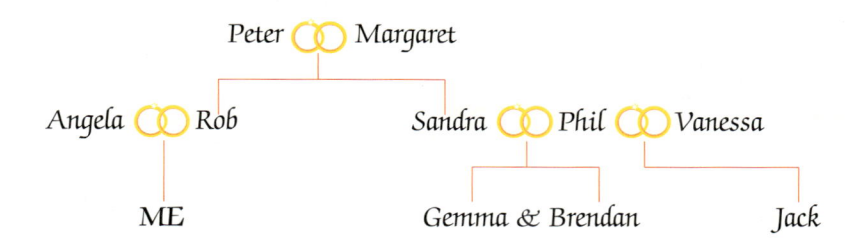

```
           Peter ⚭ Margaret
                  │
       ┌──────────┴──────────┐
Angela ⚭ Rob          Sandra ⚭ Phil ⚭ Vanessa
       │                    │              │
      ME              Gemma & Brendan     Jack
```

A Read these sentences about the family and add the missing names.

My grandfather _____ is Margaret's husband. They've got two children: Rob and _____. Rob is _____ 's uncle. Her brother _____ is his nephew. Their stepmother's name is _____.
She is Peter and _____ 's daughter-in-law. And then there's _____. He's got a half-brother and a half-sister, and one cousin: that's _____!

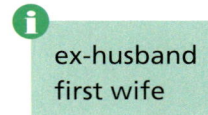

> ℹ️ ex-husband
> first wife

B Match these words with the family words in 4A. How many pairs can you make?

aunt • niece • parents • son • wife

aunt/uncle, aunt/niece

C Interview a partner. Report back to the class.

> How many members are there in your family?
> How many of them do you know?
> How often do you meet?

> I was interested / surprised to hear that ...

> I've discovered something unusual about ...

It takes all sorts — UNIT 13

D You're going to hear a mother and her daughter talking about their relationship. Who do you think said the following things? Listen and check.

1. I'm not really responsible for her now she's moved away. ☐
2. It's nice not to be financially dependent on them any more. ☐
3. She can look after herself much better than I could. ☐
4. I'm just as fond of them as I used to be. ☐
5. We're still very close to each other. ☐
6. I used to worry about her if she didn't phone home regularly. ☐

E Each sentence in 4D includes a verb that ends in a preposition (e.g. *to be responsible for*). How many of them can you use about yourself?

5 A friend is …

A Listen to some people talking about friendship and make notes. Which definition do you like best?

B What's the best way to meet people in your area?

C Pairwork. Choose one of these sets of ads. How would you complete them?

Lonely hearts

Youthful, slim, kind but poor F who likes eating out, dancing, fun, is looking for …

Curvy, good-looking, sporty but feminine F who loves to laugh wants …

Slim, dark, shy F with brown eyes who likes quiet evenings, music, art, nature, seeks …

Lonely hearts

Tall, fit, attractive M (37) who likes food, cycling, dancing is looking for …

Handsome, independent, intelligent, professional M with blue eyes, who likes eating out, red wine, music , film, theatre, current affairs seeks …

Shy, skinny artist (M) needs …

D Find a different partner who chose the other set of ads. How many of your lonely hearts can you match?

E You are going to hear two people talking about how they met. Listen and answer the questions.

1. Who put the ad in the paper?
2. Who paid for the ad?
3. Who phoned who?
4. Who sounded nice and natural?
5. What didn't Steve ask for?
6. Who suggested meeting?

F Complete these sentences, then listen again and check.

1. I wouldn't have _____ the ad in the paper if my friend hadn't _____ for it.
2. If Steve hadn't _____ "shy" in the ad, I wouldn't have _____ him.
3. I wouldn't have _____ to her for so long if she hadn't _____ so nice.
4. If he'd _____ for my address, I would have _____ the phone down.
5. If Jackie hadn't _____ nearby, I wouldn't have _____ meeting.

G Complete the box.

> **The Conditional with *would have* (Past Conditional)**
> This is used to talk about something that was possible, but didn't happen.
> - If + _____: **If** he **had asked** for my address,
> - would have + _____: I **would have put** the phone down.

past participle

Past Perfect

H Choose two of these things and write about them. What could have been different, and why?

a friend or relative
your job or hobby
something you bought or didn't buy
your home or town
a holiday or visit

If I'd taken the job in Brussels, I wouldn't have met my wife.
If my son hadn't married an American, I wouldn't be here now.

It takes all sorts

UNIT 13

6 Keeping in touch

A How do you keep in touch with your family and friends? Compare with a partner.

Greetings cards are very popular in English-speaking countries. They can be bought in newsagents and there are also many specialist shops that stock cards for every occasion. Some are blank for your own message, but there is usually a picture and a message on the outside and a further message inside so all you need to do is to add the name of the recipient and sign the card. Cards are especially popular at Christmas, when many people send dozens of them to their relatives, friends and neighbours.

B Look at these typical messages from greetings cards. Who would you send them to?

1. Many happy returns!
2. Congratulations!
3. Wishing you both every happiness!
4. Get well soon!
5. Good luck!
6. Wishing you all the best in your new home!
7. Thanks for everything!
8. Sorry!

C Choose an occasion and design a card for it. Write a personal message to go inside the card.

Hoping you'll feel better soon!
Best wishes from us both
John & Mary

> **TALKING POINT**
> "Modern communication technology keeps us all in touch with each other, and that can only be a good thing".
> Do you agree?

Checklist!

UNIT 13

Grammar

A Conditional with *will*

If I lose my key card again, I_____ have to pay for a new one.

B Conditional with *would*

If I found a credit card lying on the pavement, I_____ take it to the police station.

C Conditional with *would have*

1. If he _____ asked for my address, I would _____ put the phone down.

2. I wouldn't _____ talked to her for so long if she _____n't sounded so nice.

Phrases

A Talking about someone's appearance

1. My dad's got a round_____ face.

2. My hair was q_____ thick, but I'm r_____ bald now and a b___ overweight.

3. She's a_____ height, f_____ slim and she's got v_____ long red curly hair.

B Talking about relationships

1. Parents are responsible _____ their children.

2. Children are dependent _____ their parents.

3. Parents often worry _____ their children.

4. We all have to learn how to look _____ ourselves.

Grammar: A 'll/will, B 'd/would, C1 'd/had – 've/have, C2 have – had

Phrases: A1 (round)ish, A2 (q)uite – (r)ather – (b)it, A3 (a)verage – (f)airly – (v)ery, B1 for, B2 on, B3 about, B4 after

93

UNIT 14 A *balanced life*

1 Is it work?

A What do you think these people said?

A bit of hard _____ never hurt anybody.

Some people live to _____ and others _____ to live. It's your choice.

You know what they say: "The devil finds _____ for idle hands".

There's always too much _____ to do and not enough time to do it.

I get a lot of satisfaction out of my job. It isn't really _____ if you enjoy it, is it?

B Which of the people do you agree with, and why?

C Find someone who:
likes cooking.
doesn't like driving.
enjoys cleaning the house.
hates shopping.
doesn't mind doing DIY jobs.
likes gardening.
doesn't like answering the telephone.
enjoys washing up.

D Which of the things in 1C would you think of as work?

E A lot of people work from home nowadays. What are the advantages and disadvantages of this?

2 All work and no play …

A The title of this section is the beginning of a traditional saying. How do you think it finishes?

B Listen to some people talking about what they do when they aren't working.
What do you think their jobs are?

C What did they say?

1. I'm _____ _____ all week.
2. My husband's _____ a lot of the time.
3. You can _____ at times.
4. I'm _____ all day.
5. My wife complains that I _____ for five minutes.

D What about your typical day? What do you do to relax?

E Read this article and underline the negative aspects that are mentioned.

> **Take Back Your Time Day** is a nationwide day of action to make people aware of the time poverty they are suffering from. Millions of Americans are working longer hours than they used to and have shorter holidays than their fellow workers in Europe. Overwork threatens our health and our families; it damages the environment, weakens our communities and reduces employment. On Take Back Your Time Day thousands of Americans will take time off to say no to overwork and overstress and yes to useful, creative work, yes to spending time with their families and strengthening their communities, yes to creating new jobs and protecting the environment. Join us on Take Back Your Time Day and take time to build a more balanced America.

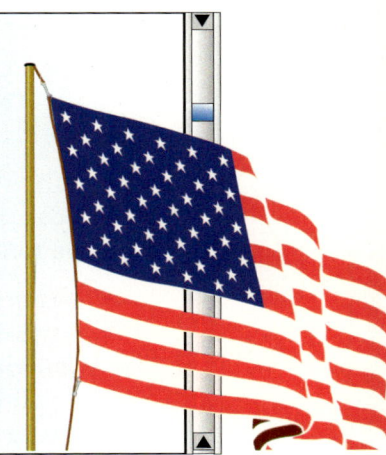

F Read the article again. Find opposites for the things you marked in 2E.

G Imagine that you're going to read the article on the radio.
Which of the words would you stress? Where would you pause?
Listen and compare, then read the article to a partner.

A balanced life   UNIT 14

95

3 Time out

A One of these people is going to sail around the world. Which one do you think it is? Why?

I'm between jobs.

I've given up my job.

I've retired.

B Listen and check.
How often do you hear these forms?   going to ☐   will ☐

C Complete the box.

> **The future: *going to* vs. *will***
> - Use ***going to*** to express things that you _____ _____: *First I'm going to get the boat in shape.*
> - Use ***will*** to express things that you think
>   1. _____:
>   *It will probably take a few more weeks.*
>   2. _____:
>   *I'll stop and explore places whenever I feel like it.*

will probably happen

intend to do

will definitely happen

D Choose one of these "dreams". Make notes about what you plan to do, hope to do and will definitely do.

- A retired policeman is going to move to the country to keep sheep.
- A middle-aged manager plans to leave her well-paid job for a six-month trip around Australia and New Zealand.
- A young man intends to spend two years building his own log cabin in the countryside before he designs and builds them for other people.
- A 60-year-old doctor wants to start writing novels. Six already planned.

E Find someone who chose one of the other dreams and interview them.

When are you going to start? How long do you think it'll take?

● **TALKING POINT**
"What is this life but full of care – we have no time to stand and stare." Do you agree?

4 No sports?

A Pairwork. How many sports can you think of which:

use a ball?
need water?
need ice or snow?
usually take place indoors?
are very expensive to do?

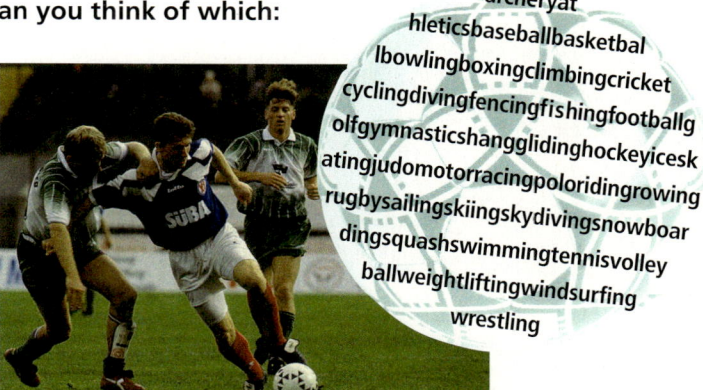

archery athletics baseball basketball bowling boxing climbing cricket cycling diving fencing fishing football golf gymnastics hanggliding hockey iceskating judo motorracing polo riding rowing rugby sailing skiing skydiving snowboarding squash swimming tennis volleyball weightlifting windsurfing wrestling

A balanced life — UNIT 14

B Pairwork. Which sports has your partner tried?

> I'm in our local hockey team.

> I went sky-diving once but I'll never do it again.

> I used to play basketball at school.

ℹ to play football, golf, tennis
to go cycling, skiing, swimming

Football has been played around the world in one form or another for centuries, but it first became an organized game when English schools and universities started to play it in the early 19th century. The standard rules of the game were drawn up at Cambridge University in 1848.

An early form of tennis was played in France in the Middle Ages, but the modern game was invented by a Major Wingfield during a Christmas party in Wales in 1873. Golf probably originated in the Netherlands around 1300. However, the game that people play today was developed in Scotland, where the world's first golf club – The Gentlemen Golfers of Edinburgh – was founded in 1744.

Other sports which originated or were standardized in Britain include boxing, cricket, hockey, rugby and squash. It is also said that a Norwegian technique for travelling across snow – called skiing – was introduced to Switzerland in the 1880s by Sir Conan Doyle, creator of the great detective Sherlock Holmes.

C Which are the most popular spectator sports in your country?
Why are they so popular?

Top spectator sports
1. _____
2. _____
3. _____
4. _____
5. _____

D Choose one of these topics make some notes about it.
Think of some questions you could ask about the other topics.

Sport & advertising

Sport & violence

Sport & health

Sport & fashion

E Ask your questions and answer the ones that are put to you.

It causes …

It makes people feel …

They want people to buy …

5 The marathon

A Read the text. What do these numbers refer to?

| 1981 | 490 | 6,255 | 1908 | 24 |

The idea of marathon races goes back to 490 B.C., when a Greek soldier called Pheidippides ran the 39 kilometres (24 miles) from Marathon to Athens with news of a victory over the Persian army. When the Olympic Games were revived in 1896, this feat was commemorated by a foot race from the Marathon Bridge to the Olympic stadium in Athens.
At the London Olympics in 1908, about three kilometres were added to the traditional marathon so that the race could finish in front of royal family's viewing box. This new distance of 42.2 km (26.2 miles) was established as the official marathon distance at the 1924 Olympics in Paris and it still is today.

A balanced life — UNIT 14

The first North American marathon was run in Boston in 1897. It wasn't until 1981 that London followed suit, but the first race in the British capital proved an instant success. More than 20,000 people applied to take part, with 7,747 accepted and 6,255 crossing the finishing line. Nowadays over 45,000 people take part and raise millions of pounds for charity.

B Compare this postcard with the text. Kyle has got some of his facts wrong!

> Dear Mum and Dad,
> I've decided to take part in the London Marathon! I've been reading about how it started in 1924. Apparently a soldier ran to Marathon to tell the Greeks about a battle they'd lost. I've agreed to do it with a friend who's collecting money for charity. We're hoping to get lots of sponsors, so please tell everyone to support me. Mind you, 26 kilometres is a long way, so I'm planning to do some running every day until April. Must go now.
> Love, Kyle

C Cover Kyle's postcard and complete these extracts.
What do the verbs have in common?

1. I've _____ to take part in the London Marathon!

2. I've _____ to do it with a friend

3. We're _____ to get lots of sponsors.

4. I'm _____ to do some running every day.

D Complete the box.

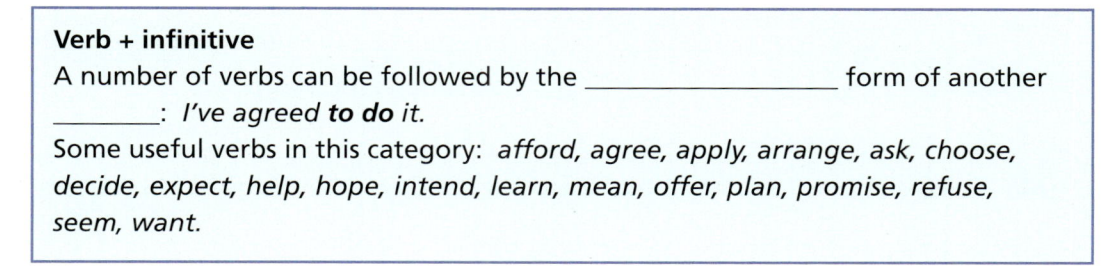

> **Verb + infinitive**
> A number of verbs can be followed by the _____ form of another _____: *I've agreed **to do** it.*
> Some useful verbs in this category: afford, agree, apply, arrange, ask, choose, decide, expect, help, hope, intend, learn, mean, offer, plan, promise, refuse, seem, want.

E Look back through this unit and find examples of the verbs in the box above. How many of them are followed by an infinitive?

6 A change is as good as a rest

A What sort of people would these holidays would appeal to, in your opinion?

1. **Help us to help them**
Have a complete change and do something really worthwhile at the same time. We are looking for people to help us give handicapped children a holiday in a family atmosphere. You will be working with experienced carers, so you don't need any skills except a cheerful nature and a love of life. We provide the food and accommodation and your reward will be happy children and very grateful parents.

2. **Make hay while the sun shines!**
Experience real country life working and relaxing on our small, homely West Country farm. At last the kids will be able to run, shout and play to their hearts' content while you try some traditional farming activities in one of the most beautiful parts of the country. Healthy farm meals with home-grown vegetables, new-laid eggs and good company.

3. **Holiday Building Group**
For years this village has had to manage without a proper community centre. We now have a unique opportunity to convert the old school into a multi-purpose building for young and old. But we won't be able to make this vital contribution to community life without your help! Interested? Contact Sarah at 18 Church Lane (665341).

4. **St Hilary's Retreat House**
Are things getting too much for you? Do you need to get away from everything for a while? We invite you to come and rethink in the warm and peaceful atmosphere of St Hilary's. You will be able to share your experiences in small group sessions or talk to our counsellors individually. We are sure that you will find something here to stimulate and encourage you.

> Present: can/can't
> Future: **will/won't be able to**

B Which of the holidays would you choose for yourself? Think of some questions you would ask the organizers before you booked it.

C Listen to someone asking for more information about one of the holidays. Which one is it? What did they say?

1. _____ the children?
2. _____ how old they are.
3. _____ the accommodation?
4. _____ a single room?
5. _____ bed linen and towels?

D Pairwork. Practise with one of the other holidays. Use the question starters in 6C.

- **TALKING POINT**
Adventure holidays, such as desert safaris, seem to be getting increasingly popular. What is the attraction of these kinds of holiday, in your view?

Checklist!

Grammar

A Futures: *going to* vs. *will*

1. First I'm _____ get the boat in shape.
2. I'm not _____ restrict myself with deadlines.
3. It _____ probably take a few more weeks.
4. I ____ stop and explore places whenever I feel like it.

B Verb + infinitive

1. I've decided _____ take part in the London Marathon!
2. We're hoping _____ get lots of sponsors.
3. I'm planning _____ do some running every day.

Phrases

A Talking about regular activities

1. I'm stuck _____ a desk all week.
2. I'm _____ my feet all day.
3. You can feel a bit cut _____ at times.
4. I'm _____ the road a lot of the time.
5. I can't sit _____ for five minutes.

B Asking for detailed information

1. Can you _____ me a bit more about the children?
2. I was _____ how old they are.
3. Can I _____ about the accommodation?
4. Is there any _____ of a single room?
5. Do you _____ bed linen and towels?

Grammar: A1 going to, A2 going to, A3 will, A4 will, B1 to, B2 to, B3 to
Phrases: A1 behind, A2 on, A3 off, A4 on, A5 still, B1 tell, B2 wondering, B3 ask, B4 chance, B5 provide

UNIT 14

UNIT 15 *Come together*

1 Languages of the world

A Pairwork. Which of these languages do you think has the most native speakers? Number them from 1 – 10.

Major Languages
- [ ] Arabic
- [ ] English
- [ ] French
- [ ] German
- [ ] Hindi
- [ ] Japanese
- [ ] Mandarin Chinese
- [ ] Portuguese
- [ ] Russian
- [ ] Spanish

B Listen and write down the numbers you hear. What do they refer to?

377 million: that's the number of people who …
6.2%: that's the percentage which …

_____   _____
_____   _____
_____   _____
_____   _____

C Listen to the recording again and check 1A. Did anything surprise you?

> I thought that …
> I didn't realize that …
> I wonder why …

D How many languages do you speak?
Do you know any words or phrases in other languages?

2 Body Language

A How can you communicate with someone whose language you don't speak?

> One thing you can do is …

> If that doesn't work, …

> As a last resort, …
> If all else fails, …

B Match the verbs and the pictures.

- ☐ to bite your lip
- ☐ to frown
- ☐ to give someone a thumbs up
- ☐ to raise your eyebrows
- ☐ to scratch your head
- ☐ to shrug your shoulders
- ☐ to smile
- ☐ to wave

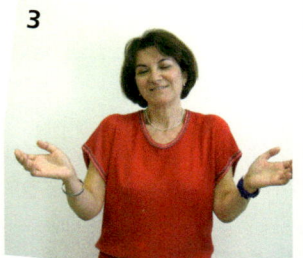

C Look at the pictures again. What messages are the people giving?

> When someone shrugs their shoulders, it (usually) means …

D Choose two of the following situations and communicate them to a partner without using words. You are:

a little tired.
pleasantly surprised.

rather bored.
delighted.

absolutely terrified.
very relieved.

Come together

UNIT 15

E Read the text. How many different ways do we communicate, according to the writer?

It's not just words, say the experts
For most of us, conversation means people talking and listening to each other. But research shows that this is only part of the story. According to communication experts, what you say is only a small part of the message that you transmit to other people.
Your tone of voice has much more impact than the words you use.
The most important thing, however, is the way you look when you are speaking. That includes your expression, your posture and the gestures you make – or don't make. In other words, we may not believe someone who says one thing, but whose body language seems to tell a different story. So if you want to make a good impression on a special occasion, it's a good idea to …

F How would you continue the text?

G Look at the text again. Mark all the examples of the definite article (*the*), then complete the box.

The definite article
Use *the* when you are talking about something _____:
The most important thing, however, is the way you look …
Don't use it when you are speaking about things in _____:
For ( ) most of us, conversation means people talking …

general
specific

H Now read this text and add definite articles where necessary.

Whatever you do, be yourself!
There are ____ many books these days which give ____ advice on how to talk, walk, dress, etc. Although they often contain ____ useful tips, it's very difficult to change ____ body language successfully. ____ problem is that if it doesn't look natural, ____ people will soon notice and probably won't trust you. ____ most important thing is to be yourself, not to worry about a lot of rules. ____ children can teach us something here. They are usually less inhibited than ____ adults, so even if they don't speak ____ same language, ____ most younger children soon make contact with ____ other children, using ____ non-verbal communication.

I Do you agree with the text?

3 I enjoy looking at them

A Think of people you know who would be interested in these events.

Southfield Community Centre
Open Poetry Slam
Saturday 8 pm
Entrance free
Refreshments available

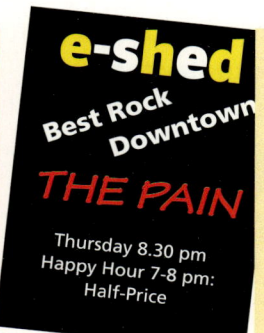

e-shed
Best Rock Downtown
THE PAIN
Thursday 8.30 pm
Happy Hour 7-8 pm: Half-Price

Hays Gallery
28-32 Broad Street
20th Century Landscape Painters
Open Daily 10 am-8 pm

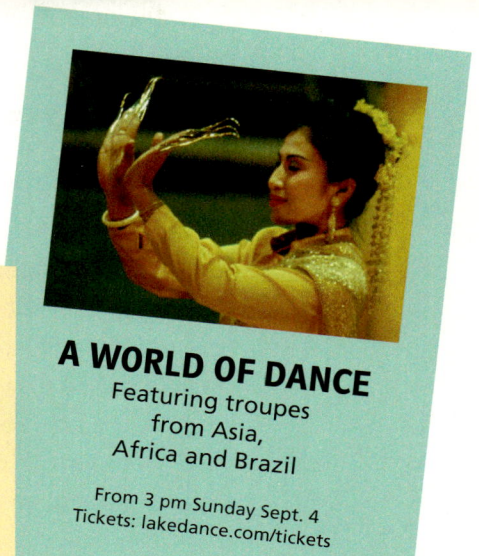

A WORLD OF DANCE
Featuring troupes from Asia, Africa and Brazil
From 3 pm Sunday Sept. 4
Tickets: lakedance.com/tickets

B You are going to hear some people talking about the events. What do you think they said? Listen and check.

1. We'll only just finish to make / making them in time for the big day!
2. One of my flatmates suggested going / to go down to the community centre.
3. I kept asking / to ask them what the songs were about.
4. To be honest, I just enjoy to look at / looking at them.

C Read this information and add verbs from 3B.

> **Verb + -ing**
> When certain verbs are followed by another verb, the second verb ends in -ing.
> Some useful verbs in this category:
> avoid, consider, delay, imagine, miss, risk, _____.

D Some verbs can be followed by either the infinitive or the -ing form, but change their meaning accordingly. Adapt these sentences so that they are true for you.

1. I **remember** go**ing** to the circus with my grandfather. It was great.
2. I must **remember to** check what time the post office closes.
3. I used to be a in a rock group, but I **stopped** play**ing** with them I got married.
4. I **stopped to** pick up the tickets for the concert on my way to work.
5. I'll never **forget** spend**ing** my first night away from home. It was on a school trip.
6. I once **forgot to** lock the car, but luckily nobody noticed. And it was in the city centre!

> ● **TALKING POINT**
> What cultural events should be financed by the local community?

Come together — UNIT 15

105

4 How long will you be able to stay?

A Number these lines in the correct order. Why was the letter written?

- [ ] turn to host it this year, so try and be here if you can. How
- [ ] and neighbours get together for a big barbecue and then
- [ ] would be really nice if you could come to stay then. We
- [ ] Pete's at college, so we can put you up for as long as you like!
- [1] David's taking his vacation in the first week of July, so it
- [ ] long will you be able to stay? We have a spare room now
- [ ] have great Fourth of July celebrations here. A lot of friends
- [ ] we all go down to the beach to watch the fireworks. It's our

B Listen to Meg's phone call and note her travel arrangements.

Arrival	_____
New York	_____
New England	_____
Departure	_____

C Now read this email. Has anything changed? How long will Meg and Jon be in the US? How long will they be able to stay with Janet and David?

> Dear Janet,
> Here are the final details of our trip. We arrive at JFK late on June 21st. We're staying in New York for a few days with Jon's cousin Nick and then he's going to show us something of New England. I hope we'll be able to get as far as Niagara Falls too – I've always wanted to see them. Nick has to be back at work on the 30th, so we could come down to you then. Our flight home leaves on the 7th, but we'll go back to NY the night before. Will that be all right for you?
> Looking forward to seeing you very soon!
> Meg and Jon

D How many ways of speaking about the future can you find in the email?

E Write an invitation to something special.
Exchange invitations with a partner, then call them and tell them your plans.

F What present would you take to Janet and David? Why?

5   Special occasions

A   What do you know about these festivals? Compare with a partner.

B   Choose one of the festivals, read the relevant text and check your ideas. Mark five useful words in the text.

Americans celebrate Independence Day on the Fourth of July every year. This is the anniversary of the day in 1776 when the Declaration of Independence from Great Britain was signed by leaders of the thirteen original colonies. On this important public holiday – which is sometimes called "America's birthday party" – many people go to the beach and have family picnics and barbecues, with organized games for the kids. In the evening there are firework displays and music.

On June 21 every year a group of white-robed people celebrate the summer solstice at Stonehenge, a 3000-year-old stone circle in southwest England. They consider themselves to be the successors of the Celtic priests known as Druids. On this day the midsummer sun rises above the so-called Heel Stone and – in clear weather – casts a shadow into the circle. Hundreds of people watch the ceremony at the monument, which some scientists believe was used as an astronomical calculator.

The festival of Halloween (originally All Hallows' Evening) on the evening of October 31st goes back to the ancient Irish festival of "Samhain" (pronounced Sa-Wain), the Feast of the Dead. It marked the end of the summer harvest season and the beginning of the harder winter months. People dressed in frightening costumes and lit turnip lanterns to keep evil spirits away. Irish emigrants took this tradition to America. Thanks to Hollywood it has now returned to Europe and is popular in a number of countries.

C   Cover the texts. Tell your partner about the festival, using the words you marked.

D   Describe another festival that you know about. When and where does it take place? Who goes to it? What happens?

Come together

UNIT 15

107

6 Thank you!

A How would you thank someone for the following things?

You have stayed with them for a few days.
They kept an eye on your home while you were away.
You have been to their home for dinner.
They have given you a present.

(phone?)   (card?)   (email?)

B Complete this thank-you letter any way you like.

Dear _____ ,

Thank you very much for the _____ stay in your _____ home. We had a _____ time and you made us feel so _____ that it was very hard to leave!

It was very _____ to meet _____ and we particularly enjoyed _____. I hadn't realized how many _____ things there are there are to _____ in your region.

Thank you too for the _____, which will have a place of honour in our _____! Do come and _____ us soon so that we can show you some of the _____ in this part of the world.

Best wishes from us both,

_____

C Compare with the rest of the class.

● **TALKING POINT**
What events in life do you think should be celebrated? Think of one celebration that was particularly important to you.

Checklist!

Grammar

A The definite article

1. _____ most important thing, however, is the way you look.
2. For _____ most of us, conversation means people talking.

B Verb + -ing / Verb + infinitive

1. I must remember ____ check the time. / I remember go_____ to the circus.
2. I stopped play_____ when I got married. / I stopped ____ pick up the tickets.
3. I once forgot ____ lock the car. / I'll never forget spend_____ my first night away from home.

C The futures

1. We _____ at JFK late on June 21st.
2. We're _____ in New York for a few days with Jon's cousin.

Phrases

A Suggesting

1. One _____ you can do is … / If that _____ work, …
2. As a _____ resort … / If all _____ fails, …

B Invitations

1. Thanks so much for _____ us.
2. How long will you be _____ to stay?
3. We have a spare room now so we can _____ you up for as long as you like!
4. Will that ____ all right for you?

C A thank-you letter

1. Thank you very _____ for the wonderful stay in your home.
2. You made us _____ very welcome.
3. We particularly _____ the Independence Day party.
4. ____ come and stay with us soon.

Grammar: A1 The, A2 –, B1 to – ing, B2 ing – to, B3 to – ing, C1 arrive, C2 staying

Phrases: A1 thing – doesn't, A2 last – else, B1 inviting, B2 able, B3 put, B4 be, C1 much, C2 feel, C3 enjoyed, C4 Do

The *On the Move Plus* Test

A **Mark the word that does not fit in the group.**
1. tactful – trustworthy – cheerful – knowledgeable – offensive
2. stir – simmer – serve – taste – roast
3. eyebrows – bald – thumb – skin – brain

B **What's the difference?**
1. whose / who's
2. used to / going to
3. oughtn't to / needn't

C **Look at these phrases. Where do you think the speakers could be?**
1. Excuse me, do you know where I can find a timetable?
2. Can I exchange it if it doesn't go with my suit?
3. It's delicious, but I really couldn't!

D **What do these things have in common? Add a word to each line.**
1. rather / fairly / quite
2. although / so that / even if
3. feel / look / sound

E **How many ways can you think of to talk about the past? When would you use them?**

F **When could you use these phrases?**
1. That must have been terrifying!
2. Thanks. I'm glad you like it.
3. Best wishes from us both,
4. Get well soon!
5. So do I.
6. Enjoy!

G **Complete these sentences**
1. She's got two children, _____ she?
2. My dad's been _____ for the same company for 25 years.
3. I _____ heard of cricket before I went to England.
4. I hope we'll be able to _____ our house redecorated soon.
5. I _____ have joined this course if I hadn't wanted to improve my English.

H **How many ways do you know to speak about the future? What's the difference between them?**

The *On the Move Plus* Poster

1 Group work. Collect some ideas for a course poster. For example:

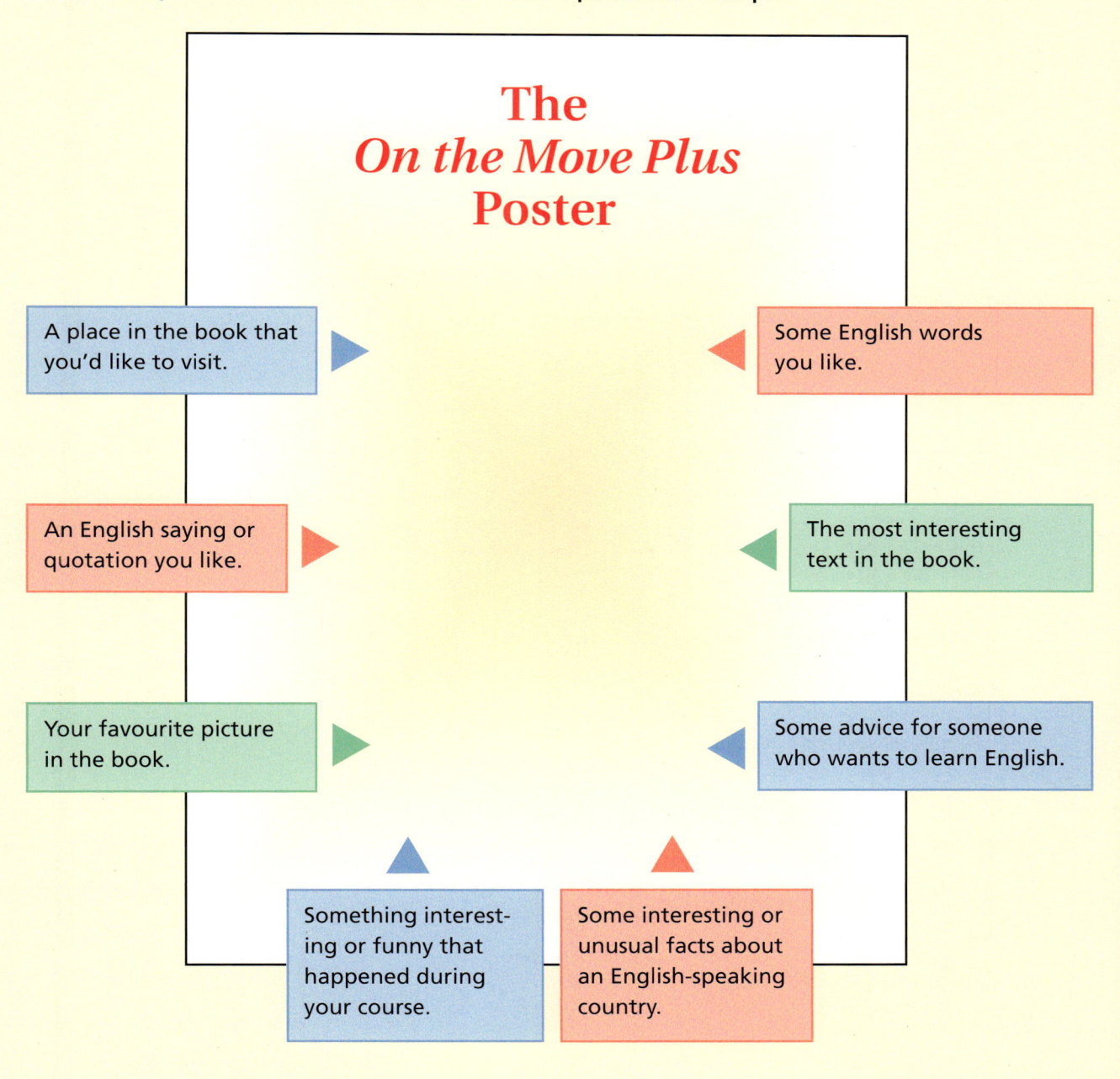

The *On the Move Plus* Poster

- A place in the book that you'd like to visit.
- Some English words you like.
- An English saying or quotation you like.
- The most interesting text in the book.
- Your favourite picture in the book.
- Some advice for someone who wants to learn English.
- Something interesting or funny that happened during your course.
- Some interesting or unusual facts about an English-speaking country.

2 Decide who is going to do what and make your poster. Give each item a title and illustrate it if possible.

3 Hang your poster on the wall so that everyone can read it.

Grammar Overview

Ein Pfeil ➤ verweist auf das Kapitel, in dem die jeweilige grammatische Struktur vorkommt bzw. behandelt wird. Eine Liste der gebräuchlichsten **unregelmäßigen Zeitwörter** finden Sie auf Seite 117.

Present Tenses Gegenwartsformen

to have got		➤ Unit 1
I/you/we/they **have got** … He/she/it **has got** …	I/you/we/they **haven't got** … He/she/it **hasn't got** …	**Have** I/you/we/they **got** …? **Has** he/she/it **got** …?

Have got bedeutet dasselbe wie *have* und wird besonders häufig in **gesprochenem** britischen bzw. australischen Englisch verwendet.

Present Continuous vs. Present Simple ➤ Unit 1

My Dad's **having** a nap.
Most people **have** a siesta after lunch.

Die *Present Continuous*-Form drückt aus, dass eine Handlung **gerade stattfindet**, im Gegensatz zur *Present Simple*-Form, die den **Normal- bzw. Dauerzustand** beschreibt. (*Present Simple* und *Present Continuous* als Zukunftsformen: siehe Seite 113.)

Past and Perfect tenses Vergangenheits- und Perfektformen

Past Continuous ➤ Unit 5

People **were** already **using** perfume by about 3000 B.C..

Das *Past Continuous* ist die Vergangenheitsform vom *Present Continuous*:
They're using it now. They were using it then.

Past Simple vs. Present Perfect ➤ Unit 5

The Egyptians **had** tattoos four thousand years **ago**.
People **have** probably always **used** make-up.
People **have decorated** their bodies **for** thousands of years / **since** 3000 B.C.

- Das *Past Simple* drückt eine **abgeschlossene Handlung** in der Vergangenheit aus. Daher ist diese Zeitform häufig in Verbindung mit Zeitangaben wie *ago, last week* usw. anzutreffen.
- Das *Present Perfect* wird häufig benutzt, um über eine Handlung in der Vergangenheit zu sprechen, deren **genauer Zeitpunkt nicht wichtig** ist, z. B. *People have probably always used make-up.*
- Das *Present Perfect* wird auch benutzt, wenn es sich um die Zeit **bis zum heutigen Tag** handelt. *For* und *since* entsprechen dem deutschen *seit* bzw. *seitdem*.

Grammar Overview

Present Perfect: Simple vs. Continuous ➤ Unit 11

We **have** decid**ed** to accept the developers' offer.
We **have been** farm**ing** this land for generations.

Das *Present Perfect Simple* wird verwendet, um ein **Ergebnis** auszudrücken.
Bei dem *Present Perfect Continuous* dagegen wird die **Kontinuität** einer Handlung betont.

Past Perfect ➤ Units 6, 10

When I arrived, the party **had** already **started**.
I wish they **had taught** us how to repair cars.

Das *Past Perfect* drückt aus, dass ein Vorgang oder Zustand weiter in der Vergangenheit zurückliegt als ein anderer. Die Form wird auch verwendet, um auszudrücken, was man sich anders gewünscht hätte.

used to ➤ Unit 1

I **used to** collect stamps.
There **didn't use to** be colour TV when we were growing up.
Did you **use to** go abroad for your holidays?

Used to drückt aus, was in der Vergangenheit **üblich** (oder nicht üblich) war.

Future forms Zukunftsformen

going to ➤ Units 2, 14

First I'm **going to** get the boat in shape.
I'm **not going to** do that.
When are you **going to** start?

Die *going to*-Zukunftsform drückt aus, das der Sprecher/die Sprecherin **etwas Bestimmtes beabsichtigt**.

Present Simple and Present Continuous as future forms ➤ Units 15

We **arrive** at JFK late on June 21.
We're **staying** in New York for a few days with Jon's cousin.

- Das *Present Simple* wird als Zukunftsform benutzt, wenn man von **Fahrplänen** bzw. **Terminplänen** spricht.
- Um sich über **feste Pläne** für die absehbare Zukunft zu äußern, verwendet man normalerweise das *Present Continuous*.

will	► Units 14, 15

It**'ll** probably take a few more weeks.
I hope we**'ll** be able to get as far as Niagara Falls.
I**'ll** stop and explore places whenever I feel like it.
I**'ll** mail you the exact details in the next day or two.

Will wird hauptsächlich bei handlungsorientierten Äußerungen verwendet, z. B. wenn man etwas **voraussagt, hofft, entscheidet** oder **verspricht**.

Conditionals Bedingungsformen

Conditional with *will* and *would*	► Unit 13

If I **lose** my key card again, I**'ll** have to buy a new one.
If I **found** a credit card, I**'d** take it to the police station.

- Bei einer **wahrscheinlichen** Bedingung, wird *will* im Folgesatz verwendet.
- Ist die Rede von einer eher **unwahrscheinlichen** Bedingung, wird *would* benutzt.
  Would wird auch bei **hypothetischen** Aussagen verwendet, z. B. *If I were you, (I'd go to the doctor).*

Conditional with *would have* (Past Conditional)	► Unit 13

If he **had asked** for my address, I **would have** put the phone down.

Das *Past Conditional* drückt aus, was hätte passieren können.

Modal verbs Modalverben

Modal verbs: *ought to, needn't, may*	► Unit 6

You **ought to** arrive a little late.	Sie sollten etwas verspätet ankommen.
You **oughtn't to** smoke without asking.	Sie sollten nicht rauchen, ohne vorher zu fragen.
You **needn't** take a gift.	Sie brauchen kein Geschenk mizutnehmen.
You **may** refuse a second helping.	Sie dürfen eine weitere Portion ablehnen.

Modal verb: *had better*	► Unit 5, Unit 6

| You**'d better** phone the lost property office. | Du solltest das Fundbüro anrufen. |
| I**'d better** not, thank you. I'm driving. | Besser nicht, ich muss fahren. |

Perfect modals	► Unit 11

I **should have** listened to the locals.	Ich hätte auf die Einheimischen hören sollen.
I **shouldn't have** drunk the water.	Ich hätte das Wasser nicht trinken dürfen.
I **would have been** terrified.	Ich hätte furchtbare Angst gehabt.
That **must have been** awful.	Das muss furchtbar gewesen sein.
They **could have been** killed.	Sie hätten getötet werden können.

Questions and answers Fragen und Antworten

Question tags ➤ Unit 10, Unit 11

It's a lovely day, **isn't it**?
It **hasn't** rained like that for ages, **has it**?

Das englische *question tag* (Frageanhängsel) entspricht dem deutschen *nicht wahr*? am Ende eines Satzes. Ist das Verb **bejaht**, wird das Anhängsel **verneint**, und umgekehrt.

Short answers ➤ Unit 2

So do I/Me too.	Ich auch.
I don't.	Ich (aber) nicht.
Neither do I./Nor me.	Ich auch nicht.
I do.	Ich schon.

Infinitive or *-ing*? Grundform oder Gerundium?

Preposition + *-ing* ➤ Unit 6

You can get enough protein **by** eat**ing** dairy products.
How **about** com**ing** for dinner the Saturday after instead?

Steht ein Verb direkt nach einer Präposition (Verhältniswort), so wird die *-ing*-Form benutzt.

Verb + infinitive vs. Verb + *-ing* ➤ Unit 14, 15

I've **decided to** take part in the London Marathon.
He **suggested** go**ing** down to the community centre.

Manchmal folgt auf ein Verb ein zweites. In diesem Fall bestimmt das erste Verb die Form des nachfolgenden Verbs. Es gibt zwei Kategorien:
- Verb + Grundform (z. B. *afford, agree, ask, choose, decide, expect, help, hope, learn, plan, want*).
- Verb + *-ing*-Form (z. B. *begin, avoid, consider, delay, finish, imagine, keep, miss, risk, suggest*).

Einige Verben **gehören beiden Kategorien** an (z. B. *begin, hate, like, love, prefer, start*).
Einige wichtige Verben (z. B. *forget, remember, stop, try*) **ändern** mit der Kategorie auch **ihre Bedeutung**.

Passiv Passiv

The Passive ➤ Unit 7

Present Simple: Commercial TV **is financed** by advertising.
Past Simple: Cigarette advertising **was banned** on TV in 1965.
Perfect: Sponsorship **has been allowed** since 1991.
Modal verbs: Private photographs **shouldn't be published**.

Wie im Deutschen haben die Verben im Englischen Aktiv- und Passivformen.
- Aktiv: *Advertising finances commercial TV.*
- Passiv: *Commercial TV is financed by advertising.*

to have something done (Causative) ➤ Unit 9

| We **had** the carpet **cleaned**. | Wir haben den Teppich reinigen lassen. |

Reported speech Indirekte Rede

Reported speech ➤ Unit 7

"There **is** a deep split in the party."	The minister said there **was** a deep split in the party.
"The heads of state **met** in Buenos Aires."	She said that the heads of state **had met** in Buenos Aires.
"I **have taken** drugs."	He admitted that he **had taken** drugs.
"The economy **will** grow by 2%."	They said that the economy **would** grow by 2%.

Reported speech: offers, commands, promises, requests ➤ Unit 9

"Would you like us to look after the children?"	They **offered to** look after the children.
"You'll have to change the glass."	She **told** us **to** change the glass in the window.
"I'll feed your cat while you're away."	He **promised to** feed our cat while we were away.
"Could you get rid of the frogs, please?"	They **asked** my father **to** get rid of the frogs.

Reported speech: questions ➤ Unit 10

| "Which of your qualifications are relevant?" | They **asked** her which of **her** qualifications were relevant. |

Irregular verbs
Unregelmäßige Zeitwörter

Infinitive	Past Simple	Past Participle	
Grundform	Vergangenheitsform	Partizip Perfekt	
be	was, were	been	sein
bear	bore	borne	tragen, ertragen
beat	beat	beaten	schlagen
become	became	become	werden
begin	began	begun	beginnen, anfangen
bend	bent	bent	beugen, sich beugen
bet	bet	bet	wetten
bind	bound	bound	binden
bite	bit	bitten	beißen
bleed	bled	bled	bluten
blow	blew	blown	wehen, blasen
break	broke	broken	brechen
bring	brought	brought	bringen, mitbringen
build	built	built	bauen
burn	burnt	burnt	brennen
buy	bought	bought	kaufen
can	could	–	können
cast	cast	cast	werfen
catch	caught	caught	fangen, ergreifen
choose	chose	chosen	wählen, auswählen
come	came	come	kommen
cost	cost	cost	kosten
cut	cut	cut	schneiden
deal (with)	dealt	dealt	sich kümmern um
dig	dug	dug	graben
do	did	done	tun
draw	drew	drawn	zeichnen, malen
drink	drank	drunk	trinken
drive	drove	driven	(Auto) fahren
eat	ate	eaten	essen
fall	fell	fallen	fallen
feed	fed	fed	füttern
feel	felt	felt	fühlen

fight	fought	fought	kämpfen
find	found	found	finden, suchen
fly	flew	flown	fliegen
forget	forgot	forgotten	vergessen
freeze	froze	frozen	frieren
get	got	got	bekommen
give	gave	given	geben
go	went	gone	gehen, fahren
grind	ground	ground	reiben, zerreiben
grow	grew	grown	wachsen
hang	hung	hung	hängen
have	had	had	haben
have got	had got	had got	haben
hear	heard	heard	hören
hide	hid	hidden	(sich) verstecken
hit	hit	hit	stoßen, schlagen
hold	held	held	halten, abhalten
hurt	hurt	hurt	schmerzen
keep	kept	kept	behalten
know	knew	known	kennen, wissen
leave	left	left	verlassen, abfahren
lend	lent	lent	leihen
let	let	let	lassen
lie	lay	lain	liegen
light	lit	lit	anzünden
lose	lost	lost	verlieren
make	made	made	machen
mean	meant	meant	meinen, bedeuten
meet	met	met	kennen lernen, treffen
pay	paid	paid	(be)zahlen
put	put	put	legen, stellen
read	read [red]	read [red]	lesen
ride	rode	ridden	reiten, Rad fahren
ring	rang	rung	anrufen, klingeln
rise	rose	risen	steigen
run	ran	run	laufen
say	said	said	sagen
see	saw	seen	sehen
seek	sought	sought	suchen
sell	sold	sold	verkaufen

Irregular verbs

send	sent	sent	senden, schicken
set	set	set	*(Sonne)* untergehen
shake	shook	shaken	schütteln
shine	shone	shone	scheinen, leuchten
shoot	shot	shot	schießen
show	showed	shown	zeigen
shut	shut	shut	schließen
sing	sang	sung	singen
sink	sank	sunk	sinken
sit	sat	sat	sitzen
sleep	slept	slept	schlafen
slide	slid	slid	rutschen
speak	spoke	spoken	sprechen, reden
spend	spent	spent	ausgeben, verbringen
spread	spread	spread	ausbreiten
stand	stood	stood	stehen
steal	stole	stolen	stehlen
stick	stuck	stuck	kleben
sting	stung	stung	stechen
swear	swore	sworn	schwören, fluchen
sweep	swept	swept	kehren
swim	swam	swum	schwimmen
swing	swung	swung	schwingen
take	took	taken	nehmen, mitnehmen
teach	taught	taught	lehren, unterrichten
tell	told	told	erzählen, sagen
think	thought	thought	denken
throw	threw	thrown	werfen
understand	understood	understood	verstehen
wake up	woke up	woken up	aufwachen
wear	wore	worn	(Kleidung) tragen
win	won	won	gewinnen
write	wrote	written	schreiben

Tapescripts

Unit 1
Lifestyle

1B

1. That's my dad. He's having a nap in our garden. In Greece most people have a siesta after lunch and then go back to work later in the afternoon.

2. This picture shows me and my family. We're having breakfast at a local restaurant. We always go out for breakfast on Sundays and I always eat pancakes. It's kind of a tradition in our family and we often meet friends and neighbours there who do the same thing.

3. Here I am at home in Ireland for the Christmas holidays. This is a local tradition – the New Year's Day swim. You can see some of my family and friends. They're swimming in the sea and it's freezing! My friend Jim, though, says it's much colder in February – he goes swimming every day of the year. He's mad!

2B

● Good morning and and welcome to "Early Bird". Today I'm talking to Angie and Kevin Bailey, the fashion designers. Angie, what time do you normally get up?
■ Well, I don't like getting up early, but I'm most energetic at about eight o'clock in the morning, so I usually get up before then. About half six most days.
● How long does it take you to wake up?
■ Oh, when I've had a shower, I feel awake straightaway.
● And what about you, Kevin?
◆ Well, I'm not really a morning person – especially in winter. It takes me ages to wake up properly then. It's much better in summer, though, when it's light outside.
● And do you have a favourite time of the week?
■ Oh, yes! Sundays. I like to have a nice long lie-in, a proper breakfast …
▲ I prefer Friday evening. There's the whole weekend ahead of you.
● Is there a time you don't like?
◆ Monday mornings! I don't know why, but I always seem to be in a bad mood …
■ Yes, you are!

3A

Sound effects: alarm clock, grandfather clock, radio alarm, timer

3B

1. I need more than one alarm clock or I don't wake up. I've got one by my bed and one over on the television, so I have to get up to turn it off. And I've got a radio alarm that switches on first.

2. I don't need a watch because I've got a good feeling for time, but I have got a couple of clocks at home. My favourite is a grandfather clock which I was given by an old friend.

3. We produce timers, for kitchen equipment, lights, central heating systems – you name it, we make it!

4. ● Have you got an electronic organizer?
■ No, I haven't got one, but my husband has. He's very forgetful so he's got one which bleeps before an appointment. Of course he's got a desk diary too and we've got a big calendar on the wall where we write everybody's birthdays and holidays and things like that.

3E

Song

5A

1. I used to collect stamps when I was a teenager, but I haven't looked at them for years now. I don't even know where they are.

2. There didn't use to be colour TV when we were growing up. It was only black and white, but we thought it was great. My brother and I used to watch "The Lone Ranger" every week. It was a western series.

3. My mother didn't get a washing machine until she was about fifty. She used to wash all our clothes by hand, and in winter she had to dry them in the kitchen.

4. Most people didn't use to go abroad for their holidays then; it was too expensive. Our family used to go camping at the seaside. We loved it because it was so different from being at home.

6B

I used to think that it would be terrible to be old, but I'm 66 now and I'm having the best time of my life. I retired four years ago and so I've got lots of time to do what I want. Of course, I'm lucky – I'm still healthy and I've also got enough money. I travel a lot nowadays and I'm learning French at the University of the Third Age. It's not really a university – it's a kind of school for people over 50. They offer lots of interesting courses in the afternoons and evenings. You can learn languages or do painting or pottery courses. And you make lots of friends with similar interests. I didn't have time when I was younger. I used to work all day and then I was tired in the evening. Now I often go out in the evening. In fact, my daughter has just bought me an answering machine because she says I'm never there when she tries to phone me!

Unit 2
From here to there

2A

1. ● Excuse me. Do you know where I can find a timetable?
   ■ No, I'm sorry. I don't know.
   ● Oh. Thanks anyway.

2. ● Can you tell me where I can buy a ticket, please?
   ■ Yes, there's a ticket office over there or you can buy one from a machine.
   ● Ah, thank you.
   ■ You're welcome.

3. ● Excuse me, do you know how this machine works?
   ■ Yes, you just touch the screen like this and then follow the instructions.
   ● Ah. I see!

4. ● Can you tell me which platform the train to Victoria leaves from, please?
   ■ Victoria? That's platform 2 – over there.
   ● Thanks.

2D

● Can I help you?
■ Er, yes, please. I'd like a return to Westfield.
● I'm sorry, there aren't any return tickets now.
■ Oh!
● You can buy a carnet, that's a book of ten single tickets, or there's the day ticket. You can use that for all the zones until three o'clock the next morning.
■ Uh huh.
● Or if you travel regularly, you can buy a monthly season ticket. That's valid until the same date the next month, so if you buy one today – what is it, the sixth? – you can use it until the fifth of next month. That's much cheaper than buying a ticket every day.
■ Right. Er, what about families? Are there any reductions for families?
● Yes, there are. Children under five travel free, and then they only pay half price until they're 15 – like senior citizens and disabled people.
■ OK.
● And there's a family ticket: two adults and up to three children can travel together between 9.15 and 3.30 and after 7 p.m. on any one day.
■ Is that for the whole system?
● Yes, but you can choose the zones too, for example if you only want to travel in the city centre, you can just buy a ticket for zones 1 and 2.

4B

1. ● Why have we stopped?
   ■ They're working on the line. There was a notice at the station.
   ● Oh, was there?
   ■ Yes. It happens all the time. I have to go to Cardiff once a week and we're always late.
   ● I thought business people did everything by e-mail these days!
   ■ Well, you can do a lot that way of course, but for some things you still need face-to-face contact.

2. ● This is the first time I've been on a real ship.
   ■ Me too. Cool, eh?

121

- Yeah. Where are you going?
- Limoges.
- Where's that?
- Er, somewhere south of Paris, I think. It's our twin town.
- Oh, yeah. Are you going there on holiday?
- No, we're on an exchange. It's arranged by our school.

3. ◆ … the weather in Delhi is fine, and the temperature this morning is 32° Celsius. Our flight is exactly on time and we should be landing in about fifteen minutes. Thank you for flying with us and we wish you a pleasant stay.
- Do you know Delhi well?
- Well, I grew up there.
- Really?
- Yes, so a trip like this isn't just meeting the customers, but a bit of a holiday too, with visits to the relatives and old school friends and so on.

4. ■ Are you getting out in Munich too?
- No, I'm going on to Vienna.
- Oh, that's a long way.
- Yes, but then I'll be back at home!
- Oh. I thought you were from England. Your English is very good.
- That's very kind of you! Actually I've just been there for four weeks on a language course, so I've had a lot of practice.

5. ● … because my sister's just moved there. I've never been to the States before.
- No, nor me. Actually you'll never believe this, but we won this trip in a competition.
- Really?
- Yes, a free flight and five days in Florida!

5B

- … because my sister's just moved there. I've never been to the States before.
- No, nor me. Actually you'll never believe this, but we won this trip in a competition.
- Really?
- Yes, a free flight and five days in Florida!
- Fantastic! What are you going to see there?
- Well, some of it's organized, but you can choose some things too. We're going to start off with a trip to Disneyworld and the next day there's a guided tour of the Space Center at Cape Canaveral.
- That'll be interesting.

- Yes. What about you?
- Well, I'm just visiting my relatives, so I don't know what we're going to do yet. Actually I'd be really interested in that underwater centre, WaterWorld.
- Me, too. You can go swimming there with the fish, but I'm not going to try that. I wouldn't feel safe!
- And the Everglades, that's in Florida too, isn't it?
- Yes, I think so, but I don't know if we're going to go there.

6A

1. Two cities for the price of one! Old Delhi with its colourful bazaars, busy streets and narrow lanes is full of historic monuments. New Delhi, by contrast, is the modern capital of India and has wide tree-lined avenues, elegant official buildings and beautiful parks. Delhi: a perfect introduction to the exotic sights and smells of India and the ideal starting point for your visit to some of India's finest tourist attractions, such as Agra and the Taj Mahal.

2. Less than two hours from London, Cardiff (Caerdyff in Welsh) is a city with an international reputation and a lively atmosphere. Cardiff's attractions include its busy commercial centre, a world-class opera house, home to the Welsh National Opera, and the Millennium Stadium for top sporting events. Its excellent shops, superb museums and its exciting nightlife all help to make the Welsh capital one of Britain's favourite cities.

3. Welcome to Miami, a cosmopolitan city with a superb climate, world-class shopping and excellent conference facilities. Miami's seven miles of beaches, three golf courses and 20 parks make it one of the world's favourite tourist destinations. Miami International Airport is the gateway to Latin America and the city has one of the fastest-growing economies in the country. With its rich mix of cultures and perfect natural setting, Miami is the city you won't want to forget.

Unit 3
Buy it!

1B

1. ● We've got some lovely red ones.
   ■ Er, I think I'd prefer yellow.
   ● Yes. How many would you like?
   ■ A dozen, please.

2. ■ Oh, yes. He hasn't read that one. I'll take that, please.
   ● Right.
   ■ Could you gift-wrap it for me, please?
   ● Yes, certainly.

3. ■ Mm, they're very nice. How much are they?
   ● They're, er, a hundred and twenty-eight fifty.
   ■ Can I exchange them if they don't match my dress?
   ● Yes, but please keep the receipt.
   ■ OK.

4. ● Good morning. Can I help you?
   ■ Er, yes please. Have you got anything for backache?
   ● Backache? You could try this. It's very good.
   ■ Uh huh.

5. ● Well, these are very good value.
   ■ Mm, but I need one with an internal modem.
   ● Ah. We haven't got any in stock, but I can order one for you.

2C

1. shopping basket
2. high quality
3. weekly shopping
4. special offer
5. excellent service
6. local store
7. low prices
8. delivery date

2E

● I don't understand why people buy online. Do you?
■ Well, I suppose it's very helpful if you live a long way from the shops, or you can't get out of the house.
◆ That's right. There aren't any good shops where I live, so I often order clothes online, but I prefer going to a shop because I like to see things before I buy them.
● Hm. I wouldn't use my credit card to shop online, although everyone says it's safe.
◆ Oh, I think it's safe and it's very convenient. My son always books his holidays online so that he doesn't have to go to the travel agent's. It's cheaper too.
■ I don't think I'd book a holiday online even if it was cheaper. Think of the risk – all that money!

3B

1. ● Customer service, good morning.
   ■ Hello, I ordered some glasses from your online service.
   ● Yes?
   ■ Well, they've just arrived and two of the glasses are missing.
   ● Oh, I'm sorry to hear that. Can I have your customer number, please?
   ■ Yes, it's 790542.
   ● One moment, please. That's Mrs Porter and it was twelve crystal glasses.
   ■ That's right. But there are only ten in the box.
   ● OK, Mrs Porter. If you'd like to return them to us, we'll replace them straight-away.

2. ● Can I help you?
   ■ Yes, please. I bought these shoes here yesterday, but they're too tight.
   ● Uh huh. Have you got your receipt, please?
   ■ Yes, here it is.
   ● OK.
   ■ Er, have you got them in a bigger size?
   ● Let's have a look … yes, here we are.
   ■ Ah, fantastic.

3. ● Excuse me. I bought this camera here yesterday and it doesn't work.
   ■ Uh huh. Let's just check the battery … no, that's OK. We'll have to send it back to the manufacturer.
   ● Have you got another one?
   ■ No, that was the last one, I'm afraid. It was a special offer.
   ● Oh.
   ■ I'll give you a credit note.

● Er, I'm leaving the country tomorrow. I'd like a refund, please.
■ Oh, OK. You'll have to go to the service department, then. It's on the fifth floor.

5A

● No, I'm not influenced by advertising, at least I don't think so. I decide what I need and then I look for the best value for money. With basic things like sugar I buy the one which is cheapest. What d'you think?
■ Well, it depends. When someone well-known advertises something, it definitely makes a difference. If it's someone who I respect, then I think the product is probably OK, too.
◆ I don't think advertising makes any difference. I mean, you don't decide to change your toothpaste because of an ad which you've just seen on TV, do you?
■ No, perhaps not, but if I can't find the things which I usually buy, then I probably buy products with names which I recognize.
◆ I know some people who only buy clothes with the right brand names, but I think that's ridiculous. You pay a lot more for a fashionable label and the quality's no better because all companies sell clothes under different names. I just choose the clothes which fit best.

6A

Well, the first thing you see when you come into the store is the fruit and the vegetables. They're on the right: all nice fresh food. The next thing in that aisle is the dairy products: butter, yoghurt and so on, and then you come to the meat counter. That's at the back of the store, opposite the tinned foods. What next? Er, there's the fish – that's between the meat and the frozen foods – and then you've got the soft drinks and the mineral water. The last thing on your right before you reach the tills, that's the wines and spirits. Right. Now, in the middle of the store you've got four rows of shelves. On the first one you'll find ...

Unit 5
You are what you wear

1C

1. What do I wear at work? Er, a blouse and skirt usually, with a jacket – or perhaps a dress when it's hot. I never dress casually. I mean, if you sell good clothes, you have to look smart yourself, don't you?

2. We all wear suits here. I know that sounds conservative, but our customers expect it. They wouldn't trust us with their money if we wore jeans. We had a trainee once who dyed his hair red. The manager sent him home to change it back to brown!

3. A skirt? You must be joking! Everyone wears what they want to here. If you feel more creative in pyjamas, well, that's OK! Most of us wear jeans and a T-shirt or sweater.

4. Well, I usually wear a T-shirt and shorts. And a tracksuit in winter. The kids think I look funny if they see me in a jacket and trousers, and sometimes they don't recognize me at all!

2C

● I'm ordering some things from this catalogue. Would you like one of these shirts?
■ Yes, that would be nice. What colour shall I have? Red?
● Well, I think blue suits you.
■ Oh, all right. I'll have a couple of blue ones, then. They'll go with my new jeans.
● Blue goes with a lot of things. What size are you?
■ Er, 44, I think.
● I'll order large. If they don't fit, we can always send them back.
■ OK.
● I'm going to order these trousers. Let's see – I think I'll get size 16 so they aren't too tight. I want them to be comfortable.
■ Yeah.
● Oh, and look at this blouse!
■ Mm, that's nice isn't it?
● It's silk – just right for the summer!
■ Yes. Why don't you order that too?
● Which colour shall I get? Green?
■ Yes, that would be nice and fresh, wouldn't it?

4B

- ● So people have always decorated themselves in some way?
- ■ Yes, even when they lived in caves, they painted their skins in different colours and wore jewellery.
- ● Really? How did they make it?
- ■ They used whatever they could find – the bones and teeth of various animals, for instance, and stones and shells from the sea.
- ● And they made these things into necklaces?
- ■ That's right; necklaces, bracelets, and so on.
- ● Do we know when people started piercing their bodies?
- ■ Not exactly, no. But they were certainly doing it by about 3000 B.C. And they were already using perfume then, too.
- ● What about tattoos? That's quite a recent thing, isn't it?
- ■ Oh, no – not at all! We're not sure exactly when it started, but we do know that the Egyptians had them four thousand years ago.
- ● Why did people start doing all these things, d'you think?
- ■ Well, the reasons haven't changed much over the years – to look more beautiful, to charm the opposite sex, to show that they were wealthy and could afford fine things. There were religious and magical reasons, too.
- ● Oh, yes?
- ■ Yes. the Aztec priests used to pierce their tongues so they could speak to the gods. And then there were health reasons. For example sailors used to believe that wearing earrings gave them better eyesight.
- ● Really?
- ■ Yes. Another reason is to show membership of a tribe or a group. The way that married people in our society usually wear rings.
- ● Ah, yes. Of course.

5B

- ● I like your scarf. Is it new?
- ■ No, I bought it on holiday last year.
- ● It's lovely. That colour really suits you.
- ■ Thanks. I'm glad you like it.

- ◆ Wow, that's a trendy mobile.
- ▼ Oh, do you like it?
- ◆ Yes, it's really neat, isn't it?
- ▼ Yes, it is. It's very practical, too.

5E

1. It lowers the cost of clothes.
2. Other children will laugh at them.
3. They started using perfume.
4. How often have you changed your hairstyle?
5. I bought it on holiday.

6B

1. ● My purse, I've lost my purse!
   - ■ Oh, dear. When did you last see it?
   - ● I don't know – I had it in town this morning.
   - ■ Well, you'd better phone the lost property office.
   - ● Yes, I will.

2. ◆ Good morning. Lost property.
   - ● Hello. I'm calling to ask if someone has found my purse. I think I lost it in town this morning.
   - ◆ A purse? Can you describe it, please?
   - ● Er, yes. It's made of black leather and it's got my initials on it: RPG.
   - ◆ Just a moment, please. No, I'm sorry. No one has handed in a purse today.
   - ● Oh.
   - ◆ You could try again this afternoon. We're open until six.
   - ● OK. Thanks. I'll call back later.

3. ● Hello. I've lost my credit card. Could you cancel it, please?
   - ▼ Right. When did you lose it, please?
   - ● I'm not sure. It was in my purse when I left home this morning, but now I can't find it.
   - ▼ Uh huh. Have you reported it to the police?
   - ● No, not yet.
   - ▼ OK. If you give me your details, we'll cancel it straightaway, but please report it to the police as soon as possible.
   - ● Yes, of course.

4. ◆ Black leather? Er, I think someone brought one in this afternoon. Yes, here we are. Can you tell me what was in it, please?
   - ● Er, my credit card, er, some cash – about a hundred and twenty, I think – er, my driving licence and and a photo of my children.
   - ◆ OK, we've got it here.
   - ● Oh, wonderful!

- ◆ Please bring some identification with you when you come to collect it.
- ● Yes, of course. Er, can you tell me who found it, please?
- ◆ Er, yes, the ice cream man in the park handed it in.
- ● Oh, I must have left it there when I bought an ice this morning!

Unit 6
Enjoy!

1B

- ● Well, I normally have breakfast at work at around seven or eight o'clock in the morning – usually a cup of decaffeinated coffee and a couple of cheese or jam rolls.
- ■ What about lunch? D'you eat in the company canteen?
- ● No, I always go out at lunchtime.
- ■ Really?
- ● Yes, with one of my colleagues. We both like spicy food, so we normally go to one of the local Asian restaurants – Indian or Thai, Persian perhaps. There's a good Turkish place near here too.
- ■ Uh huh.
- ● And in the summer we go somewhere you can sit outside.
- ■ And the rest of the day?
- ● Well, I have another coffee in my office in the afternoon.
- ■ Decaf.
- ● No, normal filter coffee and sometimes a piece of cake or a biscuit.
- ■ What time would that be?
- ● Oh, about half past three or four. And in the evening we usually have a light meal at home at eight o'clock. That's normally a salad and a sandwich with a glass of beer or red wine – French, of course.
- ■ Don't you ever eat German food?
- ● No, hardly ever – it has to be German beer, though!
- ■ And do you go out for meals in the evening, too?
- ● Not very often, no. It's difficult with two kids – expensive, too. But we sometimes go out to a local Greek restaurant on special occasions.

3C

- ■ Chicken, ham and leek pie: that sounds delicious! What ingredients do we need?
- ● For the pastry, we'll need 250 grammes of flour, 110 grammes of butter, one large egg and three tablespoons of water. And for the filling, 600 grammes of chicken …
- ■ Chicken breast or a whole chicken?
- ● It doesn't matter, but it's a lot easier if you buy chicken breast. Er, then two medium-sized leeks, a thick slice of ham and 175 milli-litres of white wine.
- ■ Which wine would you use here?
- ● Well, we always say you should use the wine that you're going to drink with the meal. But nothing too sweet. A Chardonnay is always good. And finally, 300 millilitres of milk and some salt and pepper.

3D

- ● First of all we need to preheat the oven to 180° C. Then we cut the chicken and ham in to two-centimetre cubes. Next we have to fry the chicken until it's brown all over, then add the wine and cook for another ten minutes.
- ■ But before we do that we need to taste the wine. Mm, that's good.
- ● Yes, and not too sweet. OK, now I'll fry the chicken lightly for a few minutes and then add the wine. And while the chicken's cooking we can start making the sauce. First we cut the leeks into thin slices and then we fry them in butter lightly for five to six minutes. After that we add some flour, milk, salt and pepper to make a thick sauce. Remember to keep stirring. Then we pour the leek sauce over the chicken and lastly we add the ham. And now if you could just put the mixture in that pie dish, we can get on and make the pastry.
- ■ Right.
- ● That's great. Now we need to roll out the pastry quite thickly and cover the filling with it.
- ■ Uh huh.
- ● To finish it off I always brush the pastry with a little egg to make it that wonderful golden brown colour …
- ■ Ah, yes.
- ● … and then we put the pie in the oven and bake it for 35-40 minutes. And here's one I put in the oven earlier.

- ■ Mm, that looks delicious. It smells wonderful too.
- ● Yes, it does, doesn't it? And it's so easy to make. I like to serve this with new potatoes and fresh spring vegetables. Today I've got some excellent carrots and asparagus. Would you like to join me?
- ■ Yes, please! I'll just pour the wine.

4B

- ● Would you like to come over to our house on Sunday? We're having a few friends round for a barbecue at about six.
- ■ Oh, we'd love to, but I'm afraid we can't.
- ◆ We've promised to go to my parents for the day and we won't be back till late.
- ● That's a shame! We'll have to find another time.
- ■ Yes, that would be nice.
- ▼ How about coming for dinner the Saturday after instead?
- ● Yes, why don't you come then?
- ◆ That would be great. What time?
- ● Oh, around seven.
- ■ Fine.
- ● Good. We'll look forward to seeing you then.
- ◆ Yes. Thank you.

5A

- ■ With me today is Dr Carol Billings, who has just completed a survey on the way they do things in Canada. Dr Billings, what made you do this survey?
- ● Well, we have a lot of foreigners visiting Canada and of course customs are often different from one country to another. It's sometimes difficult for them to know what they ought to do, for example when they're invited to someone's house for a meal. Should they be punctual, or should they come early ... ?
- ■ And what did you find out?
- ● Most people prefer their guests to come a little late – say up to half an hour late.
- ■ Really? And what else did you discover?
- ● Well, we asked people about gifts. Guests often think that they ought to bring one when they visit somebody. But that's not the custom here – no one expects a gift, so you needn't do that.
- ■ Uh huh.
- ● Another important thing is that you ought to tell your hosts before the meal if there's anything you don't eat. It can be very embarrassing if they've cooked lots of meat and you're a vegetarian, for example.
- ■ Yes.
- ● And then of course Canadians like to offer their guests a lot to eat – that is a custom here – but don't feel that you have to eat it all! You may say no to a second helping – that's OK.
- ■ Is there anything else that can cause problems?
- ● Smoking. It's very impolite to smoke in some one else's house without asking, you oughtn't to do that. Always ask if you may smoke, and if so, where.
- ■ Yes, that's good advice.
- ● Of course, these are all just guidelines, but we hope that they'll help a few guests to feel more confident when they're invited to someone's home.

5D

- ● Would you like to try some of this?
- ◆ Mm, yes please!

- ◆ Could you pass me the salt, please?
- ▼ Yes, of course. Here you are.

- ● Would you like some more dessert?
- ■ It's delicious, but I really couldn't!

- ▼ Can I get you another glass of wine?
- ◆ I'd better not, thank you. I'm driving.

- ◆ I'm afraid we must be going. It's getting late.
- ● Oh, d'you have to? Have another cup of coffee first.

- ■ Thank you very much for a lovely evening.
- ▼ Thank you for coming.

6A

A few years ago in Australia some students invited me to a party on Christmas Day. I arrived with my bottle at about eight thirty in the evening and then I discovered that the party had started at lunchtime and most of the guests had already left and gone to the beach. So, anyway, when I had eaten some food I joined them on the beach and went for a swim, too. It was a lovely Christmas, but now I never accept an invitation without asking exactly what time I should come!

6C

- ● Yes, it was when I was in China, some years ago.
- ■ Uh huh.
  Some people invited me out for a meal at a local restaurant. It was a great place and the food was fantastic.
- ■ So what happened?
- ● Well, we'd eaten our starters and then the waitress brought us some bowls of clear soup with pieces of lemon in it.
- ■ Uh huh.
- ● I didn't know what kind of soup it was exactly, but of course I tried it. I'd just tasted a little when I saw that everyone else was washing their fingers in it.
- ■ Oh no!
- ● Yes, I was really embarrassed!

Unit 7
The media and me

1B

- ▼ Well, the Chinese were already printing books in the ninth century.
- ● What about newspapers? When did they start?
- ■ The first real one was published in England, wasn't it?
- ◆ Yes, that's right. It was the London Gazette.
- ■ And radio, that must be the BBC.
- ◆ Uh huh, but the Americans were the first with colour TV.
- ▼ Right. The internet, too.
- ◆ Yes.

2B

1. I spend the whole day in the studio, creating the charts and maps for the programmes at lunchtime and 6.30 pm. All that work goes into one or two minutes on air.

2. It's important to read at the right speed, not too fast and not too slowly. You have to practise pronouncing the names correctly, too. People are very critical of that, quite rightly. You also have to learn to sound serious, but not emotional – the stories shouldn't sound too depressing.

3. It's no good if you aren't interested in it. After all, you spend a lot of time at the events, waiting to interview participants or commenting on games. And you have to sound enthusiastic.

4. I don't have to know all the answers myself – my producer helps me there. If I did, I'd probably sound arrogant and I wouldn't be able to sympathize with the contestants. But I enjoy finding out the answers. It's never boring.

5. These programmes are great fun. The part I like best is when the kids are actually in the studio. Sometimes they're so excited that it takes a while to calm them down, but they're great. I love it.

3B

1. Here in Britain you have to pay an annual TV licence fee, and then we subscribe to a pay-TV company too, mainly because of the sports. We pay them a monthly subscription.

2. We get about 70 different channels, I think, but I just have two or three favourite ones.

3. You notice there are more commercials in prime viewing time in the evenings – I don't think they're allowed during children's programmes earlier in the day.

4. There's always something that says the commercials are starting – End of Part 1, or something like that. They aren't allowed to show them without making a clear break.

5. I always watch the commercials – they're often better than the programmes themselves, aren't they?!

Unit 9
House and home

1A

1. ● Where's home for you?
   ■ Oh, that's difficult. I was quite glad to leave the States and I've been here for a long time now. My family and my closest friends live here, and I have French citizenship too, so I suppose this is home for me.
   ● Here? That means France?

- ■ Well, yes, this part of France, this place, where my family is, where we live.
- ● And when you go to the States on a visit, is that home?
- ■ Oh yes, of course it is. It'll always be home. It's where I was raised and spent my childhood. And when I talk about it, I always say back home. My kids don't like it, but I say, home's there and home's here.

2.
- ● I lived at home until I finished my training. Then I got a job in this city, which is two hundred miles from my hometown. At first I was terribly homesick, I was desperate to get a job nearer home.
- ■ So home for you was where your parents lived.
- ● Yes, that's right. Where I grew up, where my friends were.
- ■ And now?
- ● Well, it's changed. I've got a lot of friends here now, and a flat here in the centre of the city, which I love, and it's home for me, too. But my girlfriend lives about 20 miles away and I go there most weekends. I feel at home there, too.
- ■ Do you mean you've got more than one home?
- ● Yes, I suppose I've got three. Perhaps home isn't so important when you're young and not really settled. Of course, home is where I grew up, but it's also where I'm living at the moment. If I'm happy there, then it's home.

5B

If you watch the soaps on TV, you might think that people never get on with their neighbours, but fortunately real life is different. A recent survey found that over eighty percent of people meet their new neighbours in the first few weeks after they've moved into their new home. Nearly everyone either chats to their neighbours regularly or makes an effort to be friendly. Almost half of the people we talked to would trust their neighbours to look after their pets, and just under a third would trust their children with the neighbours. Perhaps most surprisingly, more than three quarters of the people we interviewed would trust their neighbours with a spare key to their homes.

5D

1. When we moved into our new flat, the people who lived downstairs rang the bell and offered to look after the children for us while we were sorting things out. They had two small children themselves, so that was perfect. They all had a wonderful time playing together and they've been friends ever since.

2. We had a rather difficult neighbour, but she's moved now, thank goodness. We had some trouble with her a few years ago because one of our windows looked out onto her patio. She told us to change the glass in the window and put frosted glass in there because she liked to sunbathe on the patio and she didn't want anyone to see her.

3. We'd always wanted to go on a long cruise and when my husband retired, we decided it was now or never. The only problem was our cat, but we've got a very nice neighbour who promised to feed it while we were away. And he must have fed it very well, because when we came home the cat couldn't get through the cat flap – it was too fat. We had to put it on a diet and it didn't like that at all.

4. My parents decided they'd like to have a pond in their back garden. They made a very nice one, with water lilies and reeds and so on, and put some fish in there too. Everything was fine until the next spring, when some frogs discovered the pond. Frogs can be pretty noisy and these ones spent most of the night croaking. The neighbours complained about the noise and asked my father to get rid of the frogs. He caught them all and took them down to the river, but a few days later they were back and croaking again. Now the neighbours say they're going to take them to court – my parents, that is, not the frogs.

Unit 10
Learning for life

1C

1. I learned French at school, but when I got to France I didn't understand what people were saying. It was frightening. So the first few days I didn't say anything, I just listened. And by listening carefully I gradually learned to speak myself.

2. When my little brother was about nine he taught himself to play chess. He just took a book and followed the steps from start to finish. And it worked.

3. I didn't learn to ski until I was 20. I was terrified, but my friend showed me the basics and I just copied her. She was incredibly patient.

3C

- I wish I knew more about computers. I envy these kids, they can do anything with them.
- Mm, yes, so do I. They learn a lot more than we did at school now, don't they? They didn't teach us anything practical. I mean, I wish they'd taught us how to repair cars or fill in tax forms.
- I know what you mean. In my school you couldn't do cookery unless you failed Latin. I passed, so I never learned to cook!
- We had to do Latin at our school too. I quite enjoyed it. But I wish I'd learned Spanish.
- Oh yes, I wish I spoke another language properly, don't you? Our Spanish teacher was useless.
- Yes, so was ours. Maybe we should go to evening classes and try again.
- Mm, that's an idea. But first I think I'd like to learn to dance.
- What do you mean? Tango or waltz or what?
- Anything. Ballroom dancing, really. I find it so embarrassing that I can't dance.
- Well, I'll tell what's even more embarrassing. I can't swim.
- You can't swim?
- No, we didn't have swimming at school and my parents weren't interested. Later I didn't really get the chance. And I really wish I could swim.
- Maybe we could teach you!

4E

- We have Ron Stanton here, he's a taxi driver and I'm going to ask him, Ron, what makes a good taxi driver?
- The most important thing is to be sociable, to like people. You have all sorts of different people in your taxi every day and you have to be cheerful and helpful, and not just treat them like another suitcase.
- So do you talk to all your passengers?
- Well, you have to be tactful – some don't want to talk. Some people just expect you to be polite, and others expect you to be knowledgeable about local things.
- And how well do you need to know the city?
- Like the back of your hand. We have to take an exam to prove it. You can't waste time looking at the map – it makes the passengers suspicious. You need to be honest, too, and not drive all round the houses to get to a place when there's a direct way.
- Do you need to be particularly fit?
- Yes, you do really because it's pretty tiring driving around all day. And you have to have nerves of steel, so you don't get angry with the traffic or with impatient passengers. The trouble is, you don't exactly keep fit sitting around in a taxi all day.
- No, I don't suppose you do. And what about your routine, is it fixed?
- No, no, we don't have a routine. You have to be totally flexible. You never work in the same area or the same hours two days running. You have to be prepared to get up and go out at anytime of the day or night, and in all weathers.
- So to sum up, a good taxi driver should be …
- … young, trustworthy, as fit as a fiddle, flexible, easy-going …
- That sounds like a tall order! Thanks for talking to us, Ron.
- You're welcome.

5B

- What did they ask you?
- The first question was if I had come to the interview alone.
- Oh, goodness!
- Yes, it surprised me, too. Then they asked me which of my qualifications were relevant.
- What did you say to that? Did you tell them you've got 10 GCSEs?

- Well, it was all in my CV, but I did. And I told them about my first-aid certificate, that I'd got a clean driving licence, and I'd done a secretarial diploma by distance learning. I don't know if it was relevant, but they seemed satisfied.
- Uh huh.

5C

- I don't know if it was relevant, but they seemed satisfied.
- Uh huh.
- Then they asked me if I was afraid of the dark!
- Afraid of the dark? What a strange question.
- Yes, I wasn't prepared for that at all. I was a bit nervous by then. But then they asked me the questions I had expected, like why I wanted to join the police force, and if I'd done any self-defence. And after that they wanted to know if any of my friends had ever committed a crime.
- Oh, that's nasty.
- Yes, but it's fair I suppose. I mean it probably happens to quite a lot of police officers ...

6B

There are basically three groups of people who come to our evening classes. The first group come because they want to gain new skills, for example in business studies, because they want to change their job or have a better chance of promotion. Then there are the people who come for purely social reasons: they want to get out of the house and meet other people. The people in this group often do languages or creative courses. And finally there are the people who just want to keep their minds and bodies fit.

Unit 11
The world around us

1C

- ... so United is safely through to the next round. And that's the sport, which means it's time for the weather with Christine Fulton.
- Thanks, Peter. Well, it's been another lovely autumn weekend, but the weather's changing now and winter's on the way, I'm afraid. Tomorrow will be a bit of a mixed bag. It'll be bright and sunny during the morning, but then cloud will start moving in from the west and there could be some quite heavy showers and even thunderstorms during the afternoon. Tuesday will be dry with plenty of sunshine, but it'll be rather cool for the time of year: maximum temperatures between three and five degrees Celsius. There'll also be a strong east wind which will make it feel colder. Wednesday will start frosty, so watch out for ice on the roads. And what about the rest of the week? Well, we'll probably see snow on the hills by the weekend, so it's definitely time to get your winter woollies out!

1E

- Hello, Tina.
- Oh, hello, Chris.
- It's a lovely day today, isn't it?
- Yes, it is.
- That was a terrible storm last night, wasn't it? I didn't sleep a wink!
- Nor me. They didn't forecast it, did they?
- No, they didn't. It hasn't rained like that for ages, has it?
- No. It really poured down, didn't it?
- Yes. Good for the garden, though.
- That's true.

3B

1. - Of course I was very thirsty after the journey so I drank a lot of water out of the tap. Afterwards I had terrible stomach-ache and spent the night in the bathroom.
   - Oh, no! That must have been awful.
   - Yes, it was. But it was my own fault. I shouldn't have drunk the water.

2. - Hi! How was your holiday?
   - Not so good. The island was hit by a hurricane a couple of days before we arrived.
   - No!
   - Yeah. Half the place was flattened and the rest was shut down.
   - What a shame! You must have been really disappointed.
   - You can say that again! Apparently it happens every year around this time.

- ● The travel agents should have told you when you booked.
- ■ Yes, that's what we told them. We're trying to get our money back.

3. ● They'd just got back from a walk when they saw a bear trying to get into their tent.
   ■ You're kidding! What did they do?
   ● They just hid behind their car and waited for it to go away. It was only after the food.
   ■ They didn't leave food in the tent, did they? They could have been killed!
   ● Well, bears aren't normally aggressive, but you're right. They shouldn't have stored it in the camp.

4. ● The people at the hotel said there was a risk of avalanches, but the snow looked great and the sun was shining, so I decided to go anyway. I was half-way down the slope when I heard a noise. I looked back and there was this great wall of snow coming down behind me. I only just managed to get out of the way.
   ■ I would have been terrified!
   ● Yes. I was very lucky. I should have listened to the locals.

5A

1. We have decided to accept the developers' offer. It's hard to give up land that we have been farming for generations, but we hope that this will bring new people to the area and help the local economy.

2. The number of people employed at the airport has increased by 20% in the last five years, but in the rest of the area jobs have been disappearing since the airport opened.

3. They've been trying to complete the path for years. I'd like to fight the decision, but all the other people with houses along the coast have sold their land now, so what can I do?

6A

We're in the energy business. Our main product is coal. When you say coal mine, most people probably think of underground mines, but in this area the coal is quite near the surface, so we can mine it in open-cast mines. A typical coal field stretches over several kilometres, which means we have to move roads, railways and even rivers to get at the coal. Forests are cut down and farms and villages are relocated too. An open-cast mine is basically a large, deep hole which is open to the sky. We cut the coal in the mine with excavators and transport it to power stations where it's used to produce electricity for the region. When a coal field is mined out, the mines are turned into lakes where people can swim and sail, or nature reserves for birds and so on. The forests are replanted and new farmland is created. In a few years you'd never know that there'd been a coal mine there!

Unit 13
It takes all sorts

1B

1. ● Right, thank you. And could I see your ticket, please?
   ■ Oh, sorry. There you are.
   ● Right. Thank you. Enjoy your flight.
   ■ Thanks.

2. ■ My name's Hallam.
   ● Mr Hallam ... Ah, yes. If you could just sign here, please.
   ■ OK.
   ● Thank you. And here's your room key.

3. ● Sir!
   ■ Yes?
   ● Can you come over here for a minute?
   ■ Have you found something?
   ● I think so. Look at this.
   ■ Hm! They're all over it, aren't they? Why didn't he wear gloves?

4. Sound effects

5. ● There you are, Ms Charlton.
   ■ Thanks.
   ● If you'd like to take a seat, she'll be with you in a moment.
   ■ OK.

3B

● Surnames date from about the twelfth century, don't they?
■ In England, yes.
● Where did they come from?

- Well, originally they were nicknames. If there are several people in your village called John, you need some way of identifying them, don't you? A natural way is by their appearance. You'd call them John the Brown, or John the Short. And in time these names would become just John Brown or John Short.
- Right.
- Then there are lots of people with animal names, like Bull, for instance. Someone may have been called that because he looked a bit like a bull, or behaved like one.
- ... in a china shop.
- Yes. Or perhaps he was a rather tricky character ...
- ... so they called him Fox?
- Exactly! Another way you can identify people easily is by their occupations: Baker, Farmer, Thatcher and so on. There are dozens of those.
- Right. Er, what about all those people whose surnames end with s-o-n? Johnson, for example?
- Ah yes, that's what they call a patronymic.
- Sorry?
- Patronymic. That's where you take the father's name and add "-son", so it's really John's son, Peter's son and so on. And there are short versions of these names too, like Roberts, where the "o-n" must have got lost over the years.
- Uh huh.
- Incidentally, Johnson's the second most common English surname.
- After Smith?
- Yes, that's right. Well, that brings us to the last category: the places. We've got two types here. Firstly there are the people whose surnames come from the landscape. For example, a family called Hill probably lived on a hill, or near one. Other names like that would be Field, Lake and so on.
- And the other place names?
- Well, all the names we've talked about so far are really local names, aren't they, names you'd use about someone you know. But of course people don't always stay in the same place.
- So ... ?
- So, many people have got names which must have come from an ancestor's hometown. Take someone called Richard who lived a town called Burton. When he moved to a different town, his new neighbours called him "Richard of Burton", and that's how Burton became his family's surname.
- Ah, I see.
- Someone else would be called Kent because that was the part of the country he came from. And the same is probably true of the thousands of English people whose surname is Scott.
- You mean their ancestors came from Scotland?
- Yes, they were probably people who moved south to find work.

4D

- How do you feel now that Sophie's left home?
- Well, I miss her terribly of course, but I'm not really responsible for her now she's moved away. I used to worry about her if she didn't phone home regularly, but she's got her own life to live and she can look after herself much better than I could.
- What about you, Sophie?
- Oh, I'm just as fond of of my parents as I used to be. But it's nice not to be financially dependent on them anymore. I think we're still very close to each other and when I come home I still feel it's home.

5A

- A friend is someone who's there when you need them.
- A friend? That's someone you can share a joke with.
- Someone who doesn't mind if you're busy when they call.
- A true friend is someone who doesn't care what you look like today!
- Someone whose car you can borrow.
- Well, I think a friend is someone who tells you when you're wrong.

5E

- Did you seriously expect to find a partner though the ad?
- Not really. You know how it is, it was a bit of a joke. I wouldn't have put the ad in the paper if my friend hadn't paid for it.

- ◆ It wasn't much of a joke for me – I was terrified. If Steve hadn't written 'shy' in the ad, I wouldn't have phoned him. And I was shaking on the phone.
- ● Was the first contact difficult?
- ■ Yes, the first phone call was difficult because I really am quite shy. I'm sure I wouldn't have talked to Jackie for so long if she hadn't sounded so nice – and natural.
- ◆ Something I was warned about was that he might want to know where I lived. If he'd asked for my address, I would have put the phone down straight away.
- ■ That was difficult because of course I wanted to know where she lived. If she hadn't lived nearby, I wouldn't have suggested meeting. I didn't want to spend a lot of time travelling.
- ◆ If you think about it – I was terrified and Steve wasn't really very serious to begin with, but in the end we both feel we've met our ideal partner.

Unit 14
A balanced life

2B

1. I like to get some exercise at the weekends, because I'm stuck behind a desk all week. I go running and cycling if the weather's good, and I play football with a group of friends most Sunday mornings.

2. My husband's on the road a lot of the time, so when he does get home he's happy just to be with the family, playing with the kids or taking them out somewhere. That's the most relaxing thing for him.

3. You don't meet many people in my job and you can feel a bit cut off at times, so I like to get out whenever I can, and I often go away at weekends.

4. My idea of a rest is to sit down and put my feet up with a good book or watch a nice film on TV. I'm on my feet all day at work, so I don't need anything active when I'm off duty!

5. I hate doing nothing – I always find something to do in the house or garden. My wife complains that I can't sit still for five minutes, but I feel happiest when I'm working on something.

2G

See the text on p. 95.

3B

- ● Chris, you say you've always wanted to do this. But why now?
- ■ I just felt I couldn't cope with work any more – I was actually quite ill and my friends were worried about me, so I thought: it's now or never.
- ● Uh huh. And when are you going to start?
- ■ Well, first I'm going to get the boat into shape, which will probably take a few more weeks. Then I'll decide when I'm ready, and when the weather's right, I'll go.
- ● Do you know which route you're going to take?
- ■ Oh yes, the route's all planned, but of course it'll depend on several things – my health and strength for one thing. But I'm going to start sailing southwest because of the weather at this time of year.
- ● How long do you think it'll take?
- ■ I'm not going to restrict myself with deadlines. This isn't a race, it's for pleasure, so I'll stop and explore places whenever I feel like it.
- ● OK. Well, thank you, Chris, and good luck.
- ■ Thanks.
- ● That was Chris Bromfit who is fulfilling his dream to sail around the world. And tomorrow we talk to a woman who is planning to train as a circus clown, at the age of 65!

6C

- ● Hello, I've just seen your ad in the paper.
- ■ Ah, hello.
- ● Er, can you tell me a bit more about the children?
- ■ Yes, of course. What did you want to know, exactly?
- ● Well, I was wondering how old they are.
- ■ Er, that depends on the group, but they're usually between six and fourteen.
- ● I see.
- ■ We can usually fit you in with the age group you prefer.

- OK. And can I ask about the accommodation? Do the carers live with the children?
- Yes, but we've got a separate guest house, too. We can find you a bed there if you prefer.
- Is there any chance of a single room?
- Er, we only have a few singles, but if you put that on the booking form, we'll try and keep one for you.
- Fine. Just one more question. Do you provide bed linen and towels?
- Yes, that's all there. All your meals are included too.
- Uh huh.
- If you need a special diet, we can organize that as well. But you'll find all the details in our brochure. Shall I put one in the post to you?
- Oh, yes, please. Thank you.
- Right. Could you give me your address?
- Yes, that's 42B Yorkshire Terrace, Dudley DY5 4KP.

Unit 15
Come together

1B

Recent estimates suggest that 377 million people speak English as a first language. The two largest concentrations are the USA with 251 million speakers and the UK with 56 million. This means that 6.2% of the world's population use English as their mother tongue, second only to Mandarin Chinese. The third most-spoken language is Spanish, followed by Hindi and Arabic. Portuguese, next on the list, now has more native speakers than Russian, which is spoken by about 2.7% of the world's population. French, which used to be one of the most important international languages, is now less widespread than German with its 100 million speakers and Japanese with 120 million, or about 2.0% of the world's population.

3B

1. Our daughter's dance group is appearing in the festival this weekend. Of course they all had to have special costumes, which has kept us mothers busy for weeks. I think we'll only just finish making them in time for the big day!

2. I didn't have anything planned last weekend. One of my flatmates suggested going down to the community centre. People read out their poems and we had to clap if we liked them and boo if we didn't. Poetry isn't really my thing, but it was good fun.

3. I went to a club with my teenage kids the other day. It was very loud and I couldn't hear the lyrics. I kept asking them what the songs were about. I don't think they'll ever take me again!

4. We're going to that exhibition in Broad Street tonight. I think my wife's always a bit nervous that I'm going to spend all our savings on some very expensive painting, but to be honest, I just enjoy looking at them.

4B

- Hello, Janet. This is Meg, calling from England.
- Oh, hi Meg, great to hear from you. How are you doing?
- Fine, thanks. I just wanted to thank you for your letter.
- Oh, you're welcome. Will you be able to come, do you think?
- Yes, we'd love to, if it's still all right with you.
- Sure. We're looking forward to it. Will you be here for the fourth of July?
- Yes, I hope so. We leave on June the twentieth and we're spending a few days in New York first of all, with Jon's cousin. Then we're going to tour New England with him for about a week, but after that we'll be free.
- Well, that's good, because David's on vacation the first week of July, so we'll be able to show you around a bit. When do you have to go back?
- I'm not sure. I think our flight's on the sixth. I'll mail you the exact details in the next day or two.
- Great. Well, it'll be nice to see you again.
- You too, Meg. Thanks so much for inviting us. And give our love to David.

Unit Vocabulary
Kapitel-Wörterverzeichnis

Alle neuen Wörter, die in *On the MOVE Plus* vorkommen, sind in chronologischer Reihenfolge unter der jeweiligen Kapitel- und Übungsnummer aufgenommen, z. B. 1/1A (Unit 1, Teil 1, Übung A). Wörter, die schon einmal in *On the MOVE 1 – 4* vorgekommen sind, werden hier in der Regel nicht mehr aufgeführt.

sb = somebody   sth = something   *(AE)* = amerikanisches Englisch   *(BE)* = britisches Englisch

Phonetic alphabet Lautschrift

[ː] bedeutet, dass der vorangehende Laut lang ist.
['] bedeutet, dass die folgende Silbe die Hauptbetonung erhält.
[ˌ] bedeutet, dass die folgende Silbe eine Nebenbetonung erhält.

[ɪ]	is	[iː]	meet	[eɪ]	name	[p]	post	[ʃ]	shop
[e]	hello	[ɑː]	park	[aɪ]	my	[b]	bus	[ʒ]	leisure
[æ]	at	[ɔː]	for	[ɔɪ]	boiled	[t]	to	[h]	hotel
[ʌ]	number	[uː]	afternoon	[əʊ]	no	[d]	code	[tʃ]	church
[ɒ]	office	[ɜː]	nurse	[aʊ]	town	[k]	speak	[dʒ]	Jenny
[ʊ]	good			[ɪə]	here	[g]	good	[m]	morning
[ə]	number	[ɔ̃ː]	restaurant	[eə]	where	[f]	first	[n]	nice
				[ʊə]	you're	[v]	evening	[ŋ]	long
						[θ]	thanks	[l]	left
						[ð]	this	[r]	room
						[s]	seven	[w]	waitress
						[z]	is	[j]	yes

Unit 0 *Starter*

0/1A
relative ['relətɪv] — Verwandte/r
recently ['riːsəntlɪ] — kürzlich, in der letzten Zeit

0/3A
statement ['steɪtmənt] — Aussage
mistake [mɪ'steɪk] — Fehler
to correct [tʊ kə'rekt] — korrigieren
general ['dʒenərəl] — allgemein

Unit 1 *Lifestyle*

1/1B
nap [næp] — Nickerchen
pancake ['pænkeɪk] — Pfannkuchen
a kind of tradition [ə ˌkaɪnd ˌəv trə'dɪʃn] — eine Art Tradition
freezing ['friːzɪŋ] — eisig
mad [mæd] — verrückt

1C
current ['kʌrənt] — gegenwärtig, aktuell
temporary ['tempərərɪ] — vorübergehend
routine [ruː'tiːn] — routinemäßig
regular ['regjələ] — regelmäßig

2
early bird ['ɜːlɪ ˌbɜːd] — Frühaufsteher/in
night owl ['naɪt ˌaʊl] — Nachteule

2A
energetic [enə'dʒetɪk] — fit, energisch
to feel awake [tʊ fiːl ə'weɪk] — sich wach fühlen

Unit Vocabulary

ages (It takes me ~) ['eɪdʒɪz] — ich brauche ewig
light [laɪt] — hell
lie-in (to have a ~) ['laɪ ˌɪn] — im Bett bleiben
proper ['prɒpə] — richtig
whole [həʊl] — ganz
ahead of you [ə'hed ˌəv ju:] — vor dir
to seem [tʊ si:m] — scheinen
bad mood (to be in a ~) [ˌbæd 'mu:d] — schlechte Laune haben

1/3A
stopwatch ['stɒpwɒtʃ] — Stoppuhr
radio alarm ['reɪdɪəʊ ˌə.la:m] — Radiowecker
grandfather clock [ˌgrændfɑ:ðə 'klɒk] — Standuhr
timer ['taɪmə] — Zeitschaltuhr
watch [wɒtʃ] — Armbanduhr
electronic organizer [ˌelektrɒnɪk ˌɔ:gənaɪzə] — elektronischer Terminplaner
calendar ['kæləndə] — Wand-Kalender

1/3B
to have got [tʊ hæv 'gɒt] — haben
to turn off [tʊ tɜ:n ˌɒf] — ausschalten
to switch on [tʊ swɪtʃ ˌɒn] — einschalten
feeling ['fi:lɪŋ] — Gefühl
kitchen equipment ['kɪtʃɪn ˌɪkwɪpmənt] — Küchengeräte
central heating system [ˌsentrəl 'hi:tɪŋ ˌsɪstəm] — Zentralheizungssystem
forgetful [fə'getfʊl] — vergesslich
to bleep [tʊ bli:p] — piepsen

1/3E
singer ['sɪŋə] — Sänger/in
rhythm ['rɪðəm] — Rhythmus
sky, skies [skaɪ, skaɪz] — Himmel

1/3F
pot [pɒt] — Topf
to boil [tʊ bɔɪl] — kochen

1/4
leisure ['leʒə] — Freizeit

1/4A
to collect [tʊ kə'lekt] — sammeln
stamp [stæmp] — Briefmarke
billiards ['bɪljədz] — Billard
model ['mɒdl] — Modell

1/4C
to love [tʊ lʌv] — lieben

I don't mind … [aɪ ˌdəʊnt 'maɪnd …] — Es macht mich nichts aus …
to hate [tʊ heɪt] — hassen
I can't stand … [aɪ ˌkɑ:nt ˌ'stænd] — Ich kann … nicht ertragen

1/5
I used to (collect stamps). [aɪ 'ju:st ˌtʊ] — Früher habe ich (Briefmarken gesammelt).

1/5A
I don't even know … — Ich weiß nicht einmal …
colour TV ['kʌlə ˌti:'vi:] — Farbfernsehen
to grow up [tʊ grəʊ ˌʌp] — aufwachsen
western series ['westən ˌsɪərɪz] — Western-Serie
by hand [baɪ 'hænd] — mit der Hand
to dry [tʊ draɪ] — trocknen
to go camping [tʊ gəʊ 'kæmpɪŋ] — zelten
at the seaside [ət ˌðə 'si:saɪd] — am Meer

1/5E
to pin up [tʊ pɪn ˌʌp] — anstecken, anhängen

1/6
The time of your life — die besten Jahre deines Lebens

1/6A
wrinkle ['rɪŋkl] — Falte
youth [ju:θ] — Jugend
to waste [tʊ ˌweɪst] — verschwenden
schooldays ['sku:ldeɪz] — Schulzeit

1/6B
terrible ['terəbl] — schrecklich, furchtbar
nowadays ['naʊədeɪz] — heutzutage
painting ['peɪntɪŋ] — Malerei
pottery ['pɒtərɪ] — Töpfern
answering machine ['ɑ:nsərɪŋ məˌʃi:n] — Anrufbeantworter

1/6D
retirement [rɪ'taɪəmənt] — Ruhestand

Unit 2 From here to there

2/1A
to display [tʊ dɪ'spleɪ] — zeigen

2/1B
explanation [ˌeksplə'neɪʃn] — Erklärung

137

to fasten your seat belt [tʊ ˌfɑːsn jɔː ˈsiːt ˌbelt]	sich anschnallen	**2/3B**	
to allow [tʊ əˈlaʊ]	erlauben, gestatten	to catch sight of sth [tʊ kætʃ ˈsaɪt əv]	etwas erblicken
to throw [tʊ θrəʊ]	werfen	double-decker [ˌdʌblˈdekə]	Doppeldecker-
2/1D		journey [ˈdʒɜːnɪ]	Fahrt, Reise
compartment [kəmˈpɑːtmənt]	Abteil	peak time [ˌpiːk ˈtaɪm]	Hauptverkehrszeit
passenger [ˈpæsəndʒə]	Fahrgast	to purchase [tʊ ˈpɜːtʃəs]	kaufen
to give up [tʊ gɪvˈʌp]	überlassen	to ring [tʊ rɪŋ]	anrufen
elderly (people) [ˈeldəlɪ] [ˌeldəlɪ ˈpiːpl]	ältere Leute	revolutionary [ˌrevəˈluːʃənrɪ]	revolutionär
disabled [dɪˈseɪbld]	behindert	non-stop [ˌnɒnˈstɒp]	Nonstop-
2/2A		easy-to-use [ˌiːzɪ tʊ ˈjuːz]	benutzerfreundlich
timetable [ˈtaɪmˌteɪbl]	Fahrplan	touch-screen [ˈtʌtʃskriːn]	Berührungsbildschirm
Thanks anyway.	Trotzdem vielen Dank.	first class [ˌfɜːstˈklɑːs]	erste Klasse
platform [ˈplætfɔːm]	Gleis	**2/3D**	
ticket office [ˈtɪkɪt ˌɒfɪs]	Fahrkartenschalter	to move [tʊ muːv]	sich bewegen
2/2C		just as slowly	genauso langsam
dozen [ˈdʌzn]	Dutzend	**2/4A**	
exporter [ɪkˈspɔːtə]	Exporteur	to pass the time [tʊ pɑːs ðə ˈtaɪm]	die Zeit vertreiben
to nationalize [tʊ ˈnæʃənəlaɪz]	verstaatlichen	to doze [tʊ dəʊz]	ein Nickerchen machen
to privatize [tʊ ˈpraɪvətaɪz]	privatisieren	to miss the stop [tʊ mɪs ðə ˈstɒp]	die Haltestelle verpassen
train service [ˈtreɪn ˌsɜːvɪs]	Zugverbindung	So do I. / Me too. [ˌsəʊ dʊ ˈaɪ / ˌmiː ˈtuː]	Ich auch.
to operate [tʊ ˈɒpəreɪt]	betreiben	I don't. [ˈaɪ ˌdəʊnt]	Ich (aber) nicht.
infrastructure [ˈɪnfrəˌstrʌktʃə]	Infrastruktur	Neither do I. / Nor me. [ˌnaɪðə dʊ ˈaɪ / ˌnɔː ˈmiː]	Ich auch nicht.
track [træk]	Schiene	I do. [ˈaɪ ˌduː]	Ich schon.
signal [ˈsɪgnəl]	Signal	**2/4B**	
tunnel [ˈtʌnəl]	Tunnel	ferry [ˈferɪ]	Fähre
to manage [tʊ ˈmænɪdʒ]	führen, leiten	return home [rɪˌtɜːn ˈhəʊm]	Heimkehr
the public interest [ðə ˌpʌblɪk ˈɪntrest]	das öffentliche Interesse	student exchange [ˌstjuːdənt ɪksˈtʃeɪndʒ]	Studentenaustausch
not-for-profit [ˌnɒt fə ˈprɒfɪt]	gemeinnützig	reason [ˈriːzn]	Grund
historic [hɪˈstɒrɪk]	historisch	notice [ˈnəʊtɪs]	Hinweis
to run [tʊ rʌn]	(*hier*) fahren	face-to-face [ˌfeɪs tʊ ˈfeɪs]	persönlich
a must [ə mʌst]	ein Muss	twin town [ˌtwɪn ˈtaʊn]	Partnerstadt
enthusiast [ɪnˈθjuːzɪæst]	Enthusiast/in	pleasant [ˈplezənt]	angenehm
2/2D		to get out [tʊ getˈaʊt]	aussteigen
single / return ticket [ˌsɪŋgl / rɪˌtɜːn ˈtɪkɪt]	Einzel- / Rückfahrkarte	Munich [ˈmjuːnɪk]	München
carnet [ˈkɑːneɪ]	Fahrkartenheft	Vienna [vɪˈenə]	Wien
zone [zəʊn]	Zone	to win (won, won) [tʊ wɪn (wʌn, wʌn)]	gewinnen
valid [ˈvælɪd]	gültig	competition [ˌkɒmpəˈtɪʃn]	Wettbewerb
reduction [rɪˈdʌkʃn]	Ermäßigung	**2/4C**	
senior citizen [ˌsiːnjə ˈsɪtɪzən]	Rentner/in	What's it like?	Wie ist es?

2/4D
fellow traveller	[ˌfeləʊ ˈtrævələ]	Mitreisende/r

2/5A
thrilling	[ˈθrɪlɪŋ]	aufregend
ride	[raɪd]	Fahrt
animal	[ˈænɪməl]	Tier
encounter	[ɪnˈkaʊntə]	Begegnung
killer whale	[ˈkɪlə ˌweɪl]	Killerwal, Orka
dolphin	[ˈdɒlfɪn]	Delphin/Delfin
sealion	[ˈsiːˌlaɪən]	Seelöwe
stingray	[ˈstɪŋreɪ]	Stachelrochen
to view	[tʊ vjuː]	zuschauen
launch	[lɔːntʃ]	Start, Abschuss
landing	[ˈlændɪŋ]	Landung
space shuttle	[ˈspeɪsˌʃʌtl]	Raumfähre
space station	[ˈspeɪsˌsteɪʃn]	Raumstation
alligator	[ˈælɪgeɪtə]	Alligator
to wrestle	[tʊ ˈresl]	ringen
bird	[bɜːd]	Vogel
fishing	[ˈfɪʃɪŋ]	fischen
swamp	[swɒmp]	Sumpf
buggy	[ˈbʌgɪ]	Buggy

2/5B
guided tour	[ˌgaɪdɪdˈtʊə]	Führung

2/5D
to intend	[tʊˌɪnˈtend]	beabsichtigen

2/6A
colourful	[ˈkʌləfʊl]	bunt
bazaar	[bəˈzɑː]	Basar
busy	[ˈbɪzɪ]	belebt
narrow	[ˈnærəʊ]	eng
lane	[leɪn]	Gasse
monument	[ˈmɒnjəmənt]	Denkmal, historische Gebäude
by contrast	[baɪ ˈkɒntrɑːst]	im Gegensatz
tree-lined	[ˈtriːlaɪnd]	von Bäumen gesäumt
avenue	[ˈævənjuː]	Boulevard, Allee
elegant	[ˈelɪgənt]	elegant
exotic	[ɪgˈzɒtɪk]	exotisch
sight	[saɪt]	Sehenswürdigkeit
smell	[smel]	Geruch
tourist attraction	[ˈtʊərɪstˌəˈtrækʃn]	Touristenattraktion
reputation	[ˌrepjəˈteɪʃn]	Ruf, Ansehen
commercial centre	[kəˈmɜːʃlˌsentə]	Geschäftsviertel
exciting	[ɪkˈsaɪtɪŋ]	aufregend
nightlife	[ˈnaɪtlaɪf]	Nachtleben
cosmopolitan	[ˌkɒzməˈpɒlɪtən]	kosmopolitisch
conference facilities	[ˈkɒnfərəns fəˌsɪlətɪz]	Tagungseinrichtungen
gateway	[ˈgeɪtweɪ]	Tor
to grow	[tʊ grəʊ]	wachsen
rich mix	[rɪtʃ ˈmɪks]	bunte Mischung
natural setting	[ˌnætʃərəl ˈsetɪŋ]	natürliche Lage, Umgebung

2/6C
to describe	[tʊ dɪˈskraɪb]	beschreiben
positive/ly	[ˈpɒzətɪv(lɪ)]	positiv

Unit 3 *Buy it!*

3/1B
lovely	[ˈlʌvlɪ]	schön
receipt	[rɪˈsiːt]	Quittung
value (to be good ~ for money)	[ˈvæljuː]	sein Geld wert sein
in stock	[ɪn ˈstɒk]	auf Lager

3/1C
to gift-wrap	[tʊ ˈgɪftræp]	als Geschenk verpacken
to exchange	[tʊˌɪksˈtʃeɪndʒ]	umtauschen
internal	[ɪnˈtɜːnl]	intern

3/2A
basket	[ˈbɑːskɪt]	Korb
search	[sɜːtʃ]	Suche
groceries	[ˈgrəʊsərɪz]	Lebensmittel
benefit	[ˈbenəfɪt]	Vorteil
to deliver	[tʊ dɪˈlɪvə]	liefern
to take out	[tʊ teɪkˈaʊt]	rausnehmen

3/2D
helpful	[ˈhelpfʊl]	hilfreich, nützlich
risk	[rɪsk]	Risiko

3/2E
conjunction	[kənˈdʒʌŋkʃn]	Bindewort
so	[səʊ]	daher, also
although	[ɔːlˈðəʊ]	obwohl
so that	[səʊ ðæt]	so dass
even if	[ˈiːvnˌɪf]	selbst wenn

3/2F
major	[ˈmeɪdʒə]	wichtig, bedeutend
impact	[ˈɪmpækt]	Auswirkung
habit	[ˈhæbɪt]	Gewohnheit
according to	[əˈkɔːdɪŋˌtʊ]	zufolge, gemäß, nach

consumer [kənˈsjuːmə]	Konsument/in
while [waɪl]	während

3/3A

broken [ˈbrəʊkən]	zerbrochen
damaged [ˈdæmɪdʒd]	beschädigt

3/3B

glass [glɑːs]	(Trink)Glas
to be missing [tʊ bɪ ˈmɪsɪŋ]	fehlen
crystal [ˈkrɪstl]	kristall-
tight [taɪt]	eng
battery [ˈbætəri]	Batterie
credit note [ˈkredɪt ˌnəʊt]	Gutschrift
refund (I'd like a ~, please.) [ˈriːfʌnd]	Ich hätte gern mein Geld zurück.

3/4

brilliant [ˈbrɪliənt]	genial, toll, brilliant

3/4A

aim (Who are they ~ed at?) [eɪm]	An wen sind sie gerichtet?

3/4B

clever [ˈklevə]	clever, klug
effective [ɪˈfektɪv]	effektiv, wirksam
funny [ˈfʌni]	komisch, lustig
horrible [ˈhɒrəbl]	schrecklich, grauenhaft
offensive [əˈfensɪv]	anstößig
sexist [ˈseksɪst]	sexistisch
stupid [ˈstjuːpɪd]	dumm
negative [ˈnegətɪv]	negativ

3/4C

particularly [pəˈtɪkjələli]	besonders

3/5

to influence [tʊ ˈɪnfluəns]	beeinflussen

3/5A

influence [ˈɪnfluəns]	Einfluss
to recognize [tʊ ˈrekəgnaɪz]	erkennen
well-known [ˌwelˈnəʊn]	bekannt
basic [ˈbeɪsɪk]	Grund-
to respect [tʊ rɪˈspekt]	respektieren
toothpaste [ˈtuːθpeɪst]	Zahnpaste
brand name [ˈbrænd ˌneɪm]	Markenname
ridiculous [rɪˈdɪkjələs]	lächerlich, albern
fashionable [ˈfæʃənəbl]	modisch
label [ˈleɪbl]	Etikett

3/6A

aisle [aɪl]	Gang, Korridor
shelf, shelves [ʃelf, ʃelvz]	Regal, Regale
trolley [ˈtrɒli]	Einkaufswagen
till [tɪl]	Kasse
exit [ˈeksɪt]	Ausgang
entrance [ˈentrəns]	Eingang
dairy product [ˈdeəri ˌprɒdʌkt]	Molkereiprodukt
frozen foods [ˌfrəʊzn ˈfuːdz]	Tiefkühlkost
soft drink [ˈsɒft ˌdrɪŋk]	alkoholfreies Getränk
tinned (AE: canned) foods [ˌtɪnd (ˌkænd) ˈfuːdz]	Konserven
spirits [ˈspɪrɪts]	Spirituosen
counter [ˈkaʊntə]	Theke

3/6B

cereal [ˈsɪəriəl]	Getreide
cleaning products [ˈkliːnɪŋ ˌprɒdʌkts]	Putzmittel

3/6C

washing powder [ˈwɒʃɪŋ ˌpaʊdə]	Waschpulver
the next aisle but one	der übernächste Gang
below [bɪˈləʊ]	unterhalb von

Unit 4 Revision

4/C

dice [daɪs]	Würfel

Unit 5 You are what you wear

5/1A

blouse [blaʊz]	Bluse
dress [dres]	Kleid
jacket [ˈdʒækɪt]	Jacke
shirt [ʃɜːt]	Hemd
shorts [ʃɔːts]	Shorts
skirt [skɜːt]	Rock
suit [suːt] [sjuːt]	Anzug
sweater [ˈswetə]	Pullover
tie [taɪ]	Krawatte
tracksuit [ˈtræksuːt]	Trainingsanzug
trousers [ˈtraʊzəz]	Hose

5/1B

shabby [ˈʃæbi]	schäbig
formal [ˈfɔːməl]	förmlig
casual [ˈkæʒuəl]	leger, salopp
smart [smɑːt]	fein, gepflegt
scruffy [ˈskrʌfi]	vergammelt
conservative [kənˈsɜːvətɪv]	konservativ

Unit Vocabulary

5/1C
to dress	[tʊ dres]	sich anziehen, sich kleiden
to trust	[tʊ trʌst]	anvertrauen
trainee	[ˌtreɪˈniː]	Auszubildende/r
You must be joking!	[juː ˌmʌst bɪ ˈdʒəʊkɪŋ]	Das soll wohl ein Witz sein!
to joke	[tʊ dʒəʊk]	einen Witz machen

5/1D
creative	[krɪˈeɪtɪv]	kreativ
pyjamas	[pɪˈdʒɑːməz]	Schlafanzug

5/1E
sense	[sens]	Sinn
to feel	[tʊ fiːl]	sich fühlen
to look	[tʊ lʊk]	aussehen
to smell	[tʊ smel]	riechen
to sound	[tʊ saʊnd]	sich anhören
to taste	[tʊ teɪst]	schmecken

5/1F
practical	[ˈpræktɪkl]	praktisch
comfortable/comfortably	[ˈkʌmftəbl / ˈkʌmftəblɪ]	bequem
… and that was that.		… und das war's.
First World War	[ˌfɜːst ˌwɜːld ˈwɔː]	Erster Weltkrieg
female	[ˈfiːmeɪl]	weiblich

5/1G
sightseeing	[ˈsaɪtˌsiːɪŋ]	Besichtigungen

5/2A
catalogue	[ˈkætəlɒg]	Katalog
silk	[sɪlk]	Seide
cream	[kriːm]	cremefarben
plain	[pleɪn]	Uni-
cardigan	[ˈkɑːdɪgən]	Wolljacke, Strickjacke
button	[ˈbʌtn]	Knopf
belt	[belt]	Gürtel
acrylic	[əˈkrɪlɪk]	Acryl
machine washable	[məˌʃiːn ˈwɒʃəbl]	waschmaschinenfest
beige	[beɪʒ]	Beige
burgundy	[ˈbɜːgəndɪ]	burgunderrot, weinrot
striped	[straɪpt]	gestreift
side	[saɪd]	Seiten-
pocket	[ˈpɒkɪt]	Tasche
linen	[ˈlɪnɪn]	Leinen
viscose	[ˈvɪskəʊs]	Viskose
grey	[greɪ]	grau
checked	[tʃekt]	kariert
short-sleeve(d)	[ˌʃɔːtˈsliːv(d)]	kurzärmelig
cotton	[ˈkɒtn]	Baumwolle

5/2B
material	[məˈtɪərɪəl]	Stoff
pattern	[ˈpætən]	Muster

5/2C
quantity (Abk. qty)	[ˈkwɒntətɪ]	Menge
to suit (sb)	[tʊ ˈsuːt] [tʊ ˈsjuːt]	jmd stehen, passen
to go with (sth)	[tʊ ˈgəʊ wɪð]	zu etwas passen
to fit	[tʊ fɪt]	passen (Form, Größe)
loose	[luːs]	locker

5/3
uniform	[ˈjuːnɪfɔːm]	Uniform

5/3B
to put on	[tʊ pʊt ˈɒn]	anziehen
to lower	[tʊ ˈləʊə]	reduzieren, senken
official	[əˈfɪʃl]	Beamte/r, Funktionär/in

5/3D
for / against	[fɔː / əˈgenst]	pro/contra
to judge	[tʊ dʒʌdʒ]	beurteilen
cover	[ˈkʌvə]	Umschlag, Äußeres

5/4
body decoration	[ˈbɒdɪ ˌdekəˈreɪʃn]	Körperschmuck

5/4A
perfume	[ˈpɜːfjuːm]	Parfüm
make-up	[ˈmeɪkʌp]	Make-up
jewellery	[ˈdʒuːəlrɪ]	Schmuck
tattoo	[təˈtuː]	Tattoo
piercing	[ˈpɪəsɪŋ]	Piercing
ornament	[ˈɔːnəmənt]	Ornament
valuable	[ˈvæljʊəbl]	wertvoll
precious stone	[ˌpreʃəs ˈstəʊn]	Edelstein
to attach	[tʊ əˈtætʃ]	anbringen, befestigen
skin	[skɪn]	Haut
substance	[ˈsʌbstəns]	Substanz, Stoff
appearance	[əˈpɪərəns]	Aussehen
to prick	[tʊ prɪk]	stechen
hole	[həʊl]	Loch
to fill	[tʊ fɪl]	füllen
dye	[daɪ]	Farbstoff

5/4B
cave	[keɪv]	Höhle
bone	[bəʊn]	Knochen
tooth, teeth	[tuːθ, tiːθ]	Zahn, Zähne
shell	[ʃel]	Schale
necklace	[ˈnekləs]	Halskette
bracelet	[ˈbreɪslət]	Armband
to charm	[tʊ tʃɑːm]	bezaubern

the opposite sex [ðɪˌɒpəzɪt 'seks]	das andere Geschlecht
wealthy ['welθɪ]	wohlhabend
to afford [tʊˌə'fɔːd]	sich leisten
religious [rɪ'lɪdʒəs]	religiös
magical ['mædʒɪkl]	magisch
Aztec ['æztek]	Azteke/Aztekin
priest [priːst]	Priester
tongue [tʌŋ]	Zunge
god [gɒd]	Gott
sailor ['seɪlə]	Seemann
earring ['ɪərɪŋ]	Ohrring
eyesight ['aɪsaɪt]	Sehkraft
membership ['membəʃɪp]	Mitgliedschaft
tribe [traɪb]	Volk, Stamm

5/4C
ago (4000 years ~) [ə'gəʊ]	vor 4000 Jahren
to connect [tʊ kə'nekt]	verbinden

5/4D
hairstyle ['heəstaɪl]	Haarstil
facelift ['feɪslɪft]	Gesichtsstraffung
weight (to lose / to put on ~) [weɪt]	abnehmen / zunehmen

5/5
scarf [skɑːf]	Schal

5/5A
compliment (to pay a ~) ['kɒmplɪmənt]	ein Kompliment machen

5/5B
neat [niːt]	toll, klasse
trendy ['trendɪ]	modisch
I'm glad … [aɪm 'glæd]	Ich freue mich …

5/5D
vowel ['vaʊəl]	Vokal (Selbstlaut)
consonant ['kɒnsənənt]	Konsonant (Mitlaut)
break [breɪk]	Pause

5/6
valuables ['væljʊəblz]	Wertsachen

5/6A
key [kiː]	Schlüssel
umbrella [ʌm'brelə]	Regenschirm
walkman ['wɔːkmən]	Walkman
handbag ['hændbæg]	Handtasche
purse [pɜːs]	Geldbörse
wallet ['wɒlɪt]	Brieftasche

5/6B
lost property office [ˌlɒst'prɒpətɪˌɒfɪs]	Fundbüro
loss [lɒs]	Verlust
to lose (lost, lost) [tʊ luːz (lɒst, lɒst)]	verlieren
to find (found, found) [tʊ faɪnd (faʊnd, faʊnd)]	finden
to hand in [tʊ hændˌɪn]	abgeben
to bring in (brought, brought) [tʊ brɪŋˌɪn (brɔːt, brɔːt)]	hereinbringen
identification [aɪˌdentɪfɪ'keɪʃn]	Identifikation
birth certificate ['bɜːθ səˌtɪfɪkət]	Geburtsurkunde

5/6C
to steal (stole, stolen) [tʊ stiːl (stəʊl, stəʊlən)]	stehlen
trick [trɪk]	Trick

Unit 6 Enjoy!

Enjoy! [ɪn'dʒɔɪ]	Guten Appetit!

6/1B
decaffeinated (Abk. decaf) [dɪ'kæfɪneɪtɪd ('diːkæf)]	koffeinfrei
jam [dʒæm]	Marmelade
roll [rəʊl]	Brötchen
canteen [kæn'tiːn]	Kantine
spicy ['spaɪsɪ]	würzig
Asian ['eɪʒən]	asiatisch
Indian ['ɪndɪən]	indisch
Persian ['pɜːʃən]	persisch
Thai [taɪ]	thailändisch
Turkish ['tɜːkɪʃ]	türkisch
though (It has to be German beer, ~!) [ðəʊ]	Es muss aber deutsches Bier sein!

6/1C
frequency ['friːkwənsɪ]	Häufigkeit
expression [ɪk'spreʃn]	Ausdruck

6/2
fancy (A little bit of what you ~ does you good.) ['fænsɪ]	(etwa) Man gönnt sich ja sonst nichts.
to fancy sth [tʊ 'fænsɪ ˌsʌmθɪŋ]	Lust auf etwas haben

6/2A
alternative [ɔːl'tɜːnətɪv]	Alternative
basis ['beɪsɪs]	Hauptbestandteil
diet ['daɪət]	Ernährung
amount [ə'maʊnt]	Menge
lean [liːn]	mager

Unit Vocabulary

cut [kʌt]	Stück	flour [flaʊə]	Mehl
low-fat [ˌləʊˈfæt]	fettarm	tablespoon (Abk. tbs) [ˈteɪblspuːn]	Esslöffel
portion [ˈpɔːʃn]	Portion	filling [ˈfɪlɪŋ]	Füllung

6/2B

to be rich in [tʊ bɪ rɪtʃ ɪn] — reich sein an
carbohydrate [ˌkɑːbəʊˈhaɪdreɪt] — Kohlehydrat
plenty of [ˈplentɪ əv] — reichlich
vitamin [ˈvɪtəmɪn] — Vitamin
roughage [ˈrʌfɪdʒ] — Ballaststoffe
protein [ˈprəʊtiːn] — Protein
replacement [rɪˈpleɪsmənt] — Ersatz
legume [ˈlegjuːm] — Hülsenfrucht
bean [biːn] — Bohne

6/3

recipe [ˈresɪpi] — Rezept

6/3A

sausage [ˈsɒsɪdʒ] — Wurst
apple pie [ˌæplˈpaɪ] — Apfelpastete
to fry [tʊ fraɪ] — braten
to serve [tʊ sɜːv] — servieren
chips (AE: french fries) [tʃɪps (ˌfrentʃˈfraɪz)] — Pommes frites
mashed potatoes [ˌmæʃt pəˈteɪtəʊz] — Kartoffelpüree
best before [ˌbest bɪˈfɔː] — mindestens haltbar bis
to pour [tʊ pɔː] — (darüber)gießen
saucepan [ˈsɔːspən] — Kochtopf
to empty [tʊ ˈempti] — hineingeben
to stir [tʊ stɜː] — rühren
to cover [tʊ ˈkʌvə] — abdecken
to simmer [tʊ ˈsɪmə] — köcheln
suitable [ˈsuːtəbl] [ˈsjuːtəbl] — geeignet
vegetarian [ˌvedʒɪˈteərɪən] — Vegetarier/in
to bake [tʊ beɪk] — backen
to preheat [tʊ ˌpriːˈhiːt] — vorheizen
oven [ˈʌvən] — Backofen
to store [tʊ stɔː] — lagern
dry [draɪ] — trocken

6/3B

cookery verbs [ˈkʊkəri ˌvɜːbz] — Kochverben

6/3C

ingredient [ɪnˈgriːdɪənts] — Zutat
classic [ˈklæsɪk] — klassisch
chicken [ˈtʃɪkɪn] — Hühnerfleisch
leek [liːk] — Lauch
ham [hæm] — Schinken
pastry [ˈpeɪstri] — Teig

medium-sized [ˌmiːdɪəmˈsaɪzd] — mittelgroß
thick [θɪk] — dick
slice [slaɪs] — Scheibe
delicious [dɪˈlɪʃəs] — köstlich
breast [brest] — Brust

6/3D

sauce [sɔːs] — Soße
flat pie dish [ˌflæt ˈpaɪ ˌdɪʃ] — (etwa) flache Tortenform
cube [kjuːb] — Würfel
spring vegetables [ˌsprɪŋ ˈvedʒtəblz] — junges Gemüse
asparagus [əˈspærəgəs] — Spargel
to brush [tʊ brʌʃ] — bestreichen
to cut [tʊ kʌt] — schneiden
thin [θɪn] — dünn
to roll out [tʊ rəʊl ˈaʊt] — ausrollen
golden [ˈgəʊldən] — golden

6/3F

Briton (Abk. Brit) [ˈbrɪtən (brɪt)] — Brite/Britin
to conquer [tʊ ˈkɒŋkə] — erobern
the other way round — umgekehrt
curry [ˈkʌri] — Currygericht
cook [kʊk] — Koch/Köchin
to spoil [tʊ spɔɪl] — verderben
broth [brɒθ] — Brühe

6/4A

leaf, leaves [liːf, liːvz] — Blatt, Blätter
light meal [ˌlaɪt ˈmiːl] — kleine Mahlzeit
barbecue [ˈbɑːbɪkjuː] — Grillparty
brunch (breakfast + lunch) [brʌntʃ] — Brunch

6/4B

to promise [tʊ ˈprɒmɪs] — versprechen
parent [ˈpeərənt] — Elternteil
instead [ɪnˈsted] — anstatt, stattdessen

6/5A

You ought to / oughtn't to ... [jʊ ˈɔːt tʊ / ˈɔːtnt tʊ] — Sie sollten / sollten nicht ...
You needn't ... [jʊ ˈniːdnt] — Sie brauchen nicht ...
You may ... [jʊ meɪ] — Sie dürfen ...
custom [ˈkʌstəm] — Brauch
up to half an hour [ʌp tʊ ˌhɑːf ən ˈaʊə] — bis zu einer halben Stunde
helping [ˈhelpɪŋ] — Portion

impolite [ˌɪmpəˈlaɪt]	unhöflich		7/1C	
without asking [wɪˌðaʊtˈɑːskɪŋ]	ohne zu fragen		share [ʃeə]	Aktie
			celebrity [səˈlebrətɪ]	Prominente/r
guideline [ˈɡaɪdlaɪn]	Richtlinie		scandal [ˈskændl]	Skandal
confident [ˈkɒnfɪdənt]	selbstsicher		last-minute holiday [ˌlɑːstmɪnɪt ˈhɒlɪdeɪ]	Urlaub, der kuzfristig gebucht werden kann

6/5B
host [həʊst] — Gastgeber/in
to refuse [tʊ rɪˈfjuːz] — ablehnen

6/5C
to wash up [tʊ ˌwɒʃ ˈʌp] — spülen, abwaschen

6/5D
to pass [tʊ pɑːs] — reichen
dessert [dɪˈzɜːt] — Nachspeise
I'd better not [aɪd ˈbetə nɒt] — lieber nicht

6/6
intercultural [ˌɪntəˈkʌltʃərəl] — interkulturell

6/6A
already [ɔːlˈredɪ] — schon
to go for a swim [tʊ ɡəʊ fərˌə ˈswɪm] — schwimmen gehen

6/6B
participle [pɑːˈtɪsɪpl] — Partizip, 3. Form

6/6D
clear [klɪə] — klar
lemon [ˈlemən] — Zitrone
to taste [tʊ teɪst] — (hier) probieren
embarrassing [ɪmˈbærəsɪŋ] — peinlich
enjoyable [ɪnˈdʒɔɪəbl] — angenehm

Unit 7 *The media and me*

7/1
the media age [ðə ˈmiːdɪəˌeɪdʒ] — das Medienzeitalter

7/1B
BBC (British Broadcasting Corporation) — öffentlich-rechtlicher brit. Rundfunksender
to broadcast [tʊ ˈbrɔːdkɑːst] — ausstrahlen
programme [ˈprəʊɡræm] — Sendung
military communications [ˈmɪlɪtərɪ kəˌmjuːnɪˈkeɪʃnz] — Militärkommunikationen
century (as early as the 9th ~) [ˈsentʃərɪ] — schon im 9. Jh.
CBS (Columbia Broadcasting System) — US-Rundfunksender

7/1D
household [ˈhaʊshəʊld] — Haushalt
player [ˈpleɪə] — Spieler
to miss [tʊ mɪs] — vermissen

7/2A
documentary [ˌdɒkjəˈmentərɪ] — Dokumentarfilm
quiz show [ˈkwɪzˌʃəʊ] — Quizshow
situation comedy (Abk. sitcom) [ˌsɪtjʊeɪʃn ˈkɒmədɪ] — Sitcom
soap (opera) [səʊp (ˈɒpərə)] — Seifenoper
series [ˈsɪərɪz] — Serie
to sponsor [tʊ ˈspɒnsə] — sponsern
soap manufacturer [ˈsəʊp ˌmænjəˈfæktʃərə] — Seifenhersteller/in
longest-running [ˌlɒŋɡɪstˈrʌnɪŋ] — am längsten laufend
farming community [ˈfɑːmɪŋ kəˌmjuːnətɪ] — Bauerngemeinde

7/2B
to be involved in [tʊ bɪ ɪnˈvɒlvd ɪn] — zu tun haben mit
studio [ˈstjuːdɪəʊ] — Studio
chart [tʃɑːt] — Diagramm
on air [ˌɒnˈeə] — auf Sendung
critical [ˈkrɪtɪkl] — kritisch
emotional [ɪˈməʊʃnl] — emotionell
depressing [dɪˈpresɪŋ] — deprimierend
It's no good if … — Es bringt nichts, wenn …
after all [ˌɑːftərˈɔːl] — immerhin
to comment [tʊ ˈkɒment] — kommentieren
enthusiastic [ɪnˌθjuːzɪˈæstɪk] — enthusiastisch
arrogant [ˈærəɡənt] — arrogant
to sympathize [tʊ ˈsɪmpəθaɪz] — Verständnis haben
contestant [kənˈtestənt] — Kandidat/in
to find out [tʊ faɪndˈaʊt] — erfahren, herausfinden
to be fun [tʊ bɪ fʌn] — Spaß machen
excited [ɪkˈsaɪtɪd] — aufgeregt
to calm down [tʊ kɑːmˈdaʊn] — beruhigen

7/2C
depressed	[dɪˈprest]	deprimiert
interested	[ˈɪntrəstɪd]	interresiert
bored	[bɔːd]	gelangweilt

7/3A
to pay for	[tʊ peɪ fɔː]	finanzieren
channel	[ˈtʃænl]	Sender, Kanal
commercial	[kəˈmɜːʃl]	(hier) Werbespot
spot	[spɒt]	Werbespot

7/3B
annual	[ˈænjʊəl]	jährlich
licence fee	[ˈlaɪsəns ˌfiː]	Lizenzgebühr
to subscribe to	[tʊ səbˈskraɪb tuː]	abonnieren
pay TV	[ˈpeɪtiːviː]	Pay-TV
monthly	[ˈmʌnθli]	monatlich
subscription	[səbˈskrɪpʃn]	Abonnementgebühr
prime viewing time	[ˌpraɪmˈvjuːɪŋ ˌtaɪm]	Hauptsendezeit
a clear break (without making ~)	[əˌklɪə ˈbreɪk]	(etwa) ohne es deutlich zu machen

7/3C
appropriate	[əˈprəʊpriət]	passend, geeignet
commercial television	[kəˌmɜːʃl ˈtelɪvɪʒn]	Privatfernsehen
to finance	[tʊ ˈfaɪnæns]	finanzieren
to restrict	[tʊ rɪˈstrɪkt]	einschränken
cigarette	[ˈsɪgəret, ˌsɪgərˈet]	Zigarette
to ban	[tʊ bæn]	verbieten
strictly	[ˈstrɪktli]	strikt
to regulate	[tʊ ˈregjʊleɪt]	regulieren

7/3E
package	[ˈpækɪdʒ]	Paket
full coverage	[ˌfʊl ˈkʌvərɪdʒ]	ausführliche Berichterstattung
athletics	[æθˈletɪks]	Leichtathletik
show jumping	[ˈʃəʊˌdʒʌmpɪŋ]	Springreiten
to come through	[tʊ kʌm ˈθruː]	eintreffen
aspect	[ˈæspekt]	Aspekt
history	[ˈhɪstəri]	Geschichte
freak	[friːk]	Narr/Närrin, Fanatiker/in
to be fascinated	[tʊ bɪ ˈfæsɪneɪtɪd]	fasziniert sein
informative	[ɪnˈfɔːmətɪv]	informativ
to support	[tʊ səˈpɔːt]	unterstützen

world class historian	[ˌwɜːldklɑːs hɪˈstɔːriən]	Historiker/in von Weltklasse
doorstep (on your ~)	[ˈdɔːstep]	direkt vor der Haustür
sum	[sʌm]	Summe
insight	[ˈɪnsaɪt]	Einblick
otter	[ˈɒtə]	Otter
to mate	[tʊ meɪt]	sich paaren
bird-eating spider	[ˌbɜːdiːtɪŋ ˈspaɪdə]	Vogelspinne
to guarantee	[tʊ ˌgærənˈtiː]	garantieren
feature film	[ˈfiːtʃə ˌfɪlm]	Spielfilm
No more running to the video store …		Kein Gerenne mehr zum Videoladen …
to channel hop	[tʊ ˈtʃænl ˌhɒp]	zappen
to miss	[tʊ mɪs]	verpassen
specialist	[ˈspeʃəlɪst]	spezialisiert
access	[ˈækses]	Zugang, Zugriff

7/4A
drug-related crime	[ˌdrʌgrɪˌleɪtɪd ˈkraɪm]	Drogenkriminalität
to rise	[tʊ raɪz]	steigen
dear	[dɪə]	liebe, (-r, -s); teuer

7/4B
spokeswoman	[ˈspəʊksˌwʊmən]	Sprecherin
union	[ˈjuːnjən]	Gewerkschaft
to welcome	[tʊ ˈwelkəm]	begrüßen
to solve	[tʊ sɒlv]	lösen
pay	[peɪ]	Gehalt, Gehälter
low	[ləʊ]	niedrig
figures	[ˈfɪgəz]	Zahlen, Statistiken
to fall	[tʊ fɔːl]	sinken
inner city	[ˌɪnəˈsɪti]	Stadtzentrum
violent	[ˈvaɪələnt]	gewalttätig
burglary	[ˈbɜːgləri]	Einbruch
investigation	[ɪnˌvestɪˈgeɪʃn]	Untersuchung
record	[ˈrekɔːd]	Rekord-
significant/ly	[sɪgˈnɪfɪkənt/li]	beachtlich, beträchtlich
to question	[tʊ ˈkwestʃn]	befragen
to return	[tʊ rɪˈtɜːn]	wieder besuchen, wiederkommen
in the near future		in naher Zukunft

7/5
private	[ˈpraɪvɪt]	privat
confidential	[ˌkɒnfɪˈdenʃl]	vertraulich

Unit Vocabulary

7/5A
to believe	[tʊ bɪˈliːv]	glauben
the reading public [ðə ˌriːdɪŋ ˈpʌblɪk]		die lesende Öffentlichkeit
trash	[træʃ]	Schund
sensationalism [senˈseɪʃnəlɪzm]		Sensationsmache
to inform	[tʊ ɪnˈfɔːm]	informieren
to educate [tʊ ˈedʒʊkeɪt]		bilden
chairman	[ˈtʃeəmən]	Vorsitzender
depend (It ~s on the paper.) [dɪˈpend]		Es hängt von der Zeitung ab.

7/5B
to mention	[tʊ ˈmenʃən]	erwähnen
divorce	[dɪˈvɔːs]	Scheidung
floods	[flʌdz]	Hochwasser

7/5C
journalist	[ˈdʒɜːnəlɪst]	Journalist/in
permission	[pəˈmɪʃn]	Erlaubnis
to protect	[tʊ prəˈtekt]	schützen

7/6C
to appear	[tʊ əˈpɪə]	erscheinen
drought	[draʊt]	Dürre
memory (in living ~) [ˈmemərɪ]		soweit man zurückdenken kann
to admit	[tʊ ədˈmɪt]	zugeben
runner	[ˈrʌnə]	Läufer/in
head (of state) [hed (ˌhed əv ˈsteɪt)]		(Staats)Oberhaupt
to discuss	[tʊ dɪˈskʌs]	besprechen, diskutieren
link	[lɪŋk]	Beziehung
senior	[ˈsiːnɪə]	wichtig, bedeutend
cabinet	[ˈkæbɪnət]	Kabinett
to acknowledge [tʊ əkˈnɒlɪdʒ]		zugeben
frustration	[frʌsˈtreɪʃn]	Frust
policy	[ˈpɒləsɪ]	Politik, Programm, Strategie
deep	[diːp]	tief
split	[splɪt]	Meinungsverschiedenheit
party	[ˈpɑːtɪ]	Partei

7/6D
to include	[tʊ ɪnˈkluːd]	einbeziehen, einschließen
live report	[ˌlaɪv rɪˈpɔːt]	Livebericht
correspondent [ˌkɒrɪˈspɒndənt]		Korrespondent/in
sponsorship [ˈspɒnsəʃɪp]		Sponsoring

Unit 9 *House and home*

9/1A
citizenship	[ˈsɪtɪzənʃɪp]	Staatsbürgerschaft
childhood	[ˈtʃaɪldhʊd]	Kindheit
no longer	[nəʊ ˈlɒŋgə]	nicht mehr
hometown [ˌhəʊmˈtaʊn]		Heimatstadt
not settled	[nɒt ˈsetld]	ungebunden
at home	[ət ˈhəʊm]	zuhause
girlfriend	[ˈgɜːlfrend]	Freundin
close	[kləʊs]	eng
raise (where I was ~d) [reɪz]		wo ich aufwuchs
to be homesick [tʊ bɪ ˈhəʊmsɪk]		Heimweh haben
desperate (I was ~ to) [ˈdespərət]		ich wollte unbedingt

9/2A
to brighten [tʊ ˈbraɪtən]		heller-, freundlicher machen
lightweight	[ˈlaɪtweɪt]	leicht
curtain	[ˈkɜːtən]	Vorhang; Gardine
country-style [ˌkʌntrɪˈstaɪl]		Landstil
basketwork [ˈbɑːskɪtwɜːk]		Korb-
armchair	[ˈɑːmtʃeə]	Sessel
coffee table [ˈkɒfɪ ˌteɪbl]		Beistelltisch
stylish	[ˈstaɪlɪʃ]	stilvoll
tidy	[ˈtaɪdɪ]	ordentlich
wardrobe	[ˈwɔːdrəʊb]	Kleiderschrank
functional	[ˈfʌŋkʃənəl]	funktional
steel-framed [ˌstiːlˈfreɪmd]		mit Stahlgestell
dining table [ˈdaɪnɪŋ ˌteɪbl]		Esstisch
range	[reɪndʒ]	Reihe, Palette
chest of drawers [ˌtʃest əv ˈdrɔːz]		Kommode
sofa	[ˈsəʊfə]	Sofa
to make up into a bed [tʊ meɪk ˌʌp ɪntʊ ə ˈbed]		in ein Bett unwandeln
solution	[səˈluːʃn]	Lösung
storage problem [ˈstɔːrɪdʒ ˌprɒbləm]		Platzproblem
built-in	[ˌbɪltˈɪn]	eingebaut
cupboard	[ˈkʌbəd]	Schrank
ultimate	[ˈʌltɪmət]	ultimativ
pure	[pjʊə]	rein
carpet	[ˈkɑːpɪt]	Teppich; Teppichboden

9/2B
living room [ˈlɪvɪŋ ˌruːm]		Wohnzimmer

Unit Vocabulary

9/2C
opinion	[əˈpɪnjən]	Meinung
essential	[ɪˈsenʃl]	unerlässlich

9/3A
to strip	[tʊ strɪp]	entfernen, abziehen
to install	[tʊ ɪnˈstɔːl]	installieren
to paint	[tʊ peɪnt]	anstreichen
socket	[ˈsɒkɪt]	Steckdose
wallpaper	[ˈwɔːlˌpeɪpə]	Tapete

9/3B
to redecorate	[tʊ ˌriːˈdekəreɪt]	renovieren
inconvenient	[ˌɪnkənˈviːnɪənt]	ungünstig
worn	[wɔːn]	verschlissen
cover	[ˈkʌvə]	Überzug
antique	[ænˈtiːk]	Antik-
mirror	[ˈmɪrə]	Spiegel
to hang	[tʊ hæŋ]	aufhängen
fireplace	[ˈfaɪəpleɪs]	Kamin
lampshade	[ˈlæmpʃeɪd]	Lampenschirm
a couple	[ə ˈkʌpl]	ein paar
vase	[vɑːs]	Vase
as good as new		so gut wie neu
dark	[dɑːk]	dunkel

9/3C
to do sth yourself		etwas selber tun

9/3E
to service	[tʊ ˈsɜːvɪs]	(Auto) Inspektion machen

9/3F
shower curtain	[ˈʃaʊə ˌkɜːtən]	Duschvorhang
tile	[taɪl]	Kachel; Fliese
washbasin	[ˈwɒʃˌbeɪsn]	Waschbecken
towel rail	[ˈtaʊəlˌreɪl]	Handtuchhalter
to replace	[tʊ rɪˈpleɪs]	ersetzen
to own	[tʊˌəʊn]	besitzen
rent	[rent]	Miete
landlord, landlady	[ˈlændlɔːd / ˈlændˌleɪdɪ]	Vermieter, Vermieterin
long-term loan	[ˌlɒŋtɜːm ˈləʊn]	langfristiges Darlehen
mortgage	[ˈmɔːgɪdʒ]	Hypothek
to let	[tʊ let]	vermieten
to have owned	[tʊ hævˌˈəʊnd]	besessen zu haben
lifetime	[ˈlaɪftaɪm]	Leben
tenant	[ˈtenənt]	Mieter/in
owner	[ˈəʊnə]	Besitzer
in your view	[ɪnˌjɔː vjuː]	Ihrer Meinung nach

9/4A
anywhere	[ˈenɪweə]	irgendwo

9/4B
fully-furnished	[ˌfʊlɪˈfɜːnɪʃt]	möbliert
per calendar month (Abk. pcm)	[pɜː ˌkæləndə ˈmʌnθ]	pro Kalendermonat
balcony (south-facing ~)	[ˈbælkənɪ]	Südbalkon
central location	[ˌsentrəl ləʊˈkeɪʃn]	zentrale Lage
pet	[pet]	Haustier
unfurnished	[ʌnˈfɜːnɪʃt]	nicht möbliert
terraced house	[ˈterɪstˌhaʊs]	Reihenhaus
double-glazing	[ˌdʌblˈɡleɪzɪŋ]	Doppelverglasung
for sale	[fəˈseɪl]	zum verkaufen
ground floor (AE: first floor)	[ˌɡraʊndˈflɔː (ˌfɜːstˈflɔː)]	Erdgeschoss
open-plan kitchen	[ˌəʊpnplænˈkɪtʃɪn]	amerikanische Küche
semi-detached house	[ˌsemɪdɪˈtætʃtˌhaʊs]	Doppelhaushälfte
fitted kitchen	[ˌfɪtɪdˈkɪtʃɪn]	Einbauküche
loft	[lɒft]	Dachboden
patio	[ˈpætɪəʊ]	Terrasse
covered parking space	[ˌkʌvəd ˈpɑːkɪŋˌspeɪs]	überdachter Stellplatz
detached house	[dɪˈtætʃtˌhaʊs]	freistehendes Haus
utility room	[juːˈtɪlətɪˌruːm]	Waschküche
conservatory	[kənˈsɜːvətrɪ]	Wintergarten
view	[vjuː]	Aussicht
to update	[tʊˌʌpˈdeɪt]	modernisieren

9/5B
spare key	[ˌspeə ˈkiː]	Zweitschlüssel
to get on with (sb)	[tʊ ɡetˌɒn wɪð]	sich mit jdm verstehen
fortunately	[ˈfɔːtʃənətlɪ]	glücklicherweise
to make an effort	[tʊ meɪk ənˈefət]	sich bemühen

9/5D
to feed	[tʊ fiːd]	füttern
to be away	[tʊ bɪəˈweɪ]	fort sein
to get rid of (sth)	[tʊ ɡetˌrɪdˌəv]	etwas loswerden
to sort things out	[tʊ sɔːtˌθɪŋzˈaʊt]	sich organisieren

to change [tʊ tʃeɪndʒ]	auswechseln	
frosted glass [ˌfrɒstɪd ˈglɑːs]	Milchglas	
to sunbathe [tʊ ˈsʌnbeɪð]	sonnenbaden	
cruise [kruːz]	Kreuzfahrt	
cat flap [ˈkætˌflæp]	Katzentür	
fat [fæt]	dick	
diet [ˈdaɪət]	Diät	
pond [pɒnd]	Teich	
water lily [ˈwɔːtəˌlɪlɪ]	Seerose	
reed [riːd]	Schilfgras	
frog [frɒg]	Frosch	
noisy (pretty ~) [ˈnɔɪzɪ]	ziemlich laut	
to croak [tʊ krəʊk]	quaken	
to complain [tʊ kəmˈpleɪn]	sich beschweren	
noise [nɔɪz]	Krach	
to catch [tʊ kætʃ]	fangen	
to take (sb) to court [tʊ teɪk tʊ ˈkɔːt]	jdn vor Gericht bringen	

9/6A

storm [stɔːm]	Sturm, Unwetter
earthquake [ˈɜːθkweɪk]	Erdbeben
vandalism [ˈvændəlɪzm]	Vandalismus
lightning [ˈlaɪtnɪŋ]	Blitz

9/6B

insurance policy [ɪnˈʃɔːrənsˌpɒləsɪ]	Versicherungspolice
to break (broke, broken) [tʊ breɪk (brəʊk, brəʊkn)]	zerbrechen
lawyer [ˈlɔːɪə]	Anwalt
to charge [tʊ tʃɑːdʒ]	berechnen
premium (insurance ~) [ˈpriːmɪəm]	Versicherungsbeitrag
comprehensive [ˌkɒmprɪˈhensɪv]	umfassend
cover [ˈkʌvə]	Deckung
accidental (damage) [ˌæksɪˈdentl]	Unfallsschaden
(house) contents [(ˌhaʊs) ˈkɒntents]	Hausrat
unlimited [ʌnˈlɪmɪtɪd]	unbegrenzt
legal fees [ˈliːglˌfiːz]	Anwalt- und Gerichtskosten
helpline [ˈhelplaɪn]	Hotline

9/6D

liability [ˌlaɪəˈbɪlətɪ]	Haftpflicht

Unit 10 *Learning for life*

10/1B

alone [əˈləʊn]	allein

10/1C

frightening [ˈfraɪtnɪŋ]	beängstigend
to be terrified [tʊ bɪ ˈterəfaɪd]	fürchterliche Angst haben
the basics [ðə ˈbeɪsɪks]	die Grundzüge
to copy [tʊ ˈkɒpɪ]	nachmachen
incredibly [ɪnˈkredɪblɪ]	unglaublich
patient [ˈpeɪʃənt]	geduldig

10/1D

to imitate [tʊ ˈɪmɪteɪt]	imitieren, nachmachen

10/2A

compulsory [kəmˈpʌlsərɪ]	Pflicht-
to continue [tʊ kənˈtɪnjuː]	andauern
to stay on [tʊ steɪˈɒn]	bleiben, weiter machen
to specialize [tʊ ˈspeʃəlaɪz]	sich spezialisieren
certain areas [ˌsɜːtnˈeərɪəz]	bestimmte Fächer
final examination [ˌfaɪnlˌɪgˌzæmɪˈneɪʃn]	Abschlussprüfung
subject [ˈsʌbdʒɪkt]	Fach
to provide [tʊ prəˈvaɪd]	zur Verfügung stellen
free of charge [ˌfriːəv ˈtʃɑːdʒ]	kostenlos
previously [ˈpriːvɪəslɪ]	früher, vorher
to attend [tʊ əˈtend]	besuchen
kindergarten [ˈkɪndəgɑːtn]	Kindergarten
cafeteria [ˌkæfəˈtɪərɪə]	Kantine
approximately [əˈprɒksɪmətlɪ]	ungefähr

10/2C

pupil [ˈpjuːpəl]	Schüler/in
to scrap [tʊ skræp]	abschaffen

10/3A

to be good at (sth) [tʊ bɪ ˈgʊdˌət]	gut in etwas sein
economics [ˌiːkəˈnɒmɪks]	Wirtschaftskunde
geography [dʒɪˈɒgrəfɪ]	Geografie
information technology (*Abk.* IT) [ɪnfəˌmeɪʃn tekˈnɒlədʒɪ]	Informatik
Latin [ˈlætɪn]	Latein
mathematics (*Abk.* maths, *AE:* math) [mæθˈmætɪks]	Mathematik, Mathe

Unit Vocabulary

physical education (*Abk.* PE) [ˌfɪzɪkl ˌedʒʊˈkeɪʃn]	Sport (als Schulfach)	nerves of steel [ˌnɜːvz əv ˈstiːl]	Nerven wie Drahtseile
politics [ˈpɒlətɪks]	Politik	trustworthy [ˈtrʌstˌwɜːði]	vertrauenswürdig
science [ˈsaɪəns]	Naturwissenschaften	fit as a fiddle [ˌfɪt əz ə ˈfɪdl]	fit wie ein Turnschuh
social studies [ˈsəʊʃl ˌstʌdɪz]	Sozialkunde	easy-going [ˌiːzɪ ˈgəʊɪŋ]	locker

10/3C

to wish [tʊ ˌwɪʃ]	wünschen
to repair [tʊ rɪˈpeə]	reparieren
to envy [tʊ ˌenvi]	beneiden
to fill in [tʊ ˌfɪl ˌɪn]	ausfüllen
tax form [ˈtæks ˌfɔːm]	Steuerformular
to fail [tʊ feɪl]	durchfallen
to pass [tʊ pɑːs]	bestehen
useless (he was ~) [ˈjuːsləs]	er hat nichts gebracht
ballroom dancing [ˌbɔːlruːm ˈdɑːnsɪŋ]	Gesellschaftstanz
chance [tʃɑːns]	Chance

10/4A

skill [skɪl]	Fähigkeit, Kenntnis
graduate [ˈgrædʒʊət]	Akademiker/in
nanny [ˈnæni]	Kindermädchen
to require [tʊ rɪˈkwaɪə]	brauchen
to be fond of [tʊ bɪ fɒnd ˌɒv]	mögen, lieben
to exercise [tʊ ˌeksəsaɪz]	spazieren führen
well-trained [ˌwelˈtreɪnd]	gut erzogen
receptionist [rɪˈsepʃənɪst]	Rezeptionist/in, Empfangsperson
honest [ˈɒnɪst]	ehrlich
to be good with [tʊ bɪ ˈgʊd wɪð]	gut mit umgehen können
researcher [ˈriːsɜːtʃə]	Forscher/in
editor [ˈedɪtə]	Redakteur/in
to join [tʊ dʒɔɪn]	beitreten
reliable [rɪˈlaɪəbl]	zuverlässig
to be fluent in sth [tʊ bɪ ˈfluːənt ɪn ˌsʌmθɪŋ]	etwas fließend beherrschen

10/4C

qualities [ˈkwɒlətɪz]	Eigenschaften
mother [ˈmʌðə]	Mutter
farmer [ˈfɑːmə]	Bauer/Bäuerin

10/4D

sociable [ˈsəʊʃəbl]	offen
cheerful [ˈtʃɪəfʊl]	gut drauf
tactful [ˈtæktfʊl]	taktvoll
knowledgeable [ˈnɒlɪdʒəbl]	gut informiert
like the back of your hand	wie deine Westentasche

10/4E

suitcase [ˈsuːtkeɪs] [ˈsjuːtkeɪs]	(Reise)Koffer
to prove [tʊ pruːv]	beweisen
suspicious [səˈspɪʃəs]	misstrauisch
impatient [ɪmˈpeɪʃənt]	ungeduldig
to be prepared [tʊ bɪ prɪˈpeəd]	bereit sein
two days running	zwei Tage hintereinander
That sounds like a tall order.	(*etwa*) Das ist ziemlich viel.

10/4G

to sum up [tʊ sʌm ˌʌp]	zusammenfassen
knowledge [ˈnɒlɪdʒ]	Wissen, Kenntnis
law court [ˈlɔː ˌkɔːt]	Gerichtshof
route [ruːt]	Route
candidate [ˈkændɪdət]	Kandidat/in
oral [ˈɔːrəl]	mündlich
to collect [tʊ kəˈlekt]	(*hier*) bekommen
hard-earned [ˌhɑːdˈɜːnd]	schwerverdient
licence [ˈlaɪsəns]	Schein, Lizenz
badge [bædʒ]	Schild

10/5A

qualification [ˌkwɒlɪfɪˈkeɪʃn]	Qualifikation
to take an exam [tʊ teɪk ən ɪgˈzæm]	eine Prüfung machen
theoretical [θɪəˈretɪkl]	theoretisch
degree [dɪˈgriː]	Hochschulabschluss, Diplom
to receive [tʊ rɪˈsiːv]	erhalten, bekommen
studies [ˈstʌdɪz]	Studium
A (advanced) level [ˈeɪ (ədˈvɑːnst) ˌlevl]	(*etwa*) Abitur in GB
to qualify for (sth) [tʊ ˈkwɒlɪfaɪ fə]	sich für etwas qualifizieren

10/5B

Goodness! [ˈgʊdnəs]	Du meine Güte!
relevant [ˈreləvənt]	relevant
CV [ˌsiːˈviː] (*Abk. v.* curriculum vitae)	Lebenslauf
first aid [ˌfɜːst ˈeɪd]	erste Hilfe
clean driving licence [ˌkliːn ˈdraɪvɪŋ ˌlaɪsəns]	Führerschein ohne Punkte
secretarial [ˌsekrəˈteərɪəl]	Sekretärin-

by distance learning [baɪ ˌdɪstəns ˈlɜːnɪŋ]	per Fernkurs	thunderstorm [ˈθʌndəstɔːm]	Gewitter
		round [raʊnd]	Runde
10/5C		a bit of a mixed bag [ə bɪt əv ə ˌmɪkst ˈbæg]	(etwa) durchwachsen
to be afraid of (sth) [tʊ bɪ əˈfreɪd əv]	sich vor etwas fürchten	bright [braɪt]	heiter
self-defence [ˌselfdɪˈfens]	Selbstverteidigung	strong [strɒŋ]	stark
to commit a crime [tʊ kəˌmɪt ə ˈkraɪm]	ein Verbrechen begehen	to watch out for (sth) [tʊ wɒtʃ ˈaʊt fə]	auf etwas achten
strange [streɪndʒ]	merkwürdig	winter woollies [ˌwɪntə ˈwʊlɪz]	(scherzhaft) warme Bekleidung
nervous [ˈnɜːvəs]	nervös		
nasty [ˈnɑːstɪ]	fies	**11/1D**	
fair [feə]	fair	topic [ˈtɒpɪk]	Thema
		to offend [tʊ əˈfend]	beleidigen
10/6B			
to gain [tʊ geɪn]	erwerben	**11/1E**	
promotion [prəˈməʊʃn]	Beförderung	for ages [fər ˈeɪdʒɪz]	ewig
to keep their minds fit [tʊ kiːp ðeə ˈmaɪndz ˌfɪt]	um geistig fit zu bleiben	to pour down [tʊ ˈpɔː daʊn]	schütten
		I didn't sleep a wink! [aɪ dɪdnt ˌsliːp ə ˈwɪŋk]	Ich habe kein Auge zugetan!
10/6C			
to flower [tʊ ˈflaʊə]	blühen	**11/2**	
picnic [ˈpɪknɪk]	Picknick	landscape [ˈlændskeɪp]	Landschaft
to brush up [tʊ brʌʃ ˈʌp]	auffrischen	**11/2A**	
bookkeeping [ˈbʊkˌkiːpɪŋ]	Buchführung	plateau [ˈplætəʊ]	Hochebene
		to separate [tʊ ˈsepəreɪt]	trennen
computer filing [kəmˌpjuːtə ˈfaɪlɪŋ]	Datenablage im Computer	mountain [ˈmaʊntɪn]	Berg
telephone etiquette [ˌtelɪfəʊn ˈetɪket]	Umgang am Telefon	scenery [ˈsiːnərɪ]	Landschaften
		varied [ˈveərɪd]	abwechslungsreich
psychological tips [ˌsaɪkəlɒdʒɪkl ˈtɪps]	psychologische Ratschläge	tropical [ˈtrɒpɪkl]	tropisch
		mangrove swamp [ˈmæŋgrəʊv ˌswɒmp]	Mangrovenwälder
hold [həʊld]	Griff	hill [hɪl]	Hügel
to publish [tʊ ˈpʌblɪʃ]	veröffentlichen	valley [ˈvælɪ]	Tal
oriental cookery [ˌɔːrɪentl ˈkʊkərɪ]	orientalische Küche	desert [ˈdezət]	Wüste
		surrounded by [səˈraʊndɪd baɪ]	umgeben von
aromatherapy [əˌrəʊməˈθerəpɪ]	Aromatherapie	ocean [ˈəʊʃən]	Ozean
		wildlife [ˈwaɪldlaɪf]	Tierwelt
		flora [ˈflɔːrə]	Pflanzenwelt
		mineral deposit [ˈmɪnərəl dɪˌpɒzɪts]	Mineralvorkommen

Unit 11 *The world around us*

11/1A		gold [gəʊld]	Gold
drizzle [ˈdrɪzl]	Nieselregen	diamond [ˈdaɪəmənd]	Diamant
frost [frɒst]	Frost	to range (from/to) [tʊ reɪndʒ]	von/bis … reichen
breeze [briːz]	Brise	volcano [vɒlˈkeɪnəʊ]	Vulkan
blizzard [ˈblɪzəd]	Schneesturm	lake [leɪk]	See
shower [ˈʃaʊə]	Schauer	waterfall [ˈwɔːtəfɔːl]	Wasserfall
gale [geɪl]	Wind mit Sturmstärke	rolling farmland [ˌrəʊlɪŋ ˈfɑːmlænd]	sanft ansteigendes Ackerland
hail [heɪl]	Hagel	subtropical forest [sʌbˌtrɒpɪkl ˈfɒrɪst]	subtropischer Wald
11/1C			
changeable [ˈtʃeɪndʒəbl]	wechselhaft		

Unit Vocabulary

active seismic region ['æktɪv ˌsaɪzmɪk 'riːdʒn]	seismisch aktive Region	to be disappointed [tʊ bɪ ˌdɪsə'pɔɪntɪd]	enttäuscht sein
spring [sprɪŋ]	Quelle	You can say that again!	Das kann man wohl sagen!
domestic [də'mestɪk]	Haushalts-	to get sth back	etwas zurückbekommen
substantial reserves [səbˌstænʃl rɪ'zɜːvz]	bedeutende Vorkommen	to hide (hid, hidden) [tʊ haɪd (hɪd, hɪdən)]	sich verstecken
natural gas [ˌnætʃərəl 'gæs]	Erdgas	to kill [tʊ kɪl]	töten
sea-level ['siːˌlevl]	Meeresspiegel	aggressive [ə'gresɪv]	aggressiv
plain [pleɪn]	Ebene	to store [tʊ stɔː]	(*hier*) aufbewahren
mountain range ['maʊntɪn ˌreɪndʒ]	Bergkette	camp [kæmp]	Lager
river ['rɪvə]	Fluss	anyway ['enɪweɪ]	trotzdem
hydroelectric power [ˌhaɪdrəʊɪlektrɪk 'paʊə]	Strom aus Wasserkraft	slope [sləʊp]	Hang; Piste
rainfall ['reɪnfɔːl]	Niederschlag (*Regen*)	the locals [ðə 'ləʊklz]	die Einheimischen
hurricane ['hʌrɪkən]	Orkan		
to cause [tʊ kɔːz]	verursachen		
bauxite ['bɔːksaɪt]	Bauxit		

11/2B

natural resources [ˌnætʃərəl rɪ'zɔːsɪz]	Bodenschätze

11/2C

to be closed in [tʊ bɪ kləʊzdˌ'ɪn]	eingesperrt sein

11/3A

natural disaster [ˌnætʃərəl dɪ'zɑːstə]	Naturkatastrophe
dangerous ['deɪndʒərəs]	gefährlich

11/3B

to be hit by [tʊ bɪ 'hɪtˌbaɪ]	heimgesucht werden von
bear [beə]	Bär
tent [tent]	Zelt
avalanche ['ævəlɑːntʃ]	Lawine
landslide ['lændslaɪd]	Erdrutsch
thirsty ['θɜːstɪ]	durstig
tap (*AE:* faucet) [tæp ('fɔːsɪt)]	Wasserhahn
stomach-ache ['stʌməkeɪk]	Magenschmerz
awful ['ɔːfʊl]	furchtbar, sehr schlimm
fault (it was my own ~) [fɔːlt]	ich war selber Schuld
I shouldn't have drunk the water.	Ich hätte das Wasser nicht trinken sollen.
flattened ['flætənd]	dem Erdboden gleich gemacht
shut down [ʃʌt'daʊn]	dicht gemacht
What a shame! [ˌwɒtə 'ʃeɪm]	Wie schade!

11/3D

Travel broadens the mind. ['trævl ˌbrɔːdənz ðə 'maɪnd]	Reisen bildet.

11/4A

land use ['lændˌjuːs]	Landnutzung
urban area [ˌɜːbən'eərɪə]	Stadtgebiet
agricultural activities [ˌægrɪkʌltʃərəl æk'tɪvɪtɪz]	landwirtschaftliche Aktivitäten
woodland ['wʊdlənd]	Wälder
residential [ˌrezɪ'denʃl]	Wohn-
industrial [ɪn'dʌstrɪəl]	Industrie-
transportation [ˌtrænspɔː'teɪʃn]	Transport
recreational purposes [rekrɪˌeɪʃənl 'pɜːpəsɪz]	Freizeitnutzung

11/4B

exclusive [ɪks'kluːsɪv]	exklusiv
development [dɪ'veləpmənt]	Projekt, Objekt
handful ['hændfʊl]	Handvoll
luxury ['lʌkʃərɪ]	Luxus-
automatic [ˌɔːtə'mætɪk]	Automatisch-
security [sɪ'kjʊərətɪ]	Sicherheits-
the rich [ðə 'rɪtʃ]	die Reichen
affordable [ə'fɔːdəbl]	bezahlbar
accommodation [əˌkɒmə'deɪʃn]	Unterkunft, Wohnungen
runway ['rʌnweɪ]	Start- / Landebahn
to reject; rejection [tʊ rɪ'dʒekt; rɪ'dʒekʃn]	ablehnen; Ablehnung
resident ['rezɪdənt]	Einwohner/in
unbearable [ʌn'beərəbl]	unerträglich
authorities [ɔː'θɒrətɪz]	Behörden
local council [ˌləʊkl 'kaʊnsəl]	Gemeinderat
to pass [tʊ pɑːs]	genehmigen

compulsory purchase order [kəmˌpʌlsərɪ ˈpɜːtʃəs ˌɔːdə]	Zwangsenteignung
path [pɑːθ]	Weg
to plant [tʊ plɑːnt]	pflanzen
rose bush [ˈrəʊz ˌbʌʃ]	Rosenstrauch

11/4C
gated community [ˌɡeɪtɪd kəˈmjuːnətɪ]	(*etwa*) geschlossener Wohnbezirk
private citizen [ˌpraɪvət ˈsɪtɪzən]	Privatpersonen
citizen [ˈsɪtɪzən]	Bürger/in
project [ˈprɒdʒekt]	Projekt

11/5A
developer [dɪˈveləpə]	Bauträger
offer [ˈɒfə]	Angebot
to give up [tʊ ɡɪvˌˈʌp]	aufgeben
generation [ˌdʒenəˈreɪʃn]	Generation
to decide [tʊ dɪˈsaɪd]	sich entscheiden
to farm [tʊ fɑːm]	bebauen
the local economy [ðə ˌləʊklˌɪˈkɒnəmɪ]	die hiesige Wirtschaft
to increase [tʊˌɪnˈkriːs]	steigern
to disappear [tʊ dɪsəˈpɪə]	verschwinden
to fight (sth) [tʊ ˈfaɪt]	gegen etwas kämpfen
to sell (sold, sold) [tʊ sel (səʊld, səʊld)]	verkaufen

11/5C
to save up for (sth) [tʊ seɪvˌˈʌp fə]	auf etwas sparen

11/6
(the) pros and cons [(ðə) ˌprəʊzˌənˈkɒnz]	das Pro und Kontra

11/6A
mine [maɪn]	Bergwerk
open-cast mine [ˌəʊpnkɑːst ˈmaɪn]	Tagebau
coal field [ˈkəʊlfiːld]	Kohlenrevier
energy business [ˈenədʒɪ ˌbɪznɪs]	Energiegeschäft
surface [ˈsɜːfɪs]	Oberfläche
to mine [tʊ maɪn]	gewinnen
to stretch [tʊ stretʃ]	strecken
to cut down [tʊ kʌtˌˈdaʊn]	fällen
to relocate [tʊ ˌriːləʊˈkeɪt]	umsiedeln, umlagern
excavator [ˈekskəveɪtə]	Bagger
power station [ˈpaʊəˌsteɪʃn]	Kraftwerk
mined out (when a coal field is ~) [ˌmaɪndˈaʊt]	wann das Vorkommen erschöpft ist
to turn into [tʊ tɜːnˈɪntuː]	umwandeln in
nature reserve [ˈneɪtʃəˌrɪˌzɜːv]	Naturschutzgebiet
to replant [tʊ ˌriːˈplɑːnt]	wieder aufforsten

11/6C
former [ˈfɔːmə]	ehemalig

11/6D
environmental [ɪnˌvaɪrənˈmentl]	Umwelt-
argument [ˈɑːɡjəmənt]	Argument
to counter [tʊ ˈkaʊntə]	widersprechen
anchorperson [ˈæŋkəˌpɜːsn]	Moderator/in (Fernsehen)
yard [jɑːd]	Hof, Garten

Unit 13 *It takes all sorts*

It takes all sorts.	Es gibt solche und solche.

13/1A
fingerprint [ˈfɪŋɡəprɪnt]	Fingerabdruck
signature [ˈsɪɡnətʃə]	Unterschrift

13/1B
glove [ɡlʌv]	Handschuh

13/1C
password [ˈpɑːswɜːd]	Passwort
cash card [ˈkæʃˌkɑːd]	Geldkarte
key card [ˈkiːˌkɑːd]	(elektronische) Schlüsselkarte
loyalty card [ˈlɔɪəltɪˌkɑːd]	Kundenkarte
swipe card [ˈswaɪpˌkɑːd]	Türkarte

13/1D
to lie (lay, lain) [tʊ laɪ (leɪ, leɪn)]	liegen
pavement (*AE*: sidewalk) [ˈpeɪvmənt (ˈsaɪdwɔːk)]	Bürgersteig

13/2
What does she look like?	Wie sieht sie aus?

13/2A
roundish [ˈraʊndɪʃ]	rundlich
straight hair [ˌstreɪt ˈheə]	glattes Haar

Unit Vocabulary

moustache [məˈstɑːʃ]	Schnurrbart	
I suppose … [aɪ səˈpəʊz]	Wahrscheinlich …	
overweight (he's a bit ~) [ˌəʊvəˈweɪt]	er hat etwas Übergewicht	
as long as [əzˈlɒŋ əz]	so lange wie	
ordinary [ˈɔːdənrɪ]	normal	
mousy [ˈmaʊsɪ]	mausgrau	
pale [peɪl]	hell	
beauty counselling [ˈbjuːtɪ ˌkaʊnsəlɪŋ]	Schönheitsberatung	
slim [slɪm]	schlank	
effectively [ɪˈfektɪvlɪ]	effektiv	
well-built [ˌwelˈbɪlt]	gut gebaut	
clean-shaven [ˌkliːnˈʃeɪvn]	rasiert	
fair hair [ˌfeə ˈheə]	blondes Haar	
suspect [ˈsʌspekt]	Verdächtige/r	
average height [ˌævərɪdʒ ˈhaɪt]	Durchnittsgröße	
queue [kjuː]	(Warte)Schlange	
curly [ˈkɜːlɪ]	lockig	
granny (everybody's idea of a dear old ~) [ˈgrænɪ]	wie man sich eine nette Oma vorstellt	
lined (She was very ~) [laɪnd]	Sie hatte viele Falten	
smile [smaɪl]	Lächeln	
suddenly [ˈsʌdənlɪ]	plötzlich	

13/2B

beard [bɪəd]	Bart
shoulder-length [ˌʃəʊldəˈleŋkθ]	Schulterlang
stocky [ˈstɒkɪ]	stämmig

13/2C

to modify [tʊ ˈmɒdɪfaɪ]	verändern, modifizieren

13/2D

take so much trouble with their appearance	sich so mit ihrem Aussehen beschäftigen
trouble [trʌbl]	Mühe
brain [breɪn]	Kopf, Gehirn

13/3

twin [twɪn]	Zwilling
smooth [smuːð]	glatt, weich

13/3A

nickname [ˈnɪkneɪm]	Spitzname
pet name [ˈpet ˌneɪm]	Kosename

13/3B

bull [bʊl]	Bulle, Stier
sparrow [ˈspærəʊ]	Spatz
occupation [ˌɒkjʊˈpeɪʃn]	Beruf
patronymic [ˌpætrəˈnɪmɪk]	vom Namen des Vaters abgeleiteter Name
whose [huːz]	deren, dessen
several [ˈsevərəl]	einige (-r, -s)
to behave [tʊ bɪˈheɪv]	sich benehmen
like a bull in a china shop [laɪk ə ˌbʊl ɪn ə ˈtʃaɪnə ˌʃɒp]	wie ein Elefant im Porzellanladen
tricky [ˈtrɪkɪ]	listig
fox [fɒks]	Fuchs
thatcher [ˈθætʃə]	Dachdecker/in
version [ˈvɜːʃn]	Version
common [ˈkɒmən]	(*hier*) verbreitet
ancestor [ˈænsestə]	Vorfahr/in

13/4

blood [blʌd]	Blut

13/4A

grandfather [ˈgrændˌfɑːðə]	Großvater
husband [ˈhʌzbənd]	Ehemann
uncle [ˈʌŋkl]	Onkel
brother [ˈbrʌðə]	Bruder
nephew [ˈnefjuː]	Neffe
stepmother [ˈstepˌmʌðə]	Stiefmutter
daughter-in-law [ˈdɔːtərɪnˌlɔː]	Schwiegertochter
half-brother [ˈhɑːfˌbrʌðə]	Halbbruder
sister [ˈsɪstə]	Schwester
cousin [ˈkʌzɪn]	Cousin/e
wife [waɪf]	Ehefrau

13/4B

aunt [ɑːnt]	Tante
niece [niːs]	Nichte
son [sʌn]	Sohn

13/4C

to discover [tʊ dɪˈskʌvə]	entdecken
unusual [ʌnˈjuːʒʊəl]	ungewöhnlich

13/4D

relationship [rɪˈleɪʃənʃɪp]	Beziehung
to be responsible for (sb) [tʊ bɪ rɪˈspɒnsəbl fə]	die Verantwortung für jdn haben
to be financially dependent on [tʊ bɪ faɪˌnænʃəlɪ dɪˈpendənt ɒn]	finanziell abhängig sein von
to look after (sb) [tʊ lʊkˈɑːftə]	sich um jdn kümmern
to worry about [tʊ ˈwʌrɪ əˌbaʊt]	sich sorgen um

13/5A

friendship [ˈfrendʃɪp]	Freundschaft
to share [tʊ ʃeə]	teilen

joke [dʒəʊk]	Witz
care (sb who doesn't ~) [keə]	jd, dem es egal ist
to borrow [tʊ 'bɒrəʊ]	borgen, ausleihen

13/5C

lonely hearts [ˌləʊnlɪ 'hɑːts]	einsame Herzen
youthful ['juːθʊl]	jugendlich
kind [kaɪnd]	nett, freundlich
poor [pɔː]	arm
to eat out [tʊ ˌiːt ˌaʊt]	Essen gehen
curvy ['kɜːvɪ]	weibliche Figur
good-looking [ˌɡʊd'lʊkɪŋ]	gut aussehend
sporty ['spɔːtɪ]	sportlich
feminine ['femɪnɪn]	weiblich, feminin
to laugh [tʊ lɑːf]	lachen
shy [ʃaɪ]	schüchtern
art [ɑːt]	Kunst
to seek [tʊ siːk]	suchen
tall [tɔːl]	groß
attractive [ə'træktɪv]	attraktiv
handsome ['hænsəm]	gut aussehend
independent [ˌɪndɪ'pendənt]	unabhängig
intelligent [ɪn'telɪdʒənt]	intelligent
current affairs [ˌkʌrənt ˌə'feəz]	Zeitgeschehen
skinny ['skɪnɪ]	dünn
artist ['ɑːtɪst]	Künstler/in

13/5E

to suggest [tʊ sə'dʒest]	vorschlagen
to shake [tʊ ʃeɪk]	zittern
to warn [tʊ ˌwɔːn]	warnen

13/6A

to keep in touch [tʊ kiːp ˌɪn 'tʌtʃ]	in Kontakt bleiben
greetings card ['ɡriːtɪŋz ˌkɑːd]	Grußkarte
blank [blæŋk]	leer
recipient [rɪ'sɪpɪənt]	Empfänger/in
popular ['pɒpjələ]	beliebt

13/6B

Many happy returns! [ˌmenɪ ˌhæpɪ rɪ'tɜːnz]	Herzlichen Glückwunsch zum Geburtstag!
Congratulations! [kənˌɡrætʃʊ'leɪʃnz]	Herzlichen Glückwunsch!
happiness ['hæpɪnəs]	Glück
Get well soon [ˌɡet ˌwel 'suːn]	Gute Besserung!
Good luck! [ˌɡʊd 'lʌk]	Viel Glück!

Unit 14 *A balanced life*

14/0

balanced ['bælənst]	ausgeglichen

14/1A

to hurt [tʊ hɜːt]	schmerzen
choice [tʃɔɪs]	Wahl
devil ['devəl]	Teufel
idle ['aɪdl]	faul
satisfaction [ˌsætɪs'fækʃn]	Zufriedenheit

14/1C

to clean [tʊ kliːn]	putzen, saubermachen

14/2B

to be stuck behind a desk [tʊ bɪ ˌstʌk bɪˌhaɪnd ə 'desk]	(etwa) im Büro hängen
to be on the road [tʊ bɪ ˌɒn ðə 'rəʊd]	unterwegs sein
to be cut off [tʊ bɪ kʌt'ɒf]	isoliert sein
to put your feet up [tʊ pʌt jɔː 'fiːt ˌʌp]	die Füße hochlegen
to be on your feet [tʊ bɪ ˌɒn jɔː 'fiːt]	auf den Beinen sein
duty (to be off ~) [tjuːtɪ]	nicht im Dienst sein
still [stɪl]	still

14/2E

nationwide [ˌneɪʃən'waɪd]	landesweit
action ['ækʃn]	Aktion
to be aware of (sth) [tʊ bɪ ə'weər ˌəv]	sich etwas bewusst sein
poverty ['pɒvətɪ]	Armut
to suffer from (sth) [tʊ 'sʌfə frəm]	an etwas leiden
fellow worker [ˌfeləʊ 'wɜːkə]	Mitarbeiter/in
overwork ['əʊvəwɜːk]	Überarbeitung
to threaten [tʊ 'θretn]	bedrohen
health [helθ]	Gesundheit
to weaken [tʊ 'wiːkən]	abschwächen
employment [ɪm'plɔɪmənt]	Beschäftigung
to take time off [tʊ teɪk ˌtaɪm 'ɒf]	frei nehmen
overstress ['əʊvəstres]	(etwa) zu viel Stress
to strengthen [tʊ 'streŋkθən]	verstärken

14/3B

to cope with (sth) [tʊ 'kəʊp wɪð]	mit etwas fertig werden
actually ['æktʃʊəlɪ]	eigentlich

Unit Vocabulary

boat [bəʊt]	Boot	**14/4B**	
to get (sth) into shape [tʊ ˌget ɪntʊ ˈʃeɪp]	etwas auf die Reihe kriegen	in one form or another	auf die eine oder andere Weise
strength [streŋθ]	Stärke	to draw up [tʊ drɔːˈʌp]	abfassen
deadline [ˈdedlaɪn]	Termin	the Middle Ages [ðə ˌmɪdl̩ ˈeɪdʒɪz]	das Mittelalter
race [reɪs]	Rennen	to originate [tʊˌəˈrɪdʒəneɪt]	entstehen
to explore [tʊˌɪkˈsplɔː]	entdecken	to found [tʊ faʊnd]	gründen
whenever I feel like it [wenˌevər aɪ ˈfiːlˌ laɪkˌ ɪt]	wann immer ich möchte	Norway; Norwegian [ˈnɔːweɪ, nɔːˈwiːdʒən]	Norwegen; norwegisch
to fulfil [tʊ fʊlˈfɪl]	erfüllen	creator [krɪˈeɪtə]	Erfinder/in
dream [driːm]	Traum	detective [dɪˈtektɪv]	Detektiv/in
circus clown [ˈsɜːkəsˌ klaʊn]	Zirkusclown	**14/4C**	
14/3C		spectator sport [spekˈteɪtə ˌspɔːt]	Publikumssport
to express [tʊˌɪkˈspres]	ausdrücken	**14/4D**	
14/3D		violence [ˈvaɪələns]	Gewalt
to keep sheep [tʊ kiːp ˈʃiːp]	Schafe halten	**14/5A**	
log cabin [ˌlɒgˌ ˈkæbɪn]	Blockhütte	victory [ˈvɪktərɪ]	Sieg
novel [ˈnɒvl]	Roman	army [ˈɑːmɪ]	Armee, Heer
14/3E		to revive [tʊ rɪˈvaɪv]	wiederbeleben
care [keə]	Sorgen	feat [fiːt]	(Helden)Tat
to stare [tʊ steə]	schauen	to commemorate [tʊ kəˈmeməreɪt]	gedenken
14/4A		stadium [ˈsteɪdɪəm]	Stadion
archery [ˈɑːtʃərɪ]	Bogenschießen	royal family [ˌrɔɪəlˌ ˈfæməlɪ]	königliche Familie
bowling [ˈbəʊlɪŋ]	Bowling	viewing box [ˈvjuːɪŋˌ bɒks]	Loge
ten-pin bowling [ˌtenpɪnˌ ˈbəʊlɪŋ]	Kegeln	distance [ˈdɪstəns]	Strecke
boxing [ˈbɒksɪŋ]	Boxen	to establish [tʊˌɪˈstæblɪʃ]	festlegen
climbing [ˈklaɪmɪŋ]	Bergsteigen	to follow suit [tʊˌ fɒləʊ ˈsuːt]	nachziehen
cricket [ˈkrɪkɪt]	*tradit. engl. Ballsport*	to prove a success [tʊˌ pruːvˌə səkˈses]	sich als Erfolg erweisen
cycling [ˈsaɪklɪŋ]	Radfahren	instant [ˈɪnstənt]	sofortige (-r, -s)
diving [ˈdaɪvɪŋ]	Tauchen	to apply [tʊˌəˈplaɪ]	sich anmelden
fencing [ˈfensɪŋ]	Fechten	to take part [tʊ teɪkˌ ˈpɑːt]	teilnehmen
gymnastics [dʒɪmˈnæstɪks]	Gymnastik	to cross the finishing line	die Ziellinie überqueren
hang-gliding [ˈhæŋˌglaɪdɪŋ]	Drachenfliegen	charity [ˈtʃærɪtɪ]	Wohlfahrt
ice-skating [ˈaɪsˌskeɪtɪŋ]	eislaufen	**14/5B**	
motor racing [ˈməʊtəˌreɪsɪŋ]	Autorennen	battle [ˈbætl]	Schlacht
riding [ˈraɪdɪŋ]	Reiten	sponsor [ˈspɒnsə]	Sponsor
rowing [ˈrəʊɪŋ]	Rudern	**14/5D**	
sailing [ˈseɪlɪŋ]	Segeln	to arrange [tʊˌəˈreɪndʒ]	arrangieren
skiing [ˈskiːɪŋ]	Skifahren	to expect [tʊˌɪkˈspekt]	erwarten
sky-diving [ˈskaɪˌdaɪvɪŋ]	Fallschirmspringen	to plan [tʊ plæn]	planen, vorbereiten
weightlifting [ˈweɪtˌlɪftɪŋ]	Gewichtheben		
windsurfing [ˈwɪndˌsɜːfɪŋ]	Windsurfen		

to remember [tʊ rɪˈmembə]	sich erinnern	separate [ˈsepərət]	getrennt
		chance (Is there any ~?) [tʃɑːns]	Besteht die Möglichkeit …?
		brochure [ˈbrəʊʃə]	Broschüre

14/6A

a complete change [ə kəmˌpliːt ˈtʃeɪndʒ]	etwas völlig anderes
worthwhile [ˌwɜːθˈwaɪl]	lohnend
handicapped [ˈhændɪkæpt]	behindert
experienced [ɪkˈspɪərɪənst]	erfahren
carer [ˈkeərə]	Betreuer/in
a cheerful nature [ə ˌtʃɪəfʊl ˈneɪtʃə]	ein freundliches Wesen
reward [rɪˈwɔːd]	Lohn
grateful [ˈgreɪtfʊl]	dankbar
hay [heɪ]	Heu
homely [ˈhəʊmli]	gemütlich
to their hearts' content [tʊ ðeə ˌhɑːts kənˈtent]	nach Herzenslust
home-grown [ˌhəʊmˈgrəʊn]	aus eigenem Anbau
new-laid eggs [ˌnjuːleɪd ˈegz]	frische Eier
good company [gʊd ˈkʌmpəni]	gute Gesellschaft
to manage without (sth) [tʊ ˌmænɪdʒ wɪðˈaʊt]	ohne etwas auskommen
unique [juːˈniːk]	einzigartig
opportunity [ˌɒpəˈtjuːnəti]	Chance, Möglichkeit
to convert [tʊ kənˈvɜːt]	umfunktionieren
multi-purpose [ˌmʌltiˈpɜːpəs]	Mehrzweck-
vital [ˈvaɪtl]	sehr wichtig
contribution [ˌkɒntrɪˈbjuːʃn]	Beitrag
retreat house [rɪˈtriːt ˌhaʊs]	(etwa) Haus der Besinnung
to get too much for (sb) [tʊ get ˌtuː ˈmʌtʃ fə]	jdm zu viel werden
for a while [fər ə ˈwaɪl]	für eine Weile
to rethink [tʊ ˌriːˈθɪŋk]	überdenken
peaceful [ˈpiːsfʊl]	friedlich
session [ˈseʃn]	Treffen
counsellor [ˈkaʊnsələ]	Berater/in
to stimulate [tʊ ˈstɪmjəleɪt]	stimulieren
to encourage [tʊ ɪnˈkʌrɪdʒ]	ermutigen

14/6C

bed linen [ˈbed ˌlɪnɪn]	Bettwäsche
to fit sb in [tʊ fɪt ˌsʌmbədɪ ˈɪn]	jdn einschieben

Unit 15 *Come together*

15/1A

native speaker [ˌneɪtɪv ˈspiːkə]	Muttersprachler/in
Arabic [ˈærəbɪk]	Arabisch
Hindi [ˈhɪndi]	Hindi
Mandarin Chinese [ˌmændərɪn tʃaɪˈniːz]	Mandarin (chinesische Hochsprache)

15/1B

percentage [pəˈsentɪdʒ]	Prozentsatz
estimate [ˈestɪmət]	Schätzung
concentration [ˌkɒnsənˈtreɪʃn]	Konzentration, Zentrum
mother tongue [ˌmʌðə ˈtʌŋ]	Muttersprache
influential [ˌɪnflʊˈenʃl]	einflussreich
widespread [ˈwaɪdspred]	weitverbreitet

15/1C

I didn't realize that [aɪ ˌdɪdnt ˈrɪəlaɪz ðət]	Mir war nicht bewusst, dass …
I wonder why … [aɪ ˈwʌndə ˌwaɪ]	Ich frage mich warum …

15/2

body language [ˈbɒdi ˌlæŋgwɪdʒ]	Körpersprache

15/2A

As a last resort, … [əz ə ˌlɑːst rɪˈzɔːt]	Als letzte Möglichkeit, …
If all else fails, … [ɪf ˌɔːl els ˈfeɪlz]	Wenn alle Stricke reißen, …

15/2B

to bite [tʊ baɪt]	beißen
lip [lɪp]	Lippe
to frown [tʊ fraʊn]	die Stirn runzel
thumb [θʌm]	Daumen
to raise [tʊ reɪz]	hochziehen
eyebrows [ˈaɪbraʊz]	Augenbrauen
to scratch [tʊ skrætʃ]	kratzen
to shrug your shoulders [tʊ ʃrʌg jɔː ˈʃəʊldəz]	die Achseln zucken
to wave [tʊ weɪv]	winken

15/2D

to be delighted [tʊ bi dɪˈlaɪtɪd]	entzückt sein
absolutely [ˌæbsəˈluːtli]	völlig

to be relieved [tʊ bɪ rɪˈliːvd]	erleichtert sein

15/2E
research [rɪˈsɜːtʃ]	Forschung
to transmit [tʊ trænzˈmɪt]	übermitteln
tone of voice [ˌtəʊn ˌəv ˌvɔɪs]	Ton (Stimme)
expression [ɪkˈspreʃn]	Gesichtsausdruck
gesture [ˈdʒestʃə]	Geste
posture [ˈpɒstʃə]	Körperhaltung
impression [ɪmˈpreʃn]	Eindruck
special occasion [ˌspeʃl ˌəˈkeɪʒn]	besonderer Anlass

15/2G
specific [spəˈsɪfɪk]	spezifisch

15/2H
to contain [tʊ kənˈteɪn]	enthalten
to be inhibited [tʊ bɪ ɪnˈhɪbɪtɪd]	gehemmt sein
non-verbal [ˌnɒnˈvɜːbl]	nicht gesprochen

15/3A
poetry; poem [ˈpəʊɪtri, ˈpəʊɪm]	Poesie; Gedicht
refreshments available [rɪˈfreʃmənts əˌveɪləbl]	Erfrischungen erhältlich
gallery [ˈɡæləri]	Galerie
painter [ˈpeɪntə]	Maler/in
to feature [tʊ ˈfiːtʃə]	mit
troupe [truːp]	Truppe

15/3B
to appear [tʊ əˈpɪə]	(hier) auftreten
flatmate [ˈflætmeɪt]	Mitbewohner/in
to clap [tʊ klæp]	klatschen
to boo [tʊ buː]	buhen
lyrics [ˈlɪrɪks]	(Lied)Text
exhibition [ˌeksɪˈbɪʃn]	Ausstellung
savings [ˈseɪvɪŋz]	Ersparnisse

15/3C
to avoid (sth) [tʊ əˈvɔɪd]	(etwas) meiden
to consider (sth) [tʊ kənˈsɪdə]	(etwas) überlegen
to delay [tʊ dɪˈleɪ]	zögern
to imagine [tʊ ɪˈmædʒɪn]	sich vorstellen
to keep [tʊ kiːp]	behalten

15/3D
accordingly [əˈkɔːdɪŋli]	entsprechend
luckily [ˈlʌkɪli]	glücklicherweise
to notice [tʊ ˈnəʊtɪs]	bemerken
cultural [ˈkʌltʃərəl]	Kultur-

15/4A
to put (sb) up [tʊ pʊt ˌʌp]	jdn unterbringen
vacation (BE: holiday) [veɪˈkeɪʃn (ˈhɒlɪdeɪ)]	Urlaub
spare room [ˌspeə ˈruːm]	Gästezimmer
celebration [ˌseləˈbreɪʃn]	Feier
fireworks [ˈfaɪəwɜːks]	Feuerwerk

15/4B
flight [flaɪt]	Flug

15/4F
present [ˈprezənt]	Geschenk

15/5B
to celebrate [tʊ ˈseləbreɪt]	feiern
anniversary [ˌænɪˈvɜːsəri]	Jahrestag
Declaration of Independence [ˌdekləˈreɪʃn ˌəv ˌɪndɪˈpendəns]	Unabhängigkeitserklärung
colony [ˈkɒləni]	Kolonie
white robe [ˌwaɪt ˈrəʊb]	weißes Gewand
solstice [ˈsɒlstɪs]	Sonnenwende
They consider themselves … [ðeɪ kənˈsɪdə ðəmˌselvz …]	Sie halten sich für …
successor [səkˈsesə]	Nachkommen
Celtic priests [ˌkeltɪk ˈpriːsts]	keltische Priester
known as Druids [ˌnəʊn ˌəz ˈdruːɪdz]	als Druiden bekannt
midsummer [ˌmɪdˈsʌmə]	Hochsommer
so-called [ˌsəʊˈkɔːld]	sogenannt
to cast a shadow [tʊ kɑːst ˌə ˈʃædəʊ]	einen Schatten werfen
astronomical calculator [ˌæstrəˈnɒmɪkl ˈkælkjəleɪtə]	astronomischer Rechner
goes back to [ɡəʊz ˈbæk ˌtuː]	geht zurück auf
ancient [ˈeɪntʃənt]	(sehr) alt
Feast of the Dead [ˌfiːst ˌəv ˌðə ˈded]	Totenfest
to mark [tʊ mɑːk]	kennzeichnen
harvest [ˈhɑːvɪst]	Ernte-
costume [ˈkɒstjuːm]	Kostüm
to light (lit, lit) [tʊ laɪt (lɪt, lɪt)]	anzünden
turnip [ˈtɜːnɪp]	Rübe
lantern [ˈlæntən]	Laterne

Unit Vocabulary

evil spirits [ˌiːvəl ˈspɪrɪts]	böse Geister
emigrant [ˈemɪgrənt]	Auswanderer/in

15/6A

to keep an eye on sth [tʊ kiːp ən ˈaɪ ɒn ˌsʌmθɪŋ]	auf etwas aufpassen

Alphabetical Word List
Alphabetisches Wortregister

Alle neuen Wörter, die in On the MOVE Plus vorkommen, sind hier in alphabetischer Reihenfolge aufgelistet und mit einer Verweisnummer versehen, z. B. 1/1B (Unit 1; Teil 1, Übung B).

(v) = Verb, Zeitwort sth = something *(BE)* = britisches Englisch
sb = somebody *(AE)* = amerikanisches Englisch

A
A (advanced) level *(etwa)* Abitur in GB 10/5A
absolutely völlig 15/2D
access Zugang, Zugriff 7/3E
accidental damage Unfallsschaden 9/6B
accommodation Unterkunft, Wohnungen 11/4B
according to zufolge 3/2F
accordingly entsprechend 15/3D
acknowledge *(v)* zugeben 7/6C
acrylic Acryl 5/2A
action Aktion 14/2E
active aktiv 11/2A
actually eigentlich 14/3B
admit *(v)* zugeben 7/6C
afford *(v)* sich leisten 5/4B
affordable bezahlbar 11/4B
afraid (be ~of sth) sich vor etwas fürchten 10/5C
after all immerhin 7/2B
ages (It takes me ~) ich brauche ewig 1/2A
aggressive aggressiv 11/3B
ago (4000 years ~) vor 4000 Jahren 5/4C
agricultural landwirtschaftlich 11/4A
ahead of you vor dir 1/2A
aim (to ~ sth at sb) etwas an jdn richten 3/4A
aisle Gang, Korridor 3/6A
aisle (the next ~ but one) der übernächste Gang 3/6C
alligator Alligator 2/5A
allow *(v)* erlauben, gestatten 2/1B
alone allein 10/1B
already schon 6/6A
alternative Alternative 6/2A
although obwohl 3/2E
amount Menge 6/2A
ancestor Vorfahr/in 13/3B
anchorperson Moderator/in (Fernsehen) 11/6D
ancient (sehr) alt 15/5B
animal Tier 2/5A
anniversary Jahrestag 15/5B
annual jährlich 7/3B
answering machine Anrufbeantworter 1/6B
antique Antik- 9/3B
anyway trotzdem 11/3B
anyway (Thanks ~.) Trotzdem vielen Dank. 2/2A
anywhere irgendwo 9/4A
appear *(v)* erscheinen 7/6C
appear *(v)* (hier) auftreten 15/3B
appearance Aussehen 5/4A
apple pie Apfelpastete 6/3A
apply *(v)* sich anmelden 14/5A
appropriate passend, geeignet 7/3C
approximately ungefähr 10/2A
Arabic Arabisch 15/1A
archery Bogenschießen 14/4A
argument Argument 11/6D
armchair Sessel 9/2A
army Armee, Heer 14/5A
aromatherapy Aromatherapie 10/6C
arrange *(v)* arrangieren 14/5D
arrogant arrogant 7/2B
art; artist Kunst; Künstler/in 13/5C
Asian asiatisch 6/1B
asparagus Spargel 6/3D
aspect Aspekt 7/3E
astronomical calculator astronomischer Rechner 15/5B
athletics Leichtathletik 7/3E
attach *(v)* anbringen, befestigen 5/4A
attend *(v)* besuchen 10/2A
attractive attraktiv 13/5C
aunt Tante 13/4B
authorities Behörden 11/4B
automatic Automatisch- 11/4B
available erhältlich 15/3A
avalanche Lawine 11/3B
avenue Boulevard, Allee 2/6A
average Durchnitt 13/2A
avoid sth *(v)* etwas meiden 15/3C
awake (to feel ~) sich wach fühlen 1/2A
aware (be ~of sth) sich etwas bewusst sein 14/2E
away (be ~) fort sein 9/5D
awful furchtbar, sehr schlimm 11/3B
Aztec Azteke/Aztekin 5/4B

B
badge (Namens)Schild 10/4G
bake *(v)* backen 6/3A
balanced ausgeglichen 14/0
balcony Balkon 9/4B
ballroom dancing Gesellschaftstanz 10/3C
ban *(v)* verbieten 7/3C
barbecue Grillparty 6/4A
basic Grund- 3/5A

basics (the ~) die Grundzüge 10/1C
basis Hauptbestandteil 6/2A
basket Korb 3/2A
basketwork Korb- 9/2A
battery Batterie 3/3B
battle Schlacht 14/5B
bauxite Bauxit 11/2A
bazaar Basar 2/6A
bean Bohne 6/2B
bear Bär 11/3B
beard Bart 13/2B
beauty counselling Schönheitsberatung 13/2A
bed linen Bettwäsche 14/6C
behave *(v)* sich benehmen 13/3B
beige Beige 5/2A
believe *(v)* glauben 7/5A
below unterhalb von 3/6C
belt Gürtel 5/2A
benefit Vorteil 3/2A
better not (I'd ~) lieber nicht 6/5D
billiards Billard 1/4A
bird Vogel 2/5A
birth certificate Geburtsurkunde 5/6B
bite *(v)* beißen 15/2B
blank leer 13/6A
bleep *(v)* piepsen 1/3B
blizzard Schneesturm 11/1A
blood Blut 13/4
blouse Bluse 5/1A
boat Boot 14/3B
body decoration Körperschmuck 5/4
body language Körpersprache 15/2
boil *(v)* kochen 1/3F
bone Knochen 5/4B
boo *(v)* buhen 15/3B
bookkeeping Buchführung 10/6C
bored gelangweilt 7/2C
borrow *(v)* borgen, ausleihen 13/5A
bowling Bowling 14/4A
boxing Boxen 14/4A
bracelet Armband 5/4B
brain Kopf, Gehirn 13/2D
brand name Markenname 3/5A
break *(v)* zerbrechen 9/6B

break Pause 5/5D
breast Brust 6/3C
breeze Brise 11/1A
bright heiter 11/1C
brighten *(v)* heller-, freundlicher machen 9/2A
brilliant genial, toll, brilliant 3/4
bring in *(v)* hereinbringen 5/6B
Briton *(Abk.* **Brit)** Brite/Britin 6/3F
broadcast *(v)* ausstrahlen 7/1B
broaden (Travel ~s the mind) *(v)* Reisen bildet. 11/3D
brochure Broschüre 14/6C
broken zerbrochen 3/3A
broth Brühe 6/3F
brother Bruder 13/4A
brunch Brunch 6/4A
brush *(v)* bestreichen 6/3D
brush up *(v)* auffrischen 10/6C
buggy Buggy 2/5A
built-in eingebaut 9/2A
bull Bulle, Stier 13/3B
burglary Einbruch 7/4B
burgundy burgunderrot, weinrot 5/2A
busy belebt 2/6A
button Knopf 5/2A

C

cabinet Kabinett 7/6C
cafeteria Kantine 10/2A
calendar Wand-Kalender 1/3A
calm down *(v)* beruhigen 7/2B
camp Lager 11/3B
candidate Kandidat/in 10/4G
canteen Kantine 6/1B
carbohydrate Kohlehydrat 6/2B
cardigan Wolljacke, Strickjacke 5/2A
care (sb who doesn't ~) jd, dem es egal ist 13/5A
care Sorgen 14/3E
carer Betreuer/in 14/6A
carnet Fahrkartenheft 2/2D
carpet Teppich; Teppichboden 9/2A
cash card Geldkarte 13/1C
casual leger, salopp 5/1B
cat flap Katzentür 9/5D
catalogue Katalog 5/2A
catch *(v)* fangen 9/5D

catch sight of sth *(v)* etwas erblicken 2/3B
cause *(v)* verursachen 11/2A
cave Höhle 5/4B
celebrate *(v)* feiern 15/5B
celebration Feier 15/4A
celebrity Prominente/r 7/1C
Celtic priests keltische Priester 15/5B
central heating system Zentralheizungssystem 1/3B
central location zentrale Lage 9/4B
century Jahrhundert 7/1B
cereal Getreide 3/6B
certain areas bestimmte Fächer 10/2A
chairman Vorsitzender 7/5A
chance Chance 10/3C
chance (Is there any ~ …?) Besteht die Möglichkeit …? 14/6C
change *(v)* auswechseln 9/5D
change Abwechslung 14/6A
changeable wechselhaft 11/1C
channel hop *(v)* zappen 7/3E
channel Sender, Kanal 7/3A
charge *(v)* berechnen 9/6B
charity Wohlfahrt 14/5A
charm *(v)* bezaubern 5/4B
chart Diagramm 7/2B
checked kariert 5/2A
cheerful gut drauf, freundlich 10/4D
chest of drawers Kommode 9/2A
chicken Hühnerfleisch 6/3C
childhood Kindheit 9/1A
china Porzellan 13/3B
chips *(AE:* **french fries)** Pommes frites 6/3A
choice Wahl 14/1A
cigarette Zigarette 7/3C
circus clown Zirkusclown 14/3B
citizenship Staatsbügerschaft 9/1A
clap *(v)* klatschen 15/3B
classic klassisch 6/3C
clean *(v)* putzen, saubermachen 14/1C
clean driving licence Führerschein ohne Punkte 10/5B

Alphabetical Word List

cleaning products Putzmittel 3/6B
clean-shaven rasiert 13/2A
clear klar 6/6D
clear deutlich 7/3B
clever clever, klug 3/4B
climbing Bergsteigen 14/4A
close eng 9/1A
closed in eingesperrt 11/2C
coal field Kohlenrevier 11/6A
coffee table Beistelltisch 9/2A
collect (v) sammeln 1/4A
collect (v) bekommen 10/4G
colony Kolonie 15/5B
colour TV Farbfernsehen 1/5A
colourful bunt 2/6A
come through (v) eintreffen 7/3E
comfortable/comfortably bequem 5/1F
commemorate (v) gedenken 14/5A
comment (v) kommentieren 7/2B
commercial Werbespot 7/3A
commercial centre Geschäftsviertel 2/6A
commercial television Privatfernsehen 7/3C
commit a crime (v) ein Verbrechen begehen 10/5C
common verbreitet 13/3B
communication (Tele-)Kommunikation 7/1B
company (good ~) gute Gesellschaft 14/6A
compartment Abteil 2/1D
competition Wettbewerb 2/4B
complain (v) sich beschweren 9/5D
complete komplett 14/6A
compliment (to pay a ~) ein Kompliment machen 5/5A
comprehensive umfassend 9/6B
compulsory Pflicht- 10/2A
compulsory purchase order Zwangsenteignung 11/4B
computer filing Datenablage im Computer 10/6C
concentration Konzentration, Zentrum 15/1B
conference facilities Tagungseinrichtungen 2/6A

confident selbstsicher 6/5A
confidential vertraulich 7/5
Congratulations! Herzlichen Glückwunsch! 13/6B
conjunction Bindewort 3/2E
connect (v) verbinden 5/4C
conquer (v) erobern 6/3F
conservative konservativ 5/1B
conservatory Wintergarten 9/4B
consider sth (v) etwas überlegen 15/3C
consider yourself ... (v) sich für (etwas) halten 15/5B
consonant Konsonant (Mitlaut) 5/5D
consumer Konsument/in 3/2F
contain (v) enthalten 15/H
contents (house ~) Hausrat 9/6B
contestant Kandidat/in 7/2B
continue (v) andauern 10/2A
contrast (by ~) im Gegensatz 2/6A
contribution Beitrag 14/6A
convert (v) umfunktionieren 14/6A
cook Koch/Köchin 6/3F
cookery verbs Kochverben 6/3B
cope with sth (v) mit etwas fertig werden 14/3B
copy (v) nachmachen 10/1C
correct (v) korrigieren 0/3A
correspondent Korrespondent/in 7/6D
cosmopolitan kosmopolitisch 2/6A
costume Kostüm 15/5B
cotton Baumwolle 5/2A
counsellor Berater/in 14/6A
counter (v) widersprechen 11/6D
counter Theke 3/6A
country-style Landstil 9/2A
couple paar 9/3B
cousin Cousin/e 13/4A
cover (v) abdecken 6/3A
cover Umschlag, Äußeres 5/3D
cover Überzug 9/3B
cover Deckung 9/6B
covered parking space überdachter Stellplatz 9/4B
cream cremefarben 5/2A
creative kreativ 5/1D

creator Erfinder/in 14/4B
credit note Gutschrift 3/3B
cricket *tradit. engl. Ballsport* 14/4A
crime Kriminalität 7/4A
critical kritisch 7/2B
croak (v) quaken 9/5D
cross (v) überqueren 14/5A
cruise Kreuzfahrt 9/5D
crystal kristall- 3/3B
cube Würfel 6/3D
cultural Kultur- 15/3D
cupboard Schrank 9/2A
curly lockig 13/2A
current aktuell 1/1C
current affairs Zeitgeschehen 13/5C
curry Currygericht 6/3F
curtain Vorhang; Gardine 9/2A
curvy weibliche Figur 13/5C
custom Brauch 6/5A
cut (cut, cut) (v) schneiden 6/3D
cut Stück 6/2A
cut down (v) fällen 11/6A
cut off isoliert 14/2B
CV (curriculum vitae) Lebenslauf 10/5B
cycling Radfahren 14/4A

D

dairy product Molkereiprodukt 3/6A
damaged beschädigt 3/3A
dangerous gefährlich 11/3A
dark dunkel 9/3B
daughter-in-law Schwiegertochter 13/4A
deadline Termin 14/3B
dear liebe (-r, -s); teuer 7/4A
decaffeinated (*Abk.* decaf) koffeinfrei 6/1B
decide (v) sich entscheiden 11/5A
Declaration of Independence Unabhängigkeitserklärung 15/5B
deep tief 7/6C
degree Diplom 10/5A
delay (v) zögern 15/3C
delicious köstlich 6/3C
delighted entzückt 15/2D
deliver (v) liefern 3/2A

depend on sth *(v)* von etwas abhängen 7/5A
dependent (be ~ on) abhängig sein von 13/4D
depressed deprimiert 7/2C
depressing deprimierend 7/2B
describe *(v)* beschreiben 2/6C
desert Wüste 11/2A
desperate (I was ~ to) ich wollte unbedingt 9/1A
dessert Nachspeise 6/5D
detached house freistehendes Haus 9/4B
detective Detektiv/in 14/4B
developer Bauträger 11/5A
development Projekt, Objekt 11/4B
devil Teufel 14/1A
diamond Diamant 11/2A
dice Würfel 4/C
diet Ernährung 6/2A
diet Diät 9/5D
dining table Esstisch 9/2A
disabled behindert 2/1D
disappear *(v)* verschwinden 11/5A
disappointed enttäuscht 11/3B
discover *(v)* entdecken 13/4C
discuss *(v)* besprechen, diskutieren 7/6C
display *(v)* zeigen 2/1A
distance Strecke 14/5A
distance learning Fernkurs 10/5B
diving Tauchen 14/4A
divorce Scheidung 7/5B
do sth yourself *(v)* etwas selber tun 9/3C
documentary Dokumentarfilm 7/2A
dolphin Delphin/Delfin 2/5A
domestic Haushalts- 11/2A
doorstep (on your ~) direkt vor der Haustür 7/3E
double-decker Doppeldecker- 2/3B
double-glazing Doppelverglasung 9/4B
doze *(v)* ein Nickerchen machen 2/4A
dozen Dutzend 2/2C
draw up *(v)* abfassen 14/4B
dream Traum 14/3B

dress *(v)* sich anziehen, sich kleiden 5/1C
dress Kleid 5/1A
drizzle Nieselregen 11/1A
drought Dürre 7/6C
drug Droge 7/4A
Druids Druiden 15/5B
dry *(v)* trocknen 1/5A
dry trocken 6/3A
duty (off~) nicht im Dienst 14/2B
dye Farbstoff 5/4A

E

early bird Frühaufsteher/in 1/2
earring Ohrring 5/4B
earthquake Erdbeben 9/6A
easy-going locker 10/4D
easy-to-use benutzerfreundlich 2/3B
eat out *(v)* Essen gehen 13/5C
economics Wirtschaftskunde 10/3A
editor Redakteur/in 10/4A
educate *(v)* bilden 7/5A
effective effektiv, wirksam 3/4B
elderly people ältere Leute 2/1D
electronic organizer elektronischer Terminplaner 1/3A
elegant elegant 5/1B
embarrassing peinlich 6/6D
emigrant Auswanderer/in 15/5B
emotional emotionell 7/2B
employment Beschäftigung 14/2E
empty *(v)* hineingeben 6/3A
encounter Begegnung 2/5A
encourage *(v)* ermutigen 14/6A
energetic fit, energisch 1/2A
energy business Energiegeschäft 11/6A
Enjoy! Guten Appetit! 6/0
enjoyable angenehm 6/6D
enthusiast Enthusiast/in 2/2C
enthusiastic enthusiastisch 7/2B
entrance Eingang 3/6A
environment Umwelt 14/2E
environmental Umwelt- 11/6D
envy *(v)* beneiden 10/3C
essential unerlässlich 9/2C
establish *(v)* festlegen 14/5A

estimate Schätzung 15/1B
even if selbst wenn 3/2E
evil spirits böse Geister 15/5B
ex-husband ex-Mann 13/4A
excavator Bagger 11/6A
exchange *(v)* umtauschen 3/1C
excited aufgeregt 7/2B
exciting aufregend 2/6A
exclusive exklusiv 11/4B
exercise *(v)* spazieren führen 10/4A
exhibition Ausstellung 15/3B
exit Ausgang 3/6A
exotic exotisch 2/6A
expect *(v)* erwarten 14/5D
experienced erfahren 14/6A
explanation Erklärung 2/1B
explore *(v)* entdecken 14/3B
exporter Exporteur 2/2C
express *(v)* ausdrücken 14/3C
expression Ausdruck 6/1C
expression Gesichtsausdruck 15/2E
eyebrows Augenbrauen 15/2B
eyesight Sehkraft 5/4B

F

face-to-face persönlich 2/4B
facelift Gesichtsstraffung 5/4D
fail *(v)* durchfallen 10/3C
fair fair 10/5C
fair hair blondes Haar 13/2A
fall *(v)* sinken 7/4B
fancy sth *(v)* Lust auf etwas haben 6/2
farm *(v)* bebauen 11/5A
farmer Bauer/Bäuerin 10/4C
farming community Bauerngemeinde 7/2A
farmland Ackerland 11/2A
fascinated fasziniert 7/3E
fashionable modisch 3/5A
fasten (your seat belt) *(v)* sich anschnallen 2/1B
fat dick 9/5D
fault (it was my own ~) ich war selber Schuld 11/3B
Feast of the Dead Totenfest 15/5B
feat (Helden)Tat 14/5A
feature *(v)* mit 15/3A
feature film Spielfilm 7/3E

feed *(v)* füttern 9/5D
feel *(v)* sich fühlen 5/1E
feeling Gefühl 1/3B
feet (be on your ~) auf den Beinen sein 14/2B
fellow traveller Mitreisende/r 2/4D
fellow worker Mitarbeiter/in 14/2E
female weiblich 5/1F
feminine weiblich, feminin 13/5C
fencing Fechten 14/4A
ferry Fähre 2/4B
fight sth *(v)* gegen etwas kämpfen 11/5A
figures Zahlen, Statistiken 7/4B
fill *(v)* füllen 5/4A
fill in *(v)* ausfüllen 10/3C
filling Füllung 6/3C
final examination Abschlussprüfung 10/2A
finance *(v)* finanzieren 7/3C
financial/financially finanziell 13/4D
find *(v)* finden 5/6B
find out *(v)* erfahren, herausfinden 7/2B
fingerprint Fingerabdruck 13/1A
fireplace Kamin 9/3B
fireworks Feuerwerk 15/4A
first aid erste Hilfe 10/5B
first class erste Klasse 2/3B
First World War Erster Weltkrieg 5/1F
fishing fischen 2/5A
fit *(v)* passen *(Form, Größe)* 5/2C
fit as a fiddle fit wie ein Turnschuh 10/4D
fit sb in *(v)* jdn einschieben 14/6C
fitted kitchen Einbauküche 9/4B
flat pie dish *(etwa)* flache Tortenform 6/3D
flatmate Mitbewohner/in 15/3B
to flatten dem Erdboden gleichmachen 11/3B
flight Flug 15/4B
floods Hochwasser 7/5B
flora Pflanzenwelt 11/2A

flour Mehl 6/3C
flower *(v)* blühen 10/6C
fluent (be ~ in sth) etwas fließend beherrschen 10/4A
follow suit *(v)* nachziehen 14/5A
fond (be ~ of) mögen, lieben 10/4A
for/against pro/contra 5/3D
forgetful vergesslich 1/3B
formal förmlig 5/1B
former ehemalig 11/6C
fortunately glücklicherweise 9/5B
found *(v)* gründen 14/4B
fox Fuchs 13/3B
freak Narr/Närrin, Fanatiker/in 7/3E
free of charge kostenlos 10/2A
freezing eisig 1/1B
frequency Häufigkeit 6/1C
friendship Freundschaft 13/5A
frightening beängstigend 10/1C
frog Frosch 9/5D
frost Frost 11/1A
frosted glass Milchglas 9/5D
frown *(v)* die Stirn runzeln 15/2B
frozen foods Tiefkühlkost 3/6A
frustration Frust 7/6C
fry *(v)* braten 6/3A
fulfil *(v)* erfüllen 14/3B
full coverage ausführliche Berichterstattung 7/3E
fun (be ~) Spaß machen 7/2B
functional funktional 9/2A
funny komisch, lustig 3/4B
furnished (fully ~) möbliert 9/4B

G

gain *(v)* erwerben 10/6B
gale Wind mit Sturmstärke 11/1A
gallery Galerie 15/3A
gated community *(etwa)* geschlossener Wohnbezirk 11/4C
gateway Tor 2/6A
general allgemein 0/3A
generation Generation 11/5A
geography Geografie 10/3A
gesture Geste 15/2E

get on with sb *(v)* sich mit jdm verstehen 9/5B
get out *(v)* aussteigen 2/4B
get rid of sth *(v)* etwas loswerden 9/5D
get sth back *(v)* etwas zurückbekommen 11/3B
get sth in shape *(v)* etwas auf die Reihe kriegen 14/3B
get too much for sb *(v)* jdm zu viel werden 14/6A
gift-wrap *(v)* als Geschenk verpacken 3/1C
girlfriend Freundin 9/1A
give up *(v)* überlassen 2/1D
give up *(v)* aufgeben 11/5A
glad (I'm ~) Ich freue mich 5/5B
glass (Trink)Glas 3/3B
glove Handschuh 13/1B
go back to *(v)* zurück auf etwas gehen 15/5B
go camping *(v)* zelten 1/5A
go for a swim *(v)* schwimmen gehen 6/6A
go with sth *(v)* zu etwas passen 5/2C
god Gott 5/4B
gold Gold 11/2A
golden golden 6/3D
good (be ~ at sth) gut in etwas sein 10/3A
good (be ~ with) gut mit umgehen können 10/4A
good-looking gut aussehend 13/5C
Goodness! Du meine Güte! 10/5B
graduate Akademiker/in 10/4A
grandfather Großvater 13/4A
grandfather clock Standuhr 1/3A
granny Oma 13/2A
grateful dankbar 14/6A
greetings card Grußkarte 13/6A
grey grau 5/2A
groceries Lebensmittel 3/2A
ground floor (*AE:* **first floor**) Erdgeschoss 9/4B
grow *(v)* wachsen 2/6A
grow up *(v)* aufwachsen 1/5A
guarantee *(v)* garantieren 7/3E
guided tour Führung 2/5B

Alphabetical Word List

163

guideline Richtlinie 6/5A
gymnastics Gymnastik 14/4A

H
habit Gewohnheit 3/2F
hail Hagel 11/1A
hairstyle Haarstil 5/4D
half-brother Halbbruder 13/4A
ham Schinken 6/3C
hand in (v) abgeben 5/6B
handbag Handtasche 5/6A
handful Handvoll 11/4B
handicapped behindert 14/6A
handsome gut aussehend 13/5C
hang (v) aufhängen 9/3B
hang-gliding Drachenfliegen 14/4A
happiness Glück 13/6B
hard-earned schwerverdient 10/4G
harvest Ernte- 15/5B
hate (v) hassen 1/4C
have got (v) haben 1/3B
hay Heu 14/6A
head (of state) (Staats)Oberhaupt 7/6C
health Gesundheit 14/2E
heart (to their ~s' content) nach Herzenslust 14/6A
height größe 13/2A
helpful hilfreich, nützlich 3/2CD
helping (Essen) Portion 6/5A
helpline Hotline 9/6B
hide (v) sich verstecken 11/3B
hill Hügel 11/2A
Hindi Hindi 15/1A
historian Historiker/in 7/3E
historic historisch 2/2C
history Geschichte 7/3E
hit (be ~ by) heimgesucht werden von 11/3B
hold Griff 10/6C
hole Loch 5/4A
home-grown aus eigenem Anbau 14/6A
homely gemütlich 14/6A
homesick Heimweh 9/1A
hometown Heimatstadt 9/1A
honest ehrlich 10/4A
horrible schrecklich, grauenhaft 3/4B
host Gastgeber/in 6/5B

household Haushalt 7/1D
hurricane Orkan 11/2A
hurt (v) schmerzen 14/1A
husband Ehemann 13/4A
hydroelectric power Strom aus Wasserkraft 11/2A

I
ice-skating Eislaufen 14/4A
identification Identifikation 5/6B
idle faul 14/1A
If all else fails, ... Wenn alle Stricke reißen, ... 15/2A
imagine (v) sich vorstellen 15/3C
imitate (v) imitieren, nachmachen 10/1D
impact Auswirkung 3/2F
impatient ungeduldig 10/4E
impolite unhöflich 6/5A
impression Eindruck 15/2E
include (v) einbeziehen, einschließen 7/6D
inconvenient ungünstig 9/3B
increase (v) steigern 11/5A
incredibly unglaublich 10/1C
independent unabhängig 13/5C
Indian indisch 6/1B
industrial Industrie- 11/4A
influence (v) beeinflussen 3/5
influence Einfluss 3/5A
influential einflussreich 15/1B
inform (v) informieren 7/5A
informative informativ 7/3E
infrastructure Infrastruktur 2/2C
ingredient Zutat 6/3C
inhibited gehemmt 15/2H
inner city Stadtzentrum 7/4B
insight Einblick 7/3E
install (v) installieren 9/3A
instant sofortige (-r, -s) 14/5A
instead anstatt, stattdessen 6/4B
insurance policy Versicherungspolice 9/6B
intelligent intelligent 13/5C
intend (v) beabsichtigen 2/5D
intercultural interkulturell 6/6
interested interresiert 7/2C
internal intern 3/1C

investigation Untersuchung 7/4B
involved (be ~ in) zu tun haben mit 7/2B
IT (information technology) Informatik 10/3A

J
jacket Jacke 5/1A
jam Marmelade 6/1B
jewellery Schmuck 5/4A
join (v) beitreten 10/4A
joke (v) einen Witz machen 5/1C
joke Witz 13/5A
journalist Journalist/in 7/5C
journey Fahrt, Reise 2/3B
judge (v) beurteilen 5/3D

K
keep (v) behalten 15/3C
keep an eye on sth (v) auf etwas aufpassen 15/6A
keep in touch (v) in Kontakt bleiben 13/6A
key Schlüssel 5/6A
key card (elektronische) Schlüsselkarte 13/1C
kill (v) töten 11/3B
killer whale Killerwal, Orka 2/5A
kind nett, freundlich 13/5C
kindergarten Kindergarten 10/2A
kitchen equipment Küchengeräte 1/3B
knowledge Wissen, Kenntnis 10/4G
knowledgeable gut informiert 10/4D

L
label Etikett 3/5A
lake See 11/2A
lampshade Lampenschirm 9/3B
land use Landnutzung 11/4A
landing Landung 2/5A
landlord/landlady Vermieter/Vermieterin 9/3F

landscape Landschaft 11/2
landslide Erdrutsch 11/3B
lane Gasse 2/6A
lantern Laterne 15/5B
Latin Latein 10/3A
laugh *(v)* lachen 13/5C
launch Start, Abschuss 2/5A
law court Gerichtshof 10/4G
lawyer Anwalt 9/6B
leaf, leaves Blatt, Blätter 6/4A
lean mager 6/2A
leek Lauch 6/3C
legal fees Anwalt- und Gerichtskosten 9/6B
legume Hülsenfrucht 6/2B
leisure Freizeit 1/4
lemon Zitrone 6/6D
let *(v)* vermieten 9/3F
liability Haftpflicht 9/6D
licence Schein, Lizenz 10/4G
licence fee Lizenzgebühr 7/3B
lie *(v)* liegen 13/1D
lie-in (to have a ~) im Bett bleiben 1/2A
lifetime Leben 9/3F
light *(v)* anzünden 15/5B
light hell 1/2A
light meal kleine Mahlzeit 6/4A
lightning Blitz 9/6A
lightweight leicht 9/2A
lined (She was very ~) Sie hatte viele Falten 13/2A
linen Leinen 5/2A
link Beziehung 7/6C
lip Lippe 15/2B
live report Livebericht 7/6D
living room Wohnzimmer 9/2B
local council Gemeinderat 11/4B
local economy (the ~) die hiesige Wirtschaft 11/5A
locals (the ~) die Einheimischen 11/3B
loft Dachboden 9/4B
log cabin Blockhütte 14/3D
lonely hearts einsame Herzen 13/5C
longest-running am längsten laufend 7/2A
long-term loan langfristiges Darlehen 9/3F
look *(v)* aussehen 5/1E

look after sb *(v)* sich um jdn kümmern 13/4D
look like (What does she ~?) *(v)* Wie sieht sie aus? 13/2
loose locker 5/2C
lose *(v)* verlieren 5/6B
loss Verlust 5/6B
lost property office Fundbüro 5/6B
love *(v)* lieben 1/4C
lovely schön 3/1B
low niedrig 7/4B
low-fat fettarm 6/2A
lower *(v)* reduzieren, senken 5/3B
loyalty card Kundenkarte 13/1C
luck Glück 13/6B
luckily glücklicherweise 15/3D
luxury Luxus- 11/4B
lyrics (Lied)Text 15/3B

M
machine washable waschmaschinenfest 5/2A
mad verrückt 1/1B
magical magisch 5/4B
major wichtig, bedeutend 3/2F
make an effort *(v)* sich bemühen 9/5B
make-up Make-up 5/4A
make up into a bed *(v)* in ein Bett unwandeln 9/2A
manage *(v)* führen, leiten 2/2C
manage without sth *(v)* ohne etwas auskommen 14/6A
Mandarin Chinese Mandarin *(chinesische Hochsprache)* 15/1A
mangrove swamp Mangrovenwälder 11/2A
mark *(v)* kennzeichnen 15/5B
mashed potatoes Kartoffelpüree 6/3A
mate *(v)* sich paaren 7/3E
material Stoff 5/2B
maths (mathematics) Mathematik, Mathe 10/3A
may (You ~...) Sie dürfen ... 6/5A
media age (the ~) das Medienzeitalter 7/1

medium-sized mittelgroß 6/3C
membership Mitgliedschaft 5/4B
memory Erinnerung 7/6C
mention *(v)* erwähnen 7/5B
Middle Ages (the ~) das Mittelalter 14/4B
midsummer Hochsommer 15/5B
military militärisch, Militär- 7/1B
mind (I don't ~) Es macht mich nichts aus 1/4C
mind (to keep their ~s fit) um geistig fit zu bleiben 10/6B
mine *(v)* gewinnen 11/6A
mine Bergwerk 11/6A
mined out (when a coal field is ~) wann das Vorkommen erschöpft ist 11/6A
mineral deposit Mineralvorkommen 11/2A
mirror Spiegel 9/3B
miss *(v)* vermissen 7/1D
miss *(v)* verpassen 7/3E
missing (be ~) fehlen 3/3B
mistake Fehler 0/3A
mix (rich ~) bunte Mischung 2/6A
model Modell 1/4A
modify *(v)* verändern, modifizieren 13/2C
monthly monatlich 7/3B
monument Denkmal, historische Gebäude 2/6A
mood (to be in a bad ~) schlechte Laune haben 1/2A
mortgage Hypothek 9/3F
mother Mutter 10/4C
mother tongue Muttersprache 15/1B
motor racing Autorennen 14/4A
mountain Berg 11/2A
moustache Schnurrbart 13/2A
mousy mausgrau 13/2A
move *(v)* sich bewegen 2/3D
multi-purpose Mehrzweck- 14/6A
Munich München 2/4B
must (a ~) ein Muss 2/2C

Alphabetical Word List

N

nanny Kindermädchen 10/4A
nap Nickerchen 1/1B
narrow eng 2/6A
nasty fies 10/5C
nationalize *(v)* verstaatlichen 2/2C
nationwide landesweit 14/2E
native speaker Muttersprachler/in 15/1A
natural disaster Naturkatastrophe 11/3A
natural gas Erdgas 11/2A
natural resources Bodenschätze 11/2B
natural setting natürliche Lage, Umgebung 2/6A
nature reserve Naturschutzgebiet 11/6A
neat toll, klasse 5/5B
necklace Halskette 5/4B
needn't (You ~...) Sie brauchen nicht ... 6/5A
negative negativ 3/4B
Neither do I./Nor me. Ich auch nicht. 2/4A
nephew Neffe 13/4A
nerve Nerv 10/4D
nervous nervös 10/5C
new-laid eggs frische Eier 14/6A
nickname Spitzname 13/3A
niece Nichte 13/4B
night owl Nachteule 1/2
nightlife Nachtleben 2/6A
no longer nicht mehr 9/1A
noise Krach 9/5D
noisy (pretty ~) ziemlich laut 9/5D
non-stop Nonstop- 2/3B
non-verbal *nicht gesprochen* 15/2H
Norway; Norwegian Norwegen; norwegisch 14/4B
not-for-profit gemeinnützig 2/2C
not settled ungebunden 9/1A
notice *(v)* bemerken 15/3D
notice Hinweis 2/4B
novel Roman 14/3D
nowadays heutzutage 1/6B

O

occupation Beruf 13/3B
ocean Ozean 11/2A
offend *(v)* beleidigen 11/1D
offensive anstößig 3/4B
offer Angebot 11/5A
official Beamte/r, Funktionär/in 5/3B
on air auf Sendung 7/2B
open-cast mine Tagebau 11/6A
open-plan kitchen amerikanische Küche 9/4B
operate *(v)* betreiben 2/2C
opinion Meinung 9/2C
opportunity Chance, Möglichkeit 14/6A
opposite sex (the ~) das andere Geschlecht 5/4B
oral mündlich 10/4G
ordinary normal 13/2A
oriental cookery orientalische Küche 10/6C
originate *(v)* entstehen 14/4B
ornament Ornament 5/4A
other way round (the ~) umgekehrt 6/3F
otter Otter 7/3E
ought to/oughtn't to (You ~...) Sie sollten/sollten nicht ... 6/5A
oven Backofen 6/3A
overstress *(etwa)* zu viel Stress 14/2E
overweight (he's a bit ~) er hat etwas Übergewicht 13/2A
overwork Überarbeitung 14/2E
own *(v)* besitzen 9/3F
owned (to have ~) besessen zu haben 9/3F
owner Besitzer 9/3F

P

package Paket 7/3E
paint *(v)* anstreichen 9/3A
painter Maler/in 15/3A
painting Malerei 1/6B
pale hell 13/2A
pancake Pfannkuchen 1/1B
parent Elternteil 6/4B
participle Partizip, 3. Form 6/6B
particularly besonders 3/4C
party Partei 7/6C
pass *(v)* reichen 6/5D
pass *(v)* bestehen 10/3C
pass *(v)* genehmigen 11/4B
pass the time *(v)* die Zeit vertreiben 2/4A
passenger Fahrgast 2/1D
password Passwort 13/1C
pastry Teig 6/3C
path Weg 11/4B
patient geduldig 10/1C
patio Terrasse 9/4B
patronymic vom Namen des Vaters abgeleiteter Name 13/3B
pattern Muster 5/2B
pavement (AE: sidewalk) Bürgersteig 13/1D
pay Gehalt, Gehälter 7/4B
pay for *(v)* finanzieren 7/3A
pay TV Pay-TV 7/3B
PE (physical education) Sport (als Schulfach) 10/3A
peaceful friedlich 14/6A
peak time Hauptverkehrszeit 2/3B
percentage Prozentsatz 15/1B
perfume Parfüm 5/4A
permission Erlaubnis 7/5C
Persian persisch 6/1B
pet Haustier 9/4B
pet name Kosename 13/3A
picnic Picknick 10/6C
piercing Piercing 5/4A
pin up *(v)* anstecken, anhängen 1/5E
plain *(Farbe)* Uni- 5/2A
plain Ebene 11/2A
plan *(v)* planen, vorbereiten 14/5D
plant *(v)* pflanzen 11/4B
plateau Hochebene 11/2A
platform Gleis 2/2A
player Spieler 7/1D
pleasant/ly angenehm 2/4B
plenty of reichlich 6/2B
pocket Tasche 5/2A
poem Gedicht 15/3A
poetry Poesie 15/3A
policy Politik, Programm, Strategie 7/6C
politics Politik 10/3A
pond Teich 9/5D
poor arm 13/5C

popular beliebt 13/6A
portion Portion 6/2A
positive/ly positiv 2/6C
posture Körperhaltung 15/2E
pot Topf 1/3F
pottery Töpfern 1/6B
pour *(v)* (darüber)gießen 6/3A
pour down *(v)* schütten 11/1E
poverty Armut 14/2E
power station Kraftwerk 11/6A
practical praktisch 5/1F
precious stone Edelstein 5/4A
preheat *(v)* vorheizen 6/3A
premium (insurance ~) Versicherungsbeitrag 9/6B
prepared bereit 10/4E
present Geschenk 15/4F
previously früher, vorher 10/2A
prick *(v)* stechen 5/4A
priest Priester 5/4B
prime viewing time Hauptsendezeit 7/3B
private privat 7/5
private citizen Privatpersonen 11/4C
privatize *(v)* privatisieren 2/2C
programme Sendung 7/1B
project Projekt 11/4C
promise *(v)* versprechen 6/4B
promotion Beförderung 10/6B
proper/ly richtig 1/2A
pros and cons Pro und Kontra 11/6
protect *(v)* schützen 7/5C
protein Protein 6/2B
prove *(v)* beweisen 10/4E
provide *(v)* zur Verfügung stellen 10/2A
psychological tips psychologische Ratschläge 10/6C
public interest (the ~) das öffentliche Interesse 2/2C
publish *(v)* veröffentlichen 10/6C
puchase *(v)* kaufen 2/3B
pupil Schüler/in 10/2C
pure rein 9/2A
purse Geldbörse 5/6A
put on *(v)* anziehen 5/3B
put sb up *(v)* jdn unterbringen 15/4A
put your feet up *(v)* die Füße hochlegen 14/2B
pyjamas Schlafanzug 5/1D

Q
qualification Qualifikation 10/5A
qualify for sth *(v)* sich für etwas qualifizieren 10/5A
qualities Qualitäten, Eigenschaften 10/4C
quantity *(Abk.* qty) Menge 5/2C
question *(v)* befragen 7/4B
queue (Warte)Schlange 13/2A
quiz show Quizshow 7/2A

R
race Rennen 14/3B
radio alarm Radiowecker 1/3A
rainfall Niederschlag *(Regen)* 11/2A
raise *(v)* aufziehen 9/1A
raise *(v)* hochziehen 15/2B
range from … to … *(v)* von … bis … reichen 11/2A
range Reihe, Palette 9/2A
range (mountain ~) Bergkette 11/2A
realize (I didn't ~) Mir war nicht bewusst 15/1C
reason Grund 2/4B
receipt Quittung 3/1B
receive *(v)* erhalten, bekommen 10/5A
recently kürzlich, in der letzten Zeit 0/1A
receptionist Rezeptionist/in, Empfangsperson 10/4A
recipe Rezept 6/3
recipient Empfänger/in 13/6A
recognize *(v)* erkennen 3/5A
record Rekord- 7/4B
recreational purposes Freizeitnutzung 11/4A
redecorate *(v)* renovieren 9/3B
reduction Ermäßigung 2/2D
reed Schilfgras 9/5D
refreshments Erfrischungen 15/3A

refund (I'd like a ~, please.) Ich hätte gern mein Geld zurück. 3/3B
refuse *(v)* ablehnen 6/5B
regular regelmäßig 1/1C
regulate *(v)* regulieren 7/3C
reject; rejection *(v)* ablehnen; Ablehnung 11/4B
relationship Beziehung 13/4D
relative Verwandte/r 0/1A
relevant relevant 10/5B
reliable zuverlässig 10/4A
relieved erleichtert 15/2D
religious religiös 5/4B
relocate *(v)* umsiedeln, umlagern 11/6A
remember *(v)* sich erinnern 14/5D
rent Miete 9/3F
repair *(v)* reparieren 10/3C
replace *(v)* ersetzen 9/3F
replacement Ersatz 6/2B
replant *(v)* wieder aufforsten 11/6A
reputation Ruf, Ansehen 2/6A
require *(v)* brauchen 10/4A
research Forschung 15/2E
researcher Forscher/in 10/4A
resident Einwohner/in 11/4B
residential Wohn- 11/4A
resort (As a last ~) Als letzte Möglichkeit 15/2A
respect *(v)* respektieren 3/5A
responsible (be ~ for sb) die Verantwortung für jdn haben 13/4D
restrict *(v)* einschränken 7/3C
rethink *(v)* überdenken 14/6A
retire *(v)* in Rente gehen 14/3A
retirement Ruhestand 1/6D
retreat house *(etwa)* Haus der Besinnung 14/6A
return *(v)* wieder besuchen, wiederkommen 7/4B
return home Heimkehr 2/4B
return ticket Rückfahrkarte 2/2D
returns (Many happy ~!) Herzlichen Glückwunsch zum Geburtstag! 13/6B
revive *(v)* wiederbeleben 14/5A
revolutionary revolutionär 2/3B

reward Lohn 14/6A
rhythm Rhythmus 1/3E
rich reich 6/2B
rich (the ~) die Reichen 11/4B
ride Fahrt 2/5A
ridiculous lächerlich, albern 3/5A
riding Reiten 14/4A
ring *(v)* anrufen 2/3B
rise *(v)* steigen 7/4A
risk Risiko 3/2D
river Fluss 11/2A
road (be on the ~) unterwegs sein 14/2B
roll Brötchen 6/1B
roll out *(v)* ausrollen 6/3D
rolling farmland sanft ansteigendes Ackerland 11/2A
rose bush Rosenstrauch 11/4B
roughage Ballaststoffe 6/2B
round Runde 11/1C
roundish rundlich 13/2A
route Route 10/4G
routine routinemäßig 1/1C
rowing Rudern 14/4A
royal family königliche Familie 14/5A
run *(v)* fahren 2/2C
runner Läufer/in 7/6C
running (two days ~) zwei Tage hintereinander 10/4E
runway Start-/Landebahn 11/4B

S
sailing Segeln 14/4A
sailor Seemann 5/4B
sale (for ~) zum verkaufen 9/4B
satisfaction Zufriedenheit 14/1A
savings Ersparnisse 15/3B
sauce Soße 6/3D
saucepan Kochtopf 6/3A
sausage Wurst 6/3A
save up for sth *(v)* auf etwas sparen 11/5C
scandal Skandal 7/1C
scarf Schal 5/5
scenery Landschaften 11/2A
schooldays Schulzeit 1/6A
science Naturwissenschaften 10/3A
scrap *(v)* abschaffen 10/2C

scratch *(v)* kratzen 15/2B
scruffy vergammelt 5/1B
sea-level Meeresspiegel 11/2A
sealion Seelöwe 2/5A
search Suche 3/2A
seaside die Meeresküste 1/5A
seat belt Sicherheitsgurt 2/1B
secretarial Sekretärin- 10/5B
security Sicherheits- 11/4B
seek *(v)* suchen 13/5C
seem *(v)* scheinen 1/2A
seismic seismisch 11/2A
self-defence Selbstverteidigung 10/5C
sell *(v)* verkaufen 11/5A
semi-detached house Doppelhaushälfte 9/4B
senior wichtig, bedeutend 7/6C
senior citizen Rentner/in 2/2D
sensationalism Sensationsmache 7/5A
sense Sinn 5/1E
separate *(v)* trennen 11/2A
separate getrennt 14/6C
series Serie 7/2A
serve *(v)* servieren 6/3A
service *(v)* (Auto) Inspektion machen 9/3E
session Treffen 14/6A
several einige (-r, -s) 13/3B
sexist sexistisch 3/4B
shabby schäbig 5/1B
shadow (cast a ~) einen Schatten werfen 15/5B
shake *(v)* zittern 13/5E
shame (What a ~!) Wie schade! 11/3B
share *(v)* teilen 13/5A
share Aktie 7/1C
sheep (to keep ~) Schafe halten 14/3D
shelf, shelves Regal, Regale 3/6A
shell Schale 5/4B
shirt Hemd 5/1A
shorts Shorts 5/1A
short-sleeve(d) kurzärmelig 5/2A
shoulder-length Schulterlang 13/2B
show jumping Springreiten 7/3E

shower Schauer 11/1A
shower curtain Duschvorhang 9/3F
shrug your shoulders *(v)* die Achseln zucken 15/2B
shut down *(v)* dicht machen 11/3B
shy schüchtern 13/5C
side Seiten- 5/2A
sight Sehenswürdigkeit 2/6A
sightseeing Besichtigungen 5/1G
sign *(v)* unterschreiben 13/1B
signal Signal 2/2C
signature Unterschrift 13/1A
significant/ly beachtlich, beträchtlich 7/4B
silk Seide 5/2A
simmer *(v)* köcheln 6/3A
singer Sänger/in 1/3E
single ticket Einzelfahrkarte 2/2D
sister Schwester 13/4A
sitcom Sitcom 7/2A
skiing Skifahren 14/4A
skill Fähigkeit, Kenntnis 10/4A
skin Haut 5/4A
skinny dünn 13/5C
skirt Rock 5/1A
sky, skies Himmel 1/3E
sky-diving Fallschirmspringen 14/4A
slice Scheibe 6/3C
slim schlank 13/2A
slope Hang; Piste 11/3B
smart fein, geflegt 5/1B
smell *(v)* riechen 5/1E
smell Geruch 2/6A
smile Lächeln 13/2A
smooth glatt, weich 13/3
So do I. / Me too. Ich auch. 2/4A
so daher, also 3/2E
so that so dass 3/2E
soap (opera) Seifenoper 7/2A
soap manufacturer Seifenhersteller/in 7/2A
so-called sogenannt 15/5B
sociable offen 10/4D
social studies Sozialkunde 10/3A
socket Steckdose 9/3A
sofa Sofa 9/2A

soft drink alkoholfreies Getränk 3/6A
solstice Sonnenwende 15/5B
solution Lösung 9/2A
solve *(v)* lösen 7/4B
son Sohn 13/4B
sort things out *(v)* sich organisieren 9/5D
sound *(v)* sich anhören 5/1E
space shuttle Raumfähre 2/5A
space station Raumstation 2/5A
spare key Zweitschlüssel 9/5B
spare room Gästezimmer 15/4A
sparrow Spatz 13/3B
special occasion besonderer Anlass 15/2E
specialist spezialisiert 7/3E
specialize *(v)* sich spezialisieren 10/2A
specific spezifisch 15/2G
spectator sport Publikumssport 14/4C
spicy würzig 6/1B
spider Spinne 7/3E
spirits Spirituosen 3/6A
split Meinungsverschiedenheit 7/6C
spoil *(v)* verderben 6/3F
spokesman/woman Sprecher/in 7/4B
sponsor *(v)* sponsern 7/2A
sponsor Sponsor 14/5B
sponsorship Sponsoring 7/6D
sporty sportlich 13/5C
spot Werbespot 7/3A
spring vegetables junges Gemüse 6/3D
spring Quelle 11/2A
stadium Stadion 14/5A
stamp Briefmarke 1/4A
stand (I can't ~ ...) *(v)* Ich kann ... nicht ertragen 1/4C
stare *(v)* schauen 14/3E
statement Aussage 0/3A
stay on *(v)* bleiben, weiter machen 10/2A
steal *(v)* stehlen 5/6C
steel Stahl 10/4D
steel-framed mit Stahlgestell 9/2A
stepmother Stiefmutter 13/4A
still still 14/2B
stimulate *(v)* stimulieren 14/6A

stingray Stachelrochen 2/5A
stir *(v)* rühren 6/3A
stock (in ~) auf Lager 3/1B
stocky stämmig 13/2B
stomach-ache Magenschmerz 11/3B
stop Haltestelle 2/4A
stopwatch Stoppuhr 1/3A
storage problem Platzproblem 9/2A
store *(v)* lagern 6/3A
store *(v)* aufbewahren 11/3B
storm Sturm, Unwetter 9/6A
straight hair glattes Haar 13/2A
strange merkwürdig 10/5C
strength Stärke 14/3B
strengthen *(v)* verstärken 14/2E
stretch *(v)* strecken 11/6A
strictly strikt 7/3C
strip *(v)* entfernen, abziehen 9/3A
striped gestreift 5/2A
strong stark 11/1C
stuck (be ~ behind a desk) *(etwa)* im Büro hängen 14/2B
student exchange Studentenaustausch 2/4B
studies Studium 10/5A
studio Studio 7/2B
stupid dumm 3/4B
stylish stilvoll 9/2A
subject Fach 10/2A
subscribe *(v)* abonnieren 7/3B
subscription Abonnementgebühr 7/3B
substance Substanz, Stoff 5/4A
substantial reserves bedeutende Vorkommen 11/2A
subtropical forest subtropischer Wald 11/2A
success (prove a ~) sich als Erfolg erweisen 14/5A
successor Nachkommen 15/5B
suddenly plötzlich 13/2A
suffer from sth *(v)* an etwas leiden 14/2E
suggest *(v)* vorschlagen 13/5E
suit sb *(v)* jmd stehen, passen 5/2C
suit Anzug 5/1A
suitable for vegetarians für Vegetarier geeignet 6/3A
suitcase (Reise)Koffer 10/4E

sum Summe 7/3E
sum up *(v)* zusammenfassen 10/4G
sunbathe *(v)* sonnenbaden 9/5D
support *(v)* unterstützen 7/3E
suppose (I ~ ...) Wahrscheinlich ... 13/2A
surface Oberfläche 11/6A
surrounded by umgeben von 11/2A
suspect Verdächtige/r 13/2A
suspicious misstrauisch 10/4E
swamp Sumpf 2/5A
sweater Pullover 5/1A
swipe card Türkarte 13/1C
switch on *(v)* einschalten 1/3B
sympathize *(v)* Verständnis haben 7/2B

T

tactful taktvoll 10/4D
take an exam *(v)* eine Prüfung machen 10/5A
take out *(v)* rausnehmen 3/2A
take part *(v)* teilnehmen 14/5A
take sb to court *(v)* jdn vor Gericht bringen 9/5D
take time off *(v)* frei nehmen 14/2E
take trouble with *(v)* sich Mühe geben 13/2D
tall groß 13/5C
tap (*AE*: faucet) Wasserhahn 11/3B
taste *(v)* schmecken 5/1E
taste *(v)* probieren 6/6D
tattoo Tattoo 5/4A
tax form Steuerformular 10/3C
tbs (tablespoon) Esslöffel 6/3C
telephone etiquette Umgang am Telefon 10/6C
temporary vorübergehend 1/1C
tenant Mieter/in 9/3F
ten-pin bowling Kegeln 14/4A
tent Zelt 11/3B
terraced house Reihenhaus 9/4B
terrible schrecklich, furchtbar 1/6B
terrified (be ~) fürchterliche Angst haben 10/1C

Alphabetical Word List

Thai thailändisch 6/1B
thatcher Dachdecker/in 13/3B
theoretical theoretisch 10/5A
thick dick 6/3C
thin dünn 6/3D
thirsty durstig 11/3B
though aber 6/1B
threaten (v) bedrohen 14/2E
thrilling aufregend 2/5A
throw (v) werfen 2/1B
thumb Daumen 15/2B
thunderstorm Gewitter 11/1C
ticket office Fahrkartenschalter 2/2A
tidy ordentlich 9/2A
tie Krawatte 5/1A
tight eng 3/3B
tile Kachel; Fliese 9/3F
till Kasse 3/6A
timer Zeitschaltuhr 1/3A
timetable Fahrplan 2/2A
tinned (AE: canned) foods Konserven 3/6A
tone of voice Ton (Stimme) 15/2E
tongue Zunge 5/4B
tooth, teeth Zahn, Zähne 5/4B
toothpaste Zahnpaste 3/5A
topic Thema 11/1D
touch-screen Berührungsbildschirm 2/3B
tourist attraction Touristenattraktion 2/6A
towel rail Handtuchhalter 9/3F
track Schiene 2/2C
tracksuit Trainingsanzug 5/1A
tradition Tradition 1/1B
train service Zugverbindung 2/2C
trainee Auszubildende/r 5/1C
transmit (v) übermitteln 15/2E
transportation Transport 11/4A
trash Schund 7/5A
tree-lined von Bäumen gesäumt 2/6A
trendy modisch 5/5B
tribe Volk, Stamm 5/4B
trick Trick 5/6C
tricky listig 13/3B
trolley Einkaufswagen 3/6A
tropical tropisch 11/2A
trouble Mühe 13/2D
troupe Truppe 15/3A

trousers Hose 5/1A
trust (v) anvertrauen 5/1C
trustworthy vertrauenswürdig 10/4D
tunnel Tunnel 2/2C
Turkish türkisch 6/1B
turn into (v) umwandeln in 11/6A
turn off (v) ausschalten 1/3B
turnip Rübe 15/5B
twin Zwilling 13/3
twin town Partnerstadt 2/4B

U

ultimate ultimativ 9/2A
umbrella Regenschirm 5/6A
unbearable unerträglich 11/4B
uncle Onkel 13/4A
unfurnished nicht möbliert 9/4B
uniform Uniform 5/3
union Gewerkschaft 7/4B
unique einzigartig 14/6A
unlimited unbegrenzt 9/6B
unusual ungewöhnlich 13/4C
up to half an hour bis zu einer halben Stunde 6/5A
update (v) modernisieren 9/4B
urban area Stadtgebiet 11/4A
used to (I ~ collect stamps.) Früher habe ich Briefmarken gesammelt. 1/5
useless (he was ~) er hat nichts gebracht 10/3C
utility room Waschküche 9/4B

V

vacation (BE: holiday) Urlaub 15/4A
valid gültig 2/2D
valley Tal 11/2A
valuable wertvoll 5/4A
valuables Wertsachen 5/6
value (to be good ~ for money) sein Geld wert sein 3/1B
vandalism Vandalismus 9/6A
varied abwechslungsreich 11/2A
vase Vase 9/3B
version Version 13/3B

victory Sieg 14/5A
Vienna Wien 2/4B
view (v) zuschauen 2/5A
view (in your ~) Ihrer Meinung nach 9/3F
view Aussicht 9/4B
viewing box Loge 14/5A
violence Gewalt 14/4D
violent gewalttätig 7/4B
viscose Viskose 5/2A
vital sehr wichtig 14/6A
vitamin Vitamin 6/2B
volcano Vulkan 11/2A
vowel Vokal (Selbstlaut) 5/5D

W

walkman Walkman 5/6A
wallet Brieftasche 5/6A
wallpaper Tapete 9/3A
wardrobe Kleiderschrank 9/2A
warn (v) warnen 13/5E
wash up (v) spülen, abwaschen 6/5C
washbasin Waschbecken 9/3F
washing powder Waschpulver 3/6C
waste (v) verschwenden 1/6A
watch Armbanduhr 1/3A
watch out for sth (v) auf etwas achten 11/1C
water lily Seerose 9/5D
waterfall Wasserfall 11/2A
wave (v) winken 15/2B
weaken (v) abschwächen 14/2E
wealthy wohlhabend 5/4B
weight (to lose/to put on ~) abnehmen/zunehmen 5/4D
weightlifting Gewichtheben 14/4A
welcome (v) begrüßen 7/4B
well gesund 13/6B
well-built gut gebaut 13/2A
well-known bekannt 3/5A
well-trained gut erzogen 10/4A
western series Western-Serie 1/5A
What's it like? Wie ist es? 2/4C
whenever I feel like it wann immer ich möchte 14/3B
while während 3/2F
while (for a ~) für eine Weile 14/6A

white robe weißes Gewand 15/5B
whole ganz 1/2A
whose deren; dessen 13/3B
widespread weitverbreitet 15/1B
wife Ehefrau 13/4B
wildlife Tierwelt 11/2A
win *(v)* gewinnen 2/4B
windsurfing Windsurfen 14/4A
wink (I didn't sleep a ~!) Ich habe kein Auge zugetan! 11/1E
winter woollies *(scherzhaft)* warme Bekleidung 11/1C
wish *(v)* wünschen 10/3C
without asking ohne zu fragen 6/5A
wonder (I ~ why) Ich frage mich warum 15/1C

woodland Wälder 11/4A
world class von Weltklasse 7/3E
worn verschlissen 9/3B
worry about *(v)* sich sorgen um 13/4D
worthwhile lohnend 14/6A
wrestle *(v)* ringen 2/5A
wrinkle Falte 1/6A

Y
yard Hof, Garten 11/6D
youth Jugend 1/6A
youthful jugendlich 13/5C

Z
zone Zone 2/2D

Alphabetical Word List

171

Quellennachweis

Umschlag: MEV; Stockbyte(RF) Tralee/Irland; **S. 7** 1. Zefa (H.G. Rossi), Düsseldorf; 2. Corbis (Jose Luis Pelaez), Düsseldorf; 3. Bullspress/Mirrorpix, Frankfurt **S. 8** (v. links) MEV; MEV **S. 9** (oben, v. links) MEV; Elmar Feuerbach, Remshalden; MEV; Mauritius (C. Seghers), Mittenwald; (unten, v. links) Elmar Feuerbach, Remshalden; Ernst Klett Verlag, Stuttgart; Casio Computer Co. GmbH, Norderstedt; **S. 11** (oben, v. links) GettyImages (Eyewire), München; GettyImages (Eyewire), München; DaimlerChrysler Bildarchiv, Stuttgart; GettyImages (Photodisc), München; **S. 12** (im Uhrzeigersinn) Corbis (Bettmann), Düsseldorf; British Tourist Authority, Frankfurt; Corbis (Peter Beck); Siemens AG, München; **S. 13** MEV; **S. 16** (v. links) Mauritius (ACE),) David Shallis, Weil der Stadt, Mittenwald Topham/ImageWorks; **S. 17** (v. links) Corbis RF, Düsseldorf; Corbis (David Sailors), Düsseldorf; David Shallis, Weil der Stadt; David Shallis, Weil der Stadt; **S. 18** Topham/ImageWorks **S. 19** (oben) BAA Aviation Photo Library, Hertfordshire, UK; (unten) David Shallis, Weil der Stadt; **S. 20** Deutsch Bahn AG, Berlin; **S. 21** (im Uhrzeigersinn) GettyImages (Eyewire), München; MEV; GettyImages (Eyewire), München; **S. 22** (im Uhrzeigersinn) Corbis (Bob Krist), Düsseldorf; Mauritius (Vidler), Mittenwald; Gettyimages (Photodisc), München; **S. 24** (v. links) BASF, Ludwigshafen; Gettyimages (Photodisc), München; **S. 26** Corbis RF, Düsseldorf; **S. 27** 1. Elmar Feuerbach, Remshalden ; 2. Elmar Feuerbach, Remshalden; 3. IBM Deutschland GmbH; 4. Elmar Feuerbach, Remshalden; 5. Team7 Natürlich Wohnen GmbH, Ried im Innkreis; **S. 28** (v. links) MEV; BASF, Ludwigshafen; MEV; **S. 30** MEV; **S. 32** (v. links) MEV; MEV; **S. 33** Mauritius (Macia), Mittenwald; **S. 34** (v. links) Mauritius (AGE), Mittenwald; Mauritius (The Copyright Group), Mittenwald; Corbis (Jon Feingersh), Düsseldorf; MEV; **S. 35** Corbis (Bettmann), Düsseldorf; **S. 37** (oben, v. links) Corel, Ottawa/Ontario; Corel; (unten) Corel; **S. 38** (im Uhrzeigersinn) GettyImages (Eyewire), München; MEV; Mauritius (Katzer), München; Mauritius (Bibikow), München; **S. 39** Corbis (Michael Keller), Düsseldorf; **S. 40** (im Uhrzeigersinn) MEV; MEV; MEV; MEV; **S. 42** (im Uhrzeigersinn) Corbis RF, Düsseldorf; MEV; MEV; MEV; **S. 45** GettyImages (Digital Vision), München; **S. 46** Mauritius (Benelux Press), Mittenwald; **S. 47** Mauritius (Waldkirch), Mittenwald; **S. 48** (oben) Mauritius (SST) Mittenwald; (unten) Elmar Feuerbach, Remshalden; **S. 50** (v. Links) MEV; Elmar Feuerbach, Remshalden; MEV ; Elmar Feuerbach, Remshalden; **S. 51** wdr, Köln; **S. 52** MEV; **S. 53** (v. oben) Creativ Collection, Freiburg; GettyImages (Photodisc), München; Corel, Ottawa/Ontario; MEV; Corbis (Bob Krist), Düsseldorf; **S. 55** (oben, v. links) Corel, Ottawa/Ontario; Corbis RF, Düsseldorf; Corbis RF, Düsseldorf; (unten, v. Links) MEF; Corbis RF, Düsseldorf; **S. 56** Corbis (Bob Krist), Düsseldorf; **S. 58** MEV; **S. 59** MEV; **S. 60** (v. links) Corbis (Jose Luis Pelaez), Düsseldorf; Corel, Ottawa/Ontario; **S. 61** (links – rechts) Flötotto Einrichtungssysteme, Gütersloh; Goldreif Möbelfabrik GmbH, Salzuflen; MEV; **S. 62** Mauritius (Stockimage), Mittenwald; **S. 63** (v. links) Corbis (Russel Underwood), Düsseldorf; Corbis RF, Düsseldorf; **S. 64** Corbis (Ariel Skelley), Düsseldorf; **S. 65** Corbis (Paul Barton), Düsseldorf; **S. 66** Corbis (Tom Ives), Düsseldorf; **S. 68** (v. links) Corbis (Tom Stewart), Düsseldorf; Corbis (LWA-Dann Tardif), Düsseldorf; **S. 69** (oben) Corbis (Peter Finger), Düsseldorf; (unten) Corbis (Pablo Corral V), Düsseldorf; **S. 70** Corbis (Tom Stewart), Düsseldorf; **S. 72** Corbis RF, Düsseldorf; **S. 73** Corbis (Dave Bartruff), Düsseldorf; **S. 74** (oben) Corbis (Lawrence Manning), Düsseldorf; (unten) Corel, Ottawa/Ontario; **S. 76** (v. links) GettyImages (Photodisc), München; MEV; **S. 77** Deutscher Wetterdienst, Offenbach; **S. 78** (v. oben) Corbis (Paul A. Souders), Düsseldorf; Corel, Ottawa/Ontario; Corbis (Denis Anthony Valentine), Düsseldorf; **S. 79** (im Uhrzeigersinn) Corbis (James A. Sugar), Düsseldorf; Corbis (Bettmann), Düsseldorf; MEV; Corbis (Sygma/Jacques Langevin), Düsseldorf; **S. 80** (v. links) Corbis (Nik Wheeler), Düsseldorf; MEV; **S. 81** (v. links) Corbis (Bob Krist), Düsseldorf; Corbis (David Lawrence), Düsseldorf; Corbis (Tom & Dee Ann McCarthy), Düsseldorf; **S. 82** (v. links) Vattenfall Mining, Berlin; Vattenfall Mining Berlin; **S. 84** MEV; **S. 87** (oben, v. links) MEV; MEV; (links, v. oben) MEV; MEV; (unten) MEV; **S. 88** (v. links) Corbis (Hulton-Deutsch Collection), Düsseldorf Corbis (Neal Preston), Düsseldorf; **S. 89** Kate Tranter, Gutweiler; **S. 90** (v. links) MEV; MEV; **S. 91** MEV; **S. 92** (v. links) MEV; MEV; The Spectator Limited, London; **S. 94** (links, v. oben) MEV; MEV; (rechts, v. oben) MEV; MEV; MEV; **S. 95** (oben) MEV; (unten) Elmar Feuerbach, Remshalden; **S. 96** (v. links) MEV; MEV; GettyImages (Photodisc), München; **S. 97** MEV; MEV (Hintergr.) **S. 98** (oben) Corel, Ottawa/Ontario; (unten) GettyImages (Photodisc), München; **S. 99** Corel, Ottawa/Ontario; **S. 102** MEV; **S. 103** 1-8 Elmar Feuerbach, Remshalden; **S. 104** MEV; **S. 105** Corel, Ottawa/Ontario; **S. 106** GettyImages (Photodisc), München; **S. 107** (v. Links) Mauritius (Chromosohm), Mittenwald; Corel, Ottawa/Ontario; GettyImages (Photodisc), München; **S. 110** MEV;

In einigen Fällen ist es uns trotz intensiver Bemühungen nicht gelungen, die Rechte-Inhaber zu ermitteln. Wir bitten diese, sich mit dem Verlag in Verbindung zu setzen.